SITTING ON A
KEG OF DYNAMITE

SITTING ON A
KEG OF DYNAMITE

Father Bill, Texas City, and a Disaster Foretold

JOHN NEAL PHILLIPS

UNIVERSITY OF OKLAHOMA PRESS : NORMAN

This book is published with the generous assistance
of the McCasland Foundation, Duncan, Oklahoma.

Library of Congress Cataloging-in-Publication Data

Names: Phillips, John Neal, 1949– author.
Title: Sitting on a keg of dynamite : Father Bill, Texas City, and a disaster foretold / John
    Neal Phillips.
Description: Norman : University of Oklahoma Press, [2022] | Includes bibliographical
    references and index. | Summary: "Tells several entwined stories: the life of William
    Roach, a Roman Catholic priest known affectionately as Father Bill, an outspoken
    advocate for poor and working-class citizens, fair wages, and workplace safety; the
    rapid growth and near destruction of an American industrial city; and the lax safety
    and environmental regulations that led to the worst industrial accident in US history,
    the explosion of the French vessel SS *Grandcamp* in the port of Texas City, just north
    of Galveston, Texas, in 1947. Nearly 600 people died instantly, including Father Bill"—
    Provided by publisher.
Identifiers: LCCN 2022017146 | ISBN 978-0-8061-9070-9 (paperback)
Subjects: LCSH: Roach, William Francis, 1908–1947. | *Grandcamp* (Ship) | Fires—Texas—
    Texas City—History—20th century. | Disasters—Texas—Texas City—History—20th
    century. | Industrial accidents—Texas—Texas City—History—20th century. | Texas
    City (Tex.)—History—20th century. | BISAC: BIOGRAPHY & AUTOBIOGRAPHY /
    Religious | HISTORY / United States / State & Local / Southwest (AZ, NM, OK, TX)
Classification: LCC F394.T4 P55 2022 | DDC 976.4139—dc23/eng/20220420
LC record available at https://lccn.loc.gov/2022017146

In memory of
Sister Mary William Montegut
and
Sister Mary Catherine de Ricci Laiche

CONTENTS

CONTENTS

PREFACE

Father Bill's service record in Texas, found in diocesan archives, is brief:

> Roach, William; ordained 1939; St. Mary's, Lampasas, Texas, 1940–45; St. Mary's Church, Texas City, Texas, 1946–47; died April 16, 1947, in Texas City.[1]

The entry reveals only that a man named William Roach became a priest in 1939, spent five years at St. Mary's Parish in Lampasas, Texas, was transferred to a new parish in Texas City, Texas, and died there in 1947. The brevity of the passage obscures his career, as is often the case. But the few words would have pleased the subject, Reverend William Francis Roach, or Father Bill, as he preferred. In fact, Roach would have favored no mention at all. He was not at all interested in self-promotion.[2]

But the story of how William Francis Roach journeyed from his Pennsylvania birthplace to a bustling port city in Texas is as compelling as the events leading to his death. Indeed, it is the story of two brothers, motherless identical twins, and their widowed father, forced to shunt the boys from place to place, relative to relative. It is a story of disconnection from one's family, of negative energy and negative actions redirected, first to sports, then to a serious religious calling.

The story of Father Bill and his twin, Father John, is both a road trip and a journey of deep spirituality and faith. It tells of overcoming hardships and developing the desire to help those unable to help themselves. It is a story of Catholics navigating the largely Protestant worlds of Arkansas and Texas, facing at best mild skepticism and at worst full-blown anti-Catholic hatred fomented by such groups as the Ku Klux Klan. It is the story of a man who, following the model of St. Francis of Assisi, repaired churches and even built new ones, sometimes literally with his own hands.

It is also a story of contrasts, of the rural, agrarian expanse of the Texas Hill Country juxtaposed with the booming urban industrial might of the Texas Gulf Coast immediately after World War II. It is the story of laborers struggling to win a living wage in the face of proposed open-shop and right-to-work legislation in Texas. And it is the story of a political showdown between one Texas port city and a consortium of local petrochemical industries, culminating in the worst industrial accident in US history (to date). The story is in many ways the opening act of things to come, presaging a future in which ignorance, error, and greedy interference rapidly push humankind to the point of self-extinction.

Father Bill Roach, part of a generation of socially conscious Catholic clergy speaking for those without voices, made it a point to be at the front of the stage. Possessed of a deep-rooted sincerity, Father Bill used his disarmingly affable personality and nonstop, often self-effacing sense of humor to defuse anger and promote dialogue. That was his way.

Growing up in Houston in the 1950s and 1960s, I heard many stories about the Texas City explosions of 1947 from the adults around me. My parents, who both lived and worked in Houston at the time, heard the explosions fifty miles away. My father and some of his coworkers tried to drive to Texas City to help, only to encounter hundreds of fifty-five-gallon oil drums blocking the road, blown thousands of feet through the air by the detonation of the SS *Grandcamp* on April 16, 1947.

I remember Sunday-afternoon drives with my parents to one of our favorite seafood restaurants, San Jacinto Inn, on Buffalo Bayou, twenty-five miles east of downtown Houston. Long predating construction of the freeway systems that now interlace the area, our route passed miles and miles of refineries and petro-chemical companies, particularly in Pasadena. I was fascinated by the massive, curvilinear structures and the rows of flare stacks burning off excess natural gas. My father, a pipefitter by trade, would explain how those structures functioned. And sometimes he and my mother would recall the explosions at Texas City, which caused petrochemical companies similar to the ones in Pasadena to catch fire and burn for weeks. Those stories have stayed with me for decades.

As a student attending Catholic schools, I also heard stories of a priest who was killed in the explosions. But I cannot recall anyone mentioning the priest's name—perhaps an oversight, a lack of knowledge of his name, or a failure of my memory. But the stories of this priest lingered, just like those of my parents and their friends. Eventually, these stories inspired me to do serious research about Father Bill and the Texas City explosions.

ACKNOWLEDGMENTS

I have long intended to write about the disastrous events of April 16–17, 1947. But I did not initially consider focusing on Father Bill Roach. In the course of my initial research, however, it became apparent that Father Bill was a major figure linking most of the often disparate parts of this complex story. Building on that realization, I conducted more than thirty eyewitness interviews; scoured through archives, court transcripts, and government files; and consulted numerous other primary sources. Soon, a comprehensive picture began to emerge, leading to this book. Throughout the process, I had a lot of help from some very generous people.

First and foremost, I thank Sister Mary William Montegut and Sister Mary Catherine Laiche of the Monastery of the Holy Infant Jesus in Lufkin, Texas, for their kind, humorous, and unselfish help with this project. Sister William, in particular, was a one-person juggernaut of information and support. Thanks also to Barbara Rust, director of the National Archives and Records Administration, Southwest Region, for rolling out cart after cart of written testimony attached to the *Dalehite v. United States* class action suit while always reminding me, "There's a lot more where that came from." And she was so right.

Lisa May, archivist for the Archdiocese of Galveston-Houston, was most helpful to me over a long period of time. So were Kinga Perzynska, director of the Catholic Archives of Texas, Joseph A. Casino, director, and Christine Friend, assistant archivist, for the Archdiocese of Philadelphia; Jan Brass of the Diocese of Little Rock

(Arkansas) Archives; Reverend Hilario Guajardo, pastor of Our Lady of Lourdes Catholic Church, Gatesville (Texas); Rosemary Detrich, director of the Leander (Texas) Public Library; Nancy Jones, secretary of St. Mary's Catholic Church, Lampasas (Texas); and Barbara Williams, archivist for Drexel University Medical School Archives (Pennsylvania). Father James Mancini, pastor of St. Michael's, Cherokee Village (Arkansas), shared his memories and documents related to the Roach brothers. Others who helped me track down information include Brother Ed Loch, archivist, Archdiocese of San Antonio (Texas); Jeanne Barnett, Fordham University, New York City; Anne Chamberlain and Cathy Snyder, Upper Darby High School, Upper Darby (Pennsylvania); Emily Wilson, Mount Saint Joseph's, Baltimore (Maryland); Regina Walker, Chester High School, Chester (Pennsylvania); Carol Tulba, West Catholic High School, Philadelphia (Pennsylvania) Sister Helena Mayer, archivist, Society of the Holy Child Jesus, Rosemont (Pennsylvania); and Kelly Castillo, St. Mary's Catholic Church, Texas City (Texas).

I extend special thanks to Jerry Jefferis of the Delaware County (Pennsylvania) Historical Society for all the research and footwork he did to trace the Roach brothers' childhood years. Susie Moncla, of the Moore Memorial Library in Texas City (Texas), supplied transcripts of her interviews with Dick Benedict and Curtis Trahan, among other documents. Thanks to longtime friend and fellow author Carol Roark, retired director of the Dallas History & Archives Division of the Dallas Public Library, for arranging the purchase of a number of photographs of the Texas City explosions, specifically because I was writing a book about the subject. I also extend a special thanks to Richard Meskill for sharing with me the original handwritten and typed writings of Father Bill Roach, which he received as gifts from Roach.

My editor, Alice Stanton, with whom I've worked before, deserves my utmost thanks for her insight, knowledge, and professionalism. Copyeditor Kirsteen E. Anderson is recognized for possessing an eye for detail and the ability to reshape rambling passages into coherent statements.

Thanks as well to all who took the time to recount their memories of and experiences with Father Bill Roach and the Texas City explosions.

PROLOGUE

April 16, 1947

It was a glorious spring day on Galveston Bay, cool and clear with a light breeze blowing from the northwest, a pleasant diversion from thoughts of the coming Texas summer with its legendary heat and humidity. But the weather was lost on Father Bill Roach. Not because he did not enjoy a nice bit of fair weather—there was not much of anything he could not enjoy, or at least try to make the best of. It was just that he had a lot on his mind that day, a clash of thoughts that had been with him for a number of months. Some of these thoughts he had formalized in an article published the week before in the local *Texas City Sun* newspaper. Before that, during one of his regular Sunday sermons, he had told his parishioners more. And to a select few individuals, he had already revealed much.

He stood in the sacristy of St. Mary of the Miraculous Medal, his church, the one he had been assigned to less than two years earlier as its first resident pastor. He was removing his vestments after the Wednesday morning mass—a thin figure with pale, translucent skin who walked with a slight limp and almost always flashed a ready smile, but not that day.

He stepped to the back door of the church for a smoke, the one material thing in which he indulged. Apart from books about Catholic saints, he had no possessions. He hardly slept; rarely ate. Visitors to his rectory, a small corner apartment across the street from the church, found only water in his refrigerator, and occasionally ice cream. But he smoked, a lot.

Lowering his head, he slipped the cigarette between his lips and lit it. When he straightened up to take his first drag, he saw smoke billowing in the air above the docks several blocks away. Odd-looking smoke, bright orange against the deep blue sky, thick plumes of it.

"This is it!" he said, smashing the cigarette out on the ground and heading for his car.[1]

— 1 —

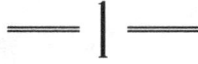

TROUBLEMAKERS

William Francis Roach and his twin brother, John Joseph, were born on the evening of Thursday, August 6, 1908, at Hahnemann Medical College of Philadelphia.[1] John arrived first, followed a few minutes later by William.[2] It was a troubled birth, the culmination of a difficult pregnancy. The newborns' mother, Helen Elizabeth Roach, knew she would give birth to twins. Her doctor had told her so. She also knew she was at risk, grave risk. Her doctor had told her this as well. After the birth she recovered only long enough to understand that her condition had become critical, that puerperal eclampsia threatened her life.[3] Still, her thoughts were of others, a trait that would emerge later in both her sons. It was on them, not herself, that she focused what energy she still could muster.[4]

Stories abound that she somehow paid a visit to the hospital chapel to pray for the infants, William and John. Yet no such chapel existed at Hahnemann in 1908.[5] Helen was by all accounts a deeply religious woman and devout Catholic. It is likely she did pray for her sons, but from her bed in ward ten—and it was in that bed, eighteen hours later, that her kidneys failed, killing her in four minutes. She was twenty-two.[6]

Her husband, William Francis Roach, though aware of this likely outcome, was suddenly faced with many changes. In a matter of hours he went from being married and childless to a widower with two infants. He took the boys home to 208 South Cecil Street, Philadelphia, and made preparations to bury his wife.

West Philadelphia and Delaware County, Pennsylvania. *Map by Carol Zuber-Mallison.*

On Saturday, August 8, 1908, a small death notice appeared in the Philadelphia *Public Ledger* announcing that a memorial would be held at 8:30 A.M. on Tuesday, the eleventh, at Roach's home, followed an hour and a half later by a solemn mass of requiem at the Church of the Transfiguration. Afterward, a brief graveside ceremony would take place at Holy Cross Cemetery, across the Schuylkill River in neighboring Delaware County.[7]

Apart from vague stories of their being shuttled between relatives, not much is known of the twins' first few years.[8] By 1916, however, they were living in the old Quaker community of Sharon Hill, Pennsylvania, just west of Philadelphia, in Delaware County. The town was not far from where their mother was buried. Their father had remarried. He and his new wife, Mabel, had by then produced two children together: Mary, age two, and Leo, an infant. Two years later another boy, Steven, would be born.[9]

Delaware County, Pennsylvania, where Bill and John Roach came of age, has a rich history. It was formed in 1789 from Chester County, one of the three original counties of William Penn's settlement.[10] The county remained sparsely populated until the late eighteenth century. During the American Revolution, Delaware County and its immediate environs became the focal point of a number of important events, including the Battle of Brandywine.[11]

Beginning in 1800 the population of Delaware County began to increase dramatically. Its location within easy reach of major cities such as Philadelphia and

Baltimore, coupled with its network of good roads, rapid streams, and navigable waterways, ensured its rapid development as an important milling center for lumber, grains, paper, tobacco, and textiles. Toward the end of the nineteenth century, a number of major industries were established, drawing large numbers of working-class immigrants to the county. Tensions emanating from nearby Philadelphia also contributed Delaware County's rapid growth in this century. Labor conflicts were foremost among the problems of the City of Brotherly Love. A cradle of the American labor movement in the early 1800s, Philadelphia became more and more anti-labor as the century progressed. Adding to the friction were clashes between religions, classes, and cultures. Protestant intolerance toward immigrants, Catholics, and Jews, coupled with white fear and mistrust of African Americans, caused members of all these groups to flee Philadelphia.[12] This flight continued into the early twentieth century.

Among those leaving Philadelphia were William F. Roach, his children, and his second wife, Mabel. In Sharon Hill, the Roaches bought a small house at 216 West Elmwood Avenue. The purchase price—one dollar—suggests a property transfer, most likely from one of Mabel's relatives, as she had several in the area. Although farming was on the decline, the region was still largely rural, quite a contrast to Philadelphia.[13]

On January 16, 1916, when the twins were seven and a half years old, a blast rattled windows and shook coffee cups in Sharon Hill. Two tons of ammonium nitrate fertilizer had exploded at the DuPont plant in Gibbstown, New Jersey, sixteen miles away, on the east side of the Delaware River. It was the first of a series of accidents involving ammonium nitrate that would rock New Jersey and Pennsylvania between 1916 and 1924.[14] The Gibbstown explosion did no damage to Sharon Hill or the house on West Elmwood, but for the young twins living there, it would prove a portent of things to come.

William and John were at best mischievous boys. Some suggest they were beyond mischievous, that they were terrible pranksters and even petty thieves at the head of a gang of six boys. There is no record of violence or trouble with the law, but their reputation as unruly pests lingered long after they left Delaware County. Reportedly, the gang was insubordinate and perpetually disruptive in town and at Holy Spirit School, the Catholic School the boys attended in Sharon Hill. Between 1916 and 1921, they and their cohorts reportedly regularly pilfered wine from the chapel sanctuary, terrorized teachers and fellow students, shoplifted candy and cigarettes from local stores, and generally ran amok with the anger of youngsters socially disconnected and unfettered by rules. Their treatment of teachers at Holy Spirit School, and in particular the principal, Mother Saint James, not only solidified the Roach brothers' reputation at the time but would come back to haunt them later.[15]

Bill and John may have been identical twins, but there were noticeable differences between them. John was slightly taller and thinner than Bill. John was also an organizer and meticulous planner, whether for good or bad, often the latter. Wheels perpetually turned in his head. As a reckless child he honed his intellect to conjure the next devious deed. Bill, on the other hand, was all about action. He would be the first to bring his brother's ideas to life. He loved nothing more than charging off and getting physically involved. Unfortunately, just like his brother's ideas, Bill's actions were usually for the worse. This trait is key to understanding how the two so often and so easily functioned as one. No one close to Bill and John could think of one without the other. The brothers even finished each other's sentences. They were the classic two-headed monster, and the monster was malevolent.[16]

The brothers looked like their father, but that is where the similarity ended. The elder Roach was quiet, almost shy, in sharp contrast to his loud, boisterous, and uncontrolled twins.[17] Their stepmother, Mabel, did not want Bill and John around. She could not cope with the boys' behavior, and she resented what they represented, constant reminders of her husband's first wife, a woman whose tragic death during childbirth cast her as a saint.

For their part, the twins bore equal resentment toward Mabel. Throughout their lives they spoke often of their birth mother, lionizing her. They rarely mentioned their stepmother or anyone else in the family. They focused instead on the mother they never knew, describing her as beautiful and deeply spiritual.[18] Their penchant for rebelliousness, disruption, and petty thievery stemmed from resentment toward the woman they felt was trying to replace their dead mother. This animosity resulted in the twins being frequently shipped to relatives and elsewhere for extended periods.

During those years the brothers grew very close, enabling them to share the load they carried. One brother never experienced anything that the other did not experience equally. Over time they developed a mechanism for combatting their mutual pain—humor. As children their humor revolved around endless practical jokes and insolent remarks, sometimes insensitive and usually at the expense of others. They were known to poke fun at themselves as well however, an aspect that increased as they got older. Indeed, as adults their humor became almost exclusively self-deprecating. Still, with or without humor, in and around Delaware

County, the prevailing feeling was that the Roach twins were troublemakers headed straight for the reformatory, or worse.

In June 1921, Bill and John were told they had both failed the fifth grade and were to be held back.[19] Instead, the Roach brothers were somehow able to transfer to Mount St. Joseph College, a prestigious boarding school in Maryland, as incoming sixth-graders. The upscale Roman Catholic facility was about five miles west of Baltimore in Irvington Township. Founded by followers of St. Xavier in 1876 as a college preparatory school, it was the second oldest Xavierian institution in the United States and was academically well respected, with an international reputation. Tuition at Mount St. Joseph College was $350 a year. At the time, the cost of sending both Bill and John Roach there exceeded the average annual income in the United States.[20]

The money to support the boys at boarding school was provided by John and Annie Clisham, the twins' maternal grandparents. John Roach once told a friend and colleague that his birth mother was from "a wealthy family."[21] He described spending summers in the home of their birth mother's parents. He was never specific, saying only that the house was large and that he and Bill played behind the grand staircase with a favorite cousin nicknamed "Short Pants." He also said that his grandfather never interacted with them. In fact, he never even spoke to the Roach brothers—ever! The twins recalled only fleeting memories of their grandfather, seated behind a large desk in a book-filled study beyond the staircase. Apart from that, they were only peripherally aware of his existence. Even less is known about their maternal grandmother, Annie Smythe Clisham. Throughout their lives, neither John nor Bill ever mentioned her.[22]

In the fall of 1921, the Roach brothers entered the sixth grade at Mount St. Joseph College. At age thirteen, they were a year older than their classmates. The total enrollment was 280 students, many of whom were from South America and Western Europe. The institution was academically demanding and distinctly cosmopolitan. The brothers studied Latin, French, German, and English, as well as business (typing and bookkeeping), math, science, and religion. There is no indication whether Bill and John were good students or bad. No accolades or academic awards, such as the annual Excellence Award or the Christian Doctrine Award, appear in their records. Yet neither do any reprimands, detentions, or letters home. They completed two years, returning to Sharon Hill in June 1923.[23]

In 1926, Bill and John's father sold the Sharon Hill house and relocated his family five-and-a-half miles north to the Lansdowne-Kirklyn area. There, the elder Roach rented an apartment at the Stratford Court on Lansdowne Avenue and, with the proceeds from the sale of his home, purchased a small filling station three miles from Lansdowne, near the intersection of Baltimore Pike and Providence Road, just east of Media.[24] Bill and John, both eighteen that year, rented a house near the intersection of Route 1 and State Road in the Drexel Hill–Upper Darby area. They both worked at their father's filling station.[25]

The twins are variously listed as students at Chester High School, seven miles southwest of Lansdowne; Upper Darby High School, north of Lansdowne; and West Catholic High School for Boys, in Philadelphia.[26] They graduated from the last in 1928, just before their twentieth birthdays.[27] While at West Catholic High School for Boys, Bill and John Roach entered a new phase of their lives. Still mischievous, the brothers found a positive way to redirect their barely controlled negative energy and anti-authoritarian disruptiveness into competitive rowing.

Competitive rowing, a tradition in Pennsylvania, dates back at least as far as the ancient Sumerians five thousand years ago. After weaving its way through Mediterranean and European cultures, the sport became well established in North America by the late eighteenth century. From the 1830s thriving permanent boat clubs have existed in Philadelphia, Boston, and New York City. The Schuylkill (Dutch for "hidden") River was nearly perfect as a rowing venue. In the 1800s the municipal water department purchased tracts of land along the banks to protect the water supply from industrial pollution and dammed the river. The resulting long, flatwater lake brought national focus on the Schuylkill River as a center for competitive rowing.[28]

In 1858, the Philadelphia clubs banded together as the Schuylkill Navy, primarily to eliminate gambling in their sport and to ensure maintenance of their amateur status. The following year the Schuylkill Navy held its first local regatta, and by 1873, it was hosting national regattas. In 1876, the club brought its first international regatta to Philadelphia. In 1896, several rowing events were to be included in the first modern Olympics, held in Athens, Greece, but were cancelled due to bad weather. Not surprisingly, the US rowing team consisted largely of Philadelphia athletes. By then so many boat clubs existed along the Schuylkill River that the area had come to be known as "boathouse row."[29]

By the late 1920s, when the Roach brothers began rowing on the Schuylkill River, boathouse row was a major world center of rowing. It was dominated by one club, the Pennsylvania Athletic Club Rowing Association, or Penn AC, of which the legendary Olympic gold medal rower Jack Kelly Sr. was a member.[30] Penn AC had originally been a Philadelphia men's social club that promoted athletics. In the nineteenth century the club approached members of the West Philadelphia

Barge Club, proposing to sponsor them if they would change their name. Thus was born Penn AC, which to date still exists at its original, historic headquarters on the Schuylkill River. Such clubs were not elitist or exclusive in the manner of class-conscious country clubs. Their mission was to promote athletics among working-class individuals. That, along with a good deal of talent, is why young men like Bill and John Roach were able to belong to one of the world's greatest rowing clubs and associate with the cream of the rowing world.

Through Penn AC, Jack Kelly Sr. established an official relationship with the athletic program of West Catholic High School to provide a competitive rowing venue for high school athletes. The school thus became a feeder to acquire talented junior rowers for Penn AC. One of those talented rowers was the Roach brothers' close friend Dan Barrow, also a West Catholic High School student. Barrow, the eldest of twelve children, was born and raised at the family home on Bailey Road, in Yeadon, but he and his family attended St. Philomena Catholic Church in neighboring Lansdowne, as did the Roach brothers.[31]

Bill and John visited Dan frequently at his home, and the Barrows made it a point to drive the few extra miles to buy gasoline at the Roach family's filling station. The Barrow household was the gathering spot for scores of people, mostly friends of the twelve Barrow children and their four cousins, who lived next door, as well as business associates of Dan's father, the owner of a construction company. Dan's mother, by all accounts an extremely friendly person, welcomed the train station atmosphere of throngs of people coming, going, and milling about. Among the most welcome visitors were the Roach brothers, who always arrived together and often just in time for breakfast, lunch, or dinner, or at least in time to grab one of the sandwiches perpetually available in the kitchen. That Bill and John were welcomed anywhere was amazing, considering their reputation—but that was in the past. The comradery, teamwork, and physical exertion of competitive rowing had radically changed the brothers.

The younger Barrow children loved it when Bill and John dropped by, getting very excited when they heard the boys' 1928 Chevrolet Woody pull up outside the house. To them Bill and John were very special because they always played games with the children, or perhaps as one of them later observed, "at least [they] pretended to play hide and seek and other games with us while they waited for Dan."[32] Still, there were genuine games of chase and piggyback rides. Everyone in the Barrow house enjoyed the twins, who were always together, inseparable.

The youngsters described the brothers as cute, always clean-shaven, with thick hair neatly combed, and wearing clothes that were "typical for young men at the time." And as a result of rigorous training for rowing, both were fit and strong. They could quite easily grab one or more of the Barrow children and lift them high into the air, or hurl them back and forth between them like footballs.[33]

Dan Barrow was recruited in 1928 from West Catholic High School for Penn AC's junior rowing program. His talent led him to become a protégé of Jack Kelly Sr. Specializing in "sweep oar," Barrow was part of the eight-oar crew that won a gold medal at the very first national high school championships. Later, Barrow joined the club's legendary senior eight-oar crew, dubbed "the Big Eight." With Barrow, that team won thirty-one consecutive races between 1929 and 1931, including the world championship in Liege, Belgium, in 1930. The team's record time in that race has, to date, never been broken, prompting the Associated Press to vote them the greatest eight-oar team of the first half of the twentieth century.[34]

Documentation of the Roach brothers' involvement in competitive rowing first appears in 1929, after high school. On July 20, John Roach was part of an eight-oar Penn AC team that defeated Undine Boat Club to win the gold in that year's Philadelphia Regatta. Later in the day, John and Bill placed second in the Junior Double Shells, narrowly outdistancing a rival boat by inches in the final stroke.[35]

During the season, every summer weekend was occupied with rowing. Crowds lined both banks of the Schuylkill River with picnic baskets and tally cards, watching races and keeping track of their favorite teams and rowers. For two years the Roach brothers were active participants in that world. Then, in 1931, something quite different would redirect their lives. From that time on, though remaining in touch with the world of rowing, their interest would only be from the sidelines.

= 2 =

PEREGRINATIO PRO DEI AMORE

Bill and John Roach arrived at their mutual decision on the same day in exactly the same way, but the process had been gradual and unique to each. For Bill, it began in the last year of high school, shortly after graduation. He started attending mass daily, something he had never done before.[1] Over time he developed a deep relationship to the faith he had known all his life but paid little attention to. Part of his newfound spirituality had to do with a polychrome statue of the Virgin Mary at St. Philomena. The Virgin was portrayed with blonde hair and blue eyes, which greatly amused both brothers, Bill in particular. He thought it incongruous that a woman from Judea two thousand years ago might resemble some Nordic goddess. Bill and John would snicker, nudge each other, and speak irreverently about "the blonde" in the corner.

Eventually, though, Bill began looking beneath the surface, beyond the hair color and even beyond the sculpture itself, to its underlying concept. Mary is an intensely appealing saint, filled with optimism and hope, very much in keeping with Bill Roach's personality. Mary has for centuries represented renewal, both physically and spiritually. Among some northern Europeans of the Gothic period, she was associated with roses, long symbolic of the hope of the coming of spring after a long winter. To the European farmers who made up the vast majority of the Christian population at the time, the changing season was supremely important. Even then, however, Mary represented not only the hope of physical renewal through the return of spring, but also the hope of spiritual renewal through the birth of her son. Renewal, birth, and rebirth are the meanings of Mary, offering assurance that cold and darkness will eventually be replaced with warmth and light.

Bill might also have thought of Mary as a symbol of selflessness, the mother who gave her son to suffer death at the hands of enemies. He recalled the stories of his mother's devotion to the Virgin Mary, of her praying to Mary in the last hours of her life, praying not for herself but for Bill and John. Something clicked inside of Bill Roach. From that moment forward, he was a changed man.

Bill's revelation triggered a brief separation between him and his brother, something that rarely occurred in their lives. Initially, John had no interest in following his brother's lead. He was devout enough, he thought, and attending St. Philomena once a week on Sundays was plenty for him. Bill's new passion for faith and spiritual rebirth puzzled John at first, but he would not remain puzzled for long.

Friends and acquaintances found Bill's initiative uncharacteristic, because they tended to think of John as more of a leader. Later, it would become clear that Bill's traits of leadership were as strong as his brother's, just less obvious, often masked behind a barrage of self-effacing humor. As the brothers grew older, though both retained ready wits, especially when they were together, John developed a more serious nature than Bill did. These subtle differences affected the direction each brother took in his respective path forward.[2]

Although it was Bill who "got religion first," as John later recalled, soon enough both brothers were attending daily mass at St. Philomena.[3] Each took the next step separately, but on the same day and at the urging of the same man. Their decision would take them away from rowing, Pennsylvania, and ultimately, their disruptive pasts. Both brothers decided to enroll in the seminary and study for the priesthood.

Bill and John both had part-time jobs as delivery truck drivers, in addition to helping out at their father's filling station. One very snowy winter day, both brothers were making deliveries in separate trucks. At different times that day, each brother happened to stop at the same small rural church for confession. The same priest heard their confessions. During both confessions there was a larger conversation that revealed a deepening sense of faith and spirituality emerging in each young man and his quandary over what to do about it. In each case the priest suggested that the confessant enter the seminary. Speaking to the second twin he added, "I don't understand this, but this is the second time today I've felt inspired to encourage someone to consider the priesthood."[4]

However, being called to study for the priesthood and actually being accepted into a seminary program were two entirely different matters for brothers of limited means in or around 1931.[5] By then the nation was in the grip of the Great Depression, an economic catastrophe that affected church organizations just as much as individuals and secular businesses.

The hard times enveloping the nation had begun in 1929, the year the Roach brothers were rowing so successfully on the Schuylkill River. On Thursday, October 24, of that year, "Black Thursday," the US stock market suffered its largest single-day sell-off in memory. Then the following Tuesday, October 29, three months to the day after Bill and John Roach placed second in the junior double shells, the bottom dropped out of the market as a panic of frenzied selling swept Wall Street. On that day, "Black Tuesday," $2 billion per hour simply vaporized, wiping out hundreds of major financial trusts.[6]

Initially, the average citizen could not imagine how the events of Black Thursday and Black Tuesday would affect them. Few Americans invested in the stock market and even fewer understood the implications of what had happened. As one auto worker asked a coworker at the time, "I ain't buying' no General Motors common [stock] . . . are you?" Of the nation's previous notable economic panics, in the 1870s, the 1890s, and 1921, only the last was within the memory of most Americans at the time. And although significant, resulting in a peak unemployment rate of nearly 12 percent, the downturn of 1921 lasted a very short time and was immediately followed by seven years of unprecedented economic prosperity. Indeed, throughout their lives, Bill and John Roach had only ever witnessed the exceptional US industrial and technological expansion of the early twentieth century. The emergence of such corporate giants as US Steel, Ford Motor Company, and Eastman Kodak combined with developments including electricity, radio, and automobiles to create a national mindset of never-ending prosperity. Even as late as September 1929, one month before the crash, incumbent President Herbert Hoover was espousing similar ideas to a group of sociologists gathered at a White House dinner.[7]

By 1931, when the Roach brothers began to search for a seminary, nearly fifty-five thousand businesses had closed and national unemployment stood at 15.9 percent, with many larger, more industrialized cities being hit even harder.[8] In New York City, eighty-two bread lines served eighty-five thousand meals daily to the homeless. In Philadelphia, evictions were averaging 1,400 a month. In March 1930, police attacked and quashed a demonstration staged by unemployed citizens of Philadelphia. Meanwhile, a group of wealthy Philadelphians, Jack Kelly Sr. among them,

contributed $29.5 million to an unemployment relief fund. No amount of charity
however, could stave off the rising numbers of displaced people in Philadelphia
and elsewhere in the United States. Nationwide, the number of transients, often
whole families, found riding illegally on the nation's freight trains numbered in
the millions.[9] Seemingly, people everywhere were on the move, moving toward
news (or rumors) of jobs that might be available in other parts of the country.

This was the world into which the Roach brothers ventured in search of a
seminary. They had no money for tuition and very little academic standing,
but they had a fierce resolve to pursue a religious life. They applied first to the
Diocese of Philadelphia, then to the Diocese of Baltimore, but were rejected at
both. Despite the Great Depression, there were so many paying applicants to
seminaries located in the eastern United States that there was little need to offer
financial aid to attract prospective priests. That was not the case elsewhere in
the country, however.

Somehow, Bill and John Roach discovered that in 1931 much of the southern
and western portions of the nation were so sparsely populated with Catholics and
Catholic clergy that the church considered them missionary territories. Consequently, many seminaries were offering free or reduced tuition to students who
were willing to uproot themselves from dioceses with significant Catholic populations and move to other, predominantly non-Catholic regions of the country. One
such program existed at St. John the Baptist Home Mission Seminary in Little
Rock, Arkansas, a state where the Catholic population amounted to little more
than 1 percent. Upon learning this, the brothers decided to leave Pennsylvania.

"Are there *any* Catholics there?" Bill joked.

"Must be. They've got a bishop." John answered.

"Is he Catholic?"

"Hope so."

"Me too."[10]

The Roach brothers traveled to Arkansas without even contacting the seminary
first. They were both impulsive, especially Bill. But before leaving Pennsylvania,
they did try to acquire at least one letter of recommendation to present to the seminary on their arrival. The twins, now approaching their twenty-third birthdays,
went back to Holy Spirit School in Sharon Hill to ask their former teacher and
principal, Mother Saint James, for a letter of recommendation. She received the
request with a great deal of suspicion, remembering the children who perpetrated
seemingly ceaseless pranks and acts of insubordination a decade earlier and
knowing little about the two grown men before her. "Recommendation for you

two!" she exclaimed. "Considering all you boys have done?" Nevertheless, and to the brothers' complete surprise, the nun composed a letter for them and placed it in a sealed envelope.[11]

In late summer 1931, Bill and John loaded their station wagon and left Delaware County, steering southwest toward Arkansas. The brothers were approaching their quest in the tradition of their ancient Irish-Celtic forebears, the tradition of *peregrinatio pro Dei amore*, vagabonds wandering for the love of God.[12] Personal salvation was at the heart of Bill and John Roach's twentieth-century peregrinatio, But when they departed for Little Rock in the late summer of 1931, they had no idea what lay ahead.

Apart from stints with various relatives as children, Bill and John Roach had never traveled very far from Delaware County. The boarding school in Baltimore was probably the farthest they had ever been from the immediate Philadelphia area. The trip to Arkansas was an eye-opening experience. If they had not already witnessed firsthand the extent of the nation's growing economic problems, the suffering must have become abundantly clear to them as they left Pennsylvania and turned southwest. In West Virginia, half of all mines had closed; in Kentucky farm income had plummeted 60 percent in two years (nearly twice the national average); and in Tennessee farm income was nearly nonexistent because erosion and overproduction had utterly ruined 14 million acres of once-prime land. The farming sector had been in dire condition since the end of World War I, after a sustaining an unprecedented level of wartime production. In hindsight, its decline can be seen as a portent of the crash of 1929.[13]

Throughout the South farmers were leaving the land and moving to large cities, some nearby, some thousands of miles away in the North. Cities including Detroit, with its auto industry, and Chicago saw armies of southerners, especially African Americans, relocate there in search of jobs. Some factory owners treated these immigrants with contempt. "The average man won't do a day's work unless he is caught and can not get out of it," said Henry Ford in March 1931. When thirty-two thousand people answered a call for job applicants at the Ford plant, company security personnel turned firehoses on the entire crowd in near-freezing temperatures. Many were hospitalized. "I know it's done them a lot of good to let them know that things are not going along too even always," Henry Ford said.[14] Insensitivity of that kind, particularly from people in positions of power, galled the Roach brothers, especially Bill. Later, he would face the same attitudes while fighting for decent wages and living conditions for poor industrial workers in Texas City.

By the time the Roach brothers arrived in Arkansas, hunger and anger were building in various communities around the state. In Tyronza, two local businessmen formed the state's first socialist movement with the specific intent of organizing the area's tenant farmers into a union. The businessmen had become outraged upon discovering that the living conditions of hogs on a nearby plantation were far better than those of the sharecroppers working there. The animals lived in an enclosed barn with a concrete floor and running water, whereas the tenant farmers were housed in substandard, one-room shacks with no plumbing, no water, and no kitchen facilities.[15]

Nearly two million southern and southwestern farmers worked on land owned by other people. A sharecropper's annual income was $312 and that of a hired laborer was only $180. Organizing could be dangerous, especially for the predominantly African American tenant farmers of rural Arkansas. Twelve years earlier an estimated seventy-five members of the Progressive Farmers and Household Workers Union of America were attacked by militant whites in eastern Arkansas. By 1931, however, people across the board, African American, Latino/a, Asian, and white, were starving and desperate.[16]

Several hundred sharecroppers and tenant farmers stormed into England, Arkansas, to demand the Red Cross reopen food stores that had suddenly closed. "Our children are crying for food and we're going to get it!" someone in the crowd yelled.[17] Scenes like these were repeated across the United States, in cities such as Minneapolis, San Francisco, Oklahoma City, and Chicago, as the Great Depression worsened. The Red Cross was not the only target. More often, grocery stores and warehouses were raided, often by women and bands of children.

"Paul Revere only woke up Concord," commented humorist Will Rogers at the time. "These birds [the food raiders] woke up America . . . you let this country get hungry and they are going to eat!"[18] Another statement by Rogers probably struck the Roach brothers as particularly poignant as they guided their station wagon through an increasingly hungry nation: "We are the first nation in the history of the world to go to the poorhouse in an automobile."[19]

As the brothers approached Little Rock, they began to focus on their impending meeting with the bishop of the Arkansas diocese. Suddenly, they remembered the letter of recommendation from Mother Saint James. With John at the wheel, Bill began digging through their belongings to retrieve the sealed envelope. He found it and sat on the passenger side of the station wagon holding it in his hand, momentarily transfixed, the wind rattling the paper as his eyes moved along the folded and glued flap. He wondered what his former teacher had written. So did

John. They were worried and suspicious. Suddenly, Bill ripped the envelope open. He pulled out the single sheaf and spread it open. A smile broke across his face as he silently scanned the words. John pressed him for information so Bill, now breaking into a laugh, read the letter aloud:

"I can not recommend these Roach twins for the seminary," Mother Saint James had written. "As far as I am concerned they have no religious or priestly vocation. . . . I would recommend anyone else but the Roach boys."[20] The letter concluded with a sincere warning to the reader to be wary of Bill and John Roach, adding that they were undoubtedly perpetrating some fraud.[21]

Both brothers laughed. Even though the letter, which they presumed they would need to gain admittance to the seminary, was utterly useless, seriously jeopardizing their whole mission, its content was the funniest thing they had encountered all day. Disregarding the consequences and with frenzied abandon, Bill ripped the letter to shreds and threw the scraps out the open window of the car, littering the streets of Little Rock. The pair was still laughing as they turned onto the grounds of St. John the Baptist Home Mission Seminary and parked in front of the old chancery building, part of a five-building complex comprising the campus.

Bill and John tumbled out of their station wagon, giggling but trying to compose themselves as they prepared to announce their arrival and pitch the idea of enrolling in the seminary with no money, no letter of introduction, and nothing to indicate a sincere religious calling. They barely had time to calm down before finding themselves in the outer office of the bishop, John Baptist Morris.[22]

In 1931, there were many areas of the diocese with no Catholic churches, no priests, and in some cases no Catholic parishioners. It was for this reason that incentives were offered to prospective clergy from outside the diocese. Still, there was no assurance that these unannounced visitors from the Northeast would gain admittance. Nevertheless, they trusted themselves to the main tenet of peregrinatio pro Dei amore, accepting without question the directive of their faith. The brothers waited for their opportunity to express their intentions to Bishop Morris.

Remembered as an affable person with a pleasant laugh and an infectious smile, Morris was also hardworking and practical. By 1931, he had done much to increase the presence of the Catholic church in Arkansas, a daunting task in this bulwark of Protestant thinking. Among other things, he was responsible for establishing a Catholic college at Little Rock. To continue his work, he needed more priests, and the key to more priests was more seminarians. Thus, after what appears to have been a relatively brief interview with the Roach brothers, Bishop Morris offered them both places at the seminary.[23]

John Roach mentioned the letter of introduction from a former teacher, but told Morris he and his brother had mislaid it. Bishop Morris told the brothers not to worry, they did not need it. The brothers' peregrinatio had led them through the open doors of the seminary. Of course, Bishop Morris desperately needed priests. Regardless, the twins impressed Morris as genuinely charming and possessed of a very real religious calling. The Roach twins, despite the attempted sabotage of Mother Saint James, were accepted.[24]

= 3 =

ARKANSAS

In 1931, St. John the Baptist Home Mission Seminary was located in the region of old Cammack Village, just northwest of downtown Little Rock. Situated at the apex of a hill overlooking a slight bend in the Arkansas River, the campus was idyllically picturesque. Little Rock was, and still is, a charming, compact city with tree-lined streets meandering up, down, and around a series of tightly clustered hills that rise on either side of the river. Despite the historic lack of a real Catholic presence in the city and throughout Arkansas, Catholics were among the earliest European visitors to the area.[1] Perhaps the earliest recorded Christian religious event in North America west of the Mississippi River took place fewer than one hundred miles from Little Rock. On June 25, 1541, Spanish explorer Hernando de Soto and his men sang a *Te Deum*, or hymn of praise, as they knelt before a cross on the western bank of the Mississippi River, which they dubbed "the Father of Waters."[2]

By the time the Roach brothers turned into the driveway of the campus of St. John's seminary and parked in front of the chancellery, Bishop Morris had been in charge of the Diocese of Little Rock for twenty-four years. Morris was only the third bishop of what was still a very new and developing diocese. He was a powerful, driven personality, the first American-born bishop of the diocese and founder of the seminary itself. Although Morris was of Irish descent, he was a native of Tennessee who brought not just a much-needed American viewpoint to his office, but also one of an American raised in the culture of the Old South, a culture whose racial attitudes he sought to change. Much of Morris's work sought to uplift the African American community through education, decent working conditions, and a living wage. This focus did not sit well with some in Arkansas.

Throughout much of his tenure, Morris battled racist, anti-Semitic, anti-immigrant, and anti-Catholic attitudes fueled by a bitter agrarian populist from Georgia named Tom Watson. Watson published the *People's Party Paper*, a white supremacist periodical that was widely read throughout the United States, particularly in the South. The prevailing sentiment articulated in the *Paper* and similar publications such as *The Menace* and its Arkansas sister magazine the *Liberator*, edited by a Baptist minister, made many minority groups, including Catholics, exceedingly unwelcome in many parts of the country, especially in Arkansas.[3]

In 1915, the Arkansas legislature passed the Convent Inspection Act. The act authorized law enforcement officials to make random searches of Catholic Church property, including schools, rectories, and convents, without cause or a search warrant, in clear violation of the US Constitution. The wave of anti-Catholicism swelled in the 1920s with the second rise of the archetypical American hate group, the Ku Klux Klan. First organized in Tennessee in 1866, during Reconstruction, the Klan had the primary goal of controlling former slaves by means of social and political terrorism. Never well organized, the original Klan as an institution had largely disappeared by the early 1870s, though the attitudes it espoused remained well entrenched in white culture, especially in the South. Its resurgence in 1915 was inspired by the release of D. W. Griffith's cinematically pivotal (and overtly racist) motion picture *Birth of a Nation*. This new version of the Klan, headquartered in Atlanta, Georgia, was very well organized. As a result it became exceedingly popular nationwide between 1915 and 1944.[4]

The local chapter of the Ku Klux Klan in Little Rock was very large—not only the largest chapter in the state, but also one of the largest in the nation. Among its leaders was the Reverend Harry Knowles of the Little Rock Disciples of Christ. Knowles was extraordinarily racist and anti-Catholic. Also fervently anti-Catholic was Little Rock resident Basil Edward Newton, who became one of the state's leading Klan lecturers.[5]

Throughout Arkansas, the Klan was particularly effective at transcending its usual limits as a purely racist organization, successfully resurrecting antiquated Victorian conventions and penetrating nearly every moral and ethical aspect of community life. The emphasis of Klan activity in the state was on political action and "law and order." Klan and pro-Klan political action committees targeted politicians who failed to fall in line with Klan policy for replacement. The practice was most potent in the early 1920s, when Klan-backed candidates swept every county and district office in and around Little Rock and took the governor's mansion as well. Elsewhere, it sufficiently frightened enough politicians to bring about much pro-Klan legislation.

The Ku Klux Klan also backed the publication of a Little Rock–based periodical called the *Arkansas Traveler*, which was especially vituperative and vitriolic in its denunciation of Catholics, Jews, immigrants, and ethnic communities. These groups, especially Catholics, were deemed responsible for the perceived moral decay of Arkansas. A Klan pamphlet distributed in Arkansas focused on Roman Catholic immigrants from Italy and Sicily. It read, in part, "Southern Europeans . . . can live on garlic and a little cheap meat. His wife—if he is married—will keep a dingy hut for him. Their religion is invariably Roman Catholic. . . . America must be kept Protestant if she wants to be kept American."[6] Despite the best efforts of the Klan, the *Arkansas Traveler*, and the *Liberator*, however, the Catholic Democratic candidate for president, Alfred E. Smith, carried the state of Arkansas in the 1928 general election.[7]

To counter the Klan's influence, Bishop Morris established as many new parishes as the diocese could support and opened a number of mission churches and schools, particularly in African American communities. By 1927, Arkansas had forty-six Catholic grade schools, seven academies, two colleges, and the St. John the Baptist seminary, with a combined total student enrollment of seven thousand. In addition, to combat the growing number of anti-Catholic publications, Morris increased the circulation of the *Guardian*, a diocesan newspaper he founded in 1911, known today as the *Arkansas Catholic*.[8]

In addition to anti-minority and anti-Catholic unrest fueled by groups like the Ku Klux Klan, an unprecedented crime wave was sweeping the nation. Murder was prevalent, particularly in the South where the homicide rate was five-and-a-half-times higher than in the rest of the nation.[9] Arkansas, in particular, was a playground and hideout for a vast cross-section of America's criminal underworld in the 1920s and 1930s, again despite the best "law and order" efforts of the Klan. It was in this vortex of hate and crime that the Roach brothers found themselves as they prepared to begin their seminary studies.[10]

The administrative heart of the Diocese of Little Rock was a complex of five buildings lining a circular drive. One of those buildings was St. John the Baptist Home Mission Seminary, located in Fitzgerald Hall on the west side of the drive, across from the chancery. The building was named for the second bishop of the diocese, Edward Fitzgerald (1867–1907), and housed both classrooms and a dormitory for the seminarians.

John and Bill Roach, as usual, were inseparable. The brothers were remembered as functioning as one person—a wildly kinetic, humorously self-effacing, mischievous entity composed of two people. Anecdotes of midnight ice-cream raids in the kitchen, or at the corner icehouse whenever supplies ran out, are numerous.

"Can't help it," one of them said. "Roaches are attracted to sweet stuff."[11]

Reprimands for leaving the seminary without permission, disrupting class, or generally wreaking havoc on fellow seminarians in the dormitory were met by the twins with laughter and mock pleas of innocence and cries for mercy. Somehow they got away with it, all of it. Their antics were more often than not annoying and juvenile, sometimes even dangerous. They once rigged a pail of water, kept on hand in case of fire, above a doorway leading into the dormitory. The brothers were trying to ensnare a fellow seminarian but caught a priest, one of their professors, instead. The trap did not work as planned. Instead of simply drenching the victim, the whole water-filled pail dropped from its perch above the door, knocking the priest over as it struck a glancing blow to his shoulder. The priest was not seriously hurt, but even the brothers realized they had gone too far. Their victim might have been killed. Such behavior would have been treated more harshly had it involved anyone else, but somehow John and Bill Roach slipped through with yet another reprimand. It was impossible to stay angry with the Roach brothers.[12]

But John and Bill Roach recognized the possibility of going too far. Fortunately, they were excellent students and well liked by the faculty, especially Father Joseph Murray. Murray, who spent his entire career on the same bluff overlooking the Arkansas River, either at the seminary or at the chancery, where he rose to the position of vicar-general, remembered the Roach brothers fondly. Despite their propensity for prankishness, Murray remembered them as "nice boys." He made more than one trip to Texas to visit them after they relocated there.[13]

The brothers also distinguished themselves elsewhere. Seminarians attending St. John the Baptist tuition-free were required to work a certain number of volunteer hours each week. John and Bill Roach helped in all areas of the seminary and even in the chancery, performing kitchen duty, janitorial services, groundskeeping, whatever was necessary. Though both worked vigorously and were apt to take the initiative in most ventures, always ready to infuse a bit of fun into every task, John stood out for his organizational skills and ability to coordinate multiple tasks into one venture. And although he remained incredibly impish in the company of his brother, John's serious side began to develop whenever he was on his own in Arkansas. Bill, forever ready to laugh, preferred engaging in hard physical labor, being hands-on, and rubbing elbows with fellow workers. These differences were not lost on seminary faculty.[14]

Another area of student life involved diocesan projects outside the seminary, including at an orphanage near Pine Bluff, Arkansas, forty-two miles southeast of Little Rock. One of Bishop Morris' projects, the orphanage opened in 1932 and, like many of the bishop's undertakings, it served primarily the African American community. Orphaned children were housed, schooled, and placed with African American families. The venture was never very successful and had to close after only a few years. Most African Americans in Arkansas were of Protestant faiths and never fully accepted the idea of working with Catholics. However, there were other reasons for the orphanage's ultimate demise, the Ku Klux Klan among them. Ironically, Klan propaganda accounted for much of the African American community's negative attitude toward the orphanage and the Catholics who operated it.[15]

On at least one occasion the Klan's opposition to the orphanage manifested in physical form. Seminarians working off their tuition served at the orphanage on a rotating basis by making daytrips on holidays and weekends, usually accompanied by one of the priests on the seminary faculty. Unsurprisingly, John and Bill Roach typically preferred to work together. On one of their trips to Pine Bluff, the accompanying priest noticed that a car seemed to appear from nowhere and had been following them since they crossed into Jefferson County.

"So what?" Bill asked. When the priest explained that outlaws and bandits often preyed on motorists, Bill's mood changed. "The Klan doesn't like us either," the priest added. "Probably nothing, though."

In Pine Bluff, the priest pulled over and stopped in a very visible, very public place. The car behind them appeared at first to be doing the same, slowing to a near-stop perhaps twenty yards away. But then it picked up speed, swung around them, and continued around a corner. Two men were inside, neither of whom looked their way as they passed. The priest put the car in gear, turned around, and continued on to the orphanage, five miles outside of town in the opposite direction.

"Shouldn't we tell the police?" John asked.

"It's nothing," the priest said.

After working all day at the orphanage, the trio started back to Little Rock in the dark. A few miles northeast of Pine Bluff, headlights appeared on the road behind them. A car was closing in fast. The priest slowed to let the car pass. As the vehicle came abreast of theirs, a blur of fluttering white robes could be seen filling the interior. The passing car then swerved, narrowly missing the driver's side front quarter panel of the diocesan car. Instinctively, the priest jerked the wheel to avoid a collision. The maneuver sent the car skidding along the gravel shoulder and slipping briefly into the shallow, dry drainage ditch running parallel to the road before it straightened out and eventually glided back onto the road. By then the other car was gone. The whole incident had passed in a matter of seconds.

John asked again whether they should contact the sheriff or local police. "'Love your enemy,'" the priest quoted with a tinge of sarcasm. "Isn't that what Matthew says? No, trust me. It won't do any good [to contact authorities]." He went on to explain that since the occupants of the other car had been wearing their gowns and hoods, they only meant to scare them. It would have been more dangerous if they had not cared whether they could be identified. "They won't be back," he said.[16]

The incident strengthened the Roach brothers' resolve to serve the public, not only the orphans, but also minorities and workers' rights groups, whether diocesan-sponsored or not. One organization the brothers sympathized with was the Share Croppers Union (SCU). Indeed, individual churches and other religious organizations, both Catholic and Protestant, contributed money and labor to support the union. Nationally known writers including Father John LaFarge Jr. (1880–1963), staff writer for *America* magazine, and pro-labor journalist Dorothy Day (1897–1980), supported the SCU as well.[17] Particularly active in eastern and southern Arkansas, the SCU was largely African American but had a large white membership as well. One of hundreds of socialist organizations that appeared during the Depression, it sought to prevent landowners from cheating sharecroppers out of their legal share of the profits of their work, a practice that was rampant at the time.[18]

The Roach brothers were developing a strong sense of social responsibility and evolving academically at the seminary. Theirs was part of a much larger, national experience, an experience rooted in the bitterness of the lost generation of World War I and reinforced by the dire economic hopelessness of the Great Depression. Much of the literature of the time reflects this experience. The work of F. Scott Fitzgerald exposed a frenetic materialism raging in the 1920s, perpetrated by characters bent on consuming much more than they could ever hope to replace. *Oil*, by Upton Sinclair, also focused on rabid materialism and unthinking conformity. William Faulkner, wounded in combat during World War I, wrote fiction framed within the very real origins of southern culture and its inevitable extinction. Meanwhile, John Steinbeck revealed the effects of the Great Depression on the most vulnerable of the nation's population. The Roach brothers' growing social awareness reflected the culture of their time.

At the close of the Roach brothers' second full year of classes, their time in Arkansas ended abruptly. The Great Depression was harming not only farmers and working-class individuals but a number of organizations as well, including the Diocese of Little Rock. Toward the end of May 1933, it was apparent that the diocese could no longer support seminarians who were enrolled in the work-study program. It was announced that beginning in the fall semester, all seminarians would be required to pay full tuition. John and Bill Roach, with no resources and no savings, were forced to drop out of St. John the Baptist Home Mission Seminary.

Packing was easy. The brothers owned next to nothing. What they did have, mostly textbooks and biographies of saints, they gave to fellow seminarians. They even donated their car to the diocese. Before being dropped off at the train station for the trip back to Pennsylvania, Bill decided to do one last thing. On the south side of Fitzgerald Hall, by either leaning out of a second-floor window or using a ladder, he painted a single word in large block letters: ROACH.[19] The painted word remained for decades, to the utter confusion of most future seminarians and diocesan workers, who had no idea of its history.

= 4 =
FROM JOHN TO MARY

John and Bill Roach spent the summer of 1933 in Pennsylvania, living with their family at the Stratford Court Apartments and working at their father's filling station. They spent much of their spare time with their old friend Dan Barrow, whose world-champion eight-oar crew from Penn AC had disbanded the year before. Dan's siblings recalled accompanying their older brother to collect the twins at the filling station, which they remembered as being so small it resembled "a kid's playhouse."[1]

Boathouse row along the Schuylkill River was a gathering place that summer. The Barrow family spent nearly every weekend on the riverbanks, watching race after race.[2] Since the breakup of his famed crew, Barrow had switched to single-shell sculling. Indeed, he was training for the 1936 Olympics, scheduled to take place in Berlin. The Roach brothers also worked out on the river that summer, but only for fun. Their focus was no longer athletic. While Dan Barrow looked eastward, toward the Olympics in Europe, the Roach brothers were again drawn to the Southwest.

Being unable to pursue seminary studies did not dampen the brothers' desire to become priests. On hearing the news that they would have to leave Little Rock, John and Bill began searching for another diocese that was not only in dire need of priests but willing to accept them, free of charge, into its seminary program. Father Murray, one of their professors at St. John's seminary and a native of Texarkana, suggested the brothers approach the Diocese of Galveston, in Texas.

It was a huge, sprawling clerical province, much of it mission territory. It seemed a likely choice and one that especially appealed to Bill. He had long been fascinated by the frontier history of Texas and all the folklore associated with that part of the world.[3] Over the summer in Pennsylvania, John made the final decision. He said, "Well, let's go down to Galveston and ask Bishop Byrne if he will take us."[4] They would arrive unannounced, just as they had done at Little Rock. The strategy had worked then, it might work again.

Father Murray was also familiar with St. Mary's Seminary, in La Porte, Texas. Its reputation by then was such that a number of dioceses were sending their seminarians there, particularly for their final year of theology.[5] Toward the end of the summer of 1933, the Roach brothers loaded their meager possessions into a car they had somehow acquired and prepared to embark on the 1,500-mile journey to the Texas Gulf Coast.

Texas was and still is a land of incredible contrasts. Geographically, its territory encompasses thick forests, rolling plains, semi-arid hill country, primeval basins, mountains, rivers, and more than four hundred miles of coastline along the Gulf of Mexico. It is a largely Spanish-English bilingual state. In addition, the European settlement and development of Texas in colonial times is inexorably linked to Spain and the Roman Catholic Church.[6]

The earliest recorded European visitors to what later became Texas were Álvar Núñez Cabeza de Vaca and three fellow explorers who traversed the area between 1528 and 1535. All four were Catholics from Spain. By the late seventeenth century, Catholic Spain controlled most of Texas, although René-Robert Cavelier, sieur de La Salle, did establish a French Catholic mission church on the Texas coast during this period.

During the eighteenth century, the Vatican assigned religious authority over the Texas territory west of the Pecos River to the Diocese of Durango, headquartered in Durango, Viceroyalty of New Spain (later Mexico). The region east of the Pecos was assigned to the Diocese of Guadalajara, in Guadalajara.

In 1779, the Vatican reassigned the religious governance of Texas east of the Pecos River to the Diocese of Linares o Nuevo León, in Monterrey. Then, largely because of the separation of Mexico from New Spain (1821), followed by the Texas revolution (1836) and the new republic's subsequent annexation by the United States (1845), the Vatican created the Diocese of Galveston on May 4, 1847. Its boundaries, carved from the Diocese of Linares o Nuevo León, were deliberately left undefined because the United States and Mexico were then at war and the location of the Texas border was disputed.[7]

The first bishop of the new diocese, Jean Marie Odin (1847–61), was of great interest to Bill Roach. An energetic and capable administrator, Odin felt quite at home on the back of a horse traversing the enormous expanse of his diocese, all 360,000 square miles of it. Odin's territory stretched from the Rio Grande to the northern Great Plains and included all or part of the future states of Oklahoma, New Mexico, Kansas, Colorado, and Wyoming. Twenty thousand Catholics and a dozen established churches were sprinkled throughout this vast space, served by Odin and a dozen other clergymen, collectively called "saddle priests" because of their principal means of transport.[8] The determination of Odin and his "saddle priests" filled Bill Roach with a sense of romance. From the moment he arrived in Texas, Bill was determined to emulate them. He told more than one person of his desire to become a "cowboy priest."[9]

By the time the Roach brothers crossed the low, two-mile causeway from the mainland to Galveston Island, in late August or early September 1933, the territory of the state of Texas had been reduced by 100,000 square miles and the diocese that once covered much of the state had itself been subdivided. Nevertheless, the Diocese of Galveston was still large, stretching east to the Sabine River, north to Nacogdoches, and west to the Texas Hill Country, north of Austin. As John and Bill knew, there were not enough priests to serve such a vast area. They counted on this fact weighing in their favor as they guided their old Ford, variously described as a Model A or a Model T, down Broadway toward the diocesan offices and their unannounced visit with Christopher E. Byrne, the fourth bishop of the Diocese of Galveston.[10]

Palatial Gulf Coast–style mansions lined either side of the avenue, their foundations raised above sea level to protect them from hurricanes, their yards a mix of brilliant flowers and exotic-looking trees, such as palms, magnolias, and enormous live oaks with great strands of Spanish moss sagging from their branches like grayish-white church veils. Not far away, along streets radiating from Broadway, stood the not-so-palatial homes of working-class and poor Galvestonians. These were smaller, much smaller, exhibiting varying degrees of disrepair and peeling paint but with the same mix of flowers and trees. The Great Depression had depleted household budgets, but not the island's lush vegetation.

The air was thick with salty humidity. The brutal late-summer sun evaporating surface water from the Gulf of Mexico, just a few blocks to the south, and from Galveston Bay to the north created a moist, hot blanket that clung to the streets and, indeed, to the whole island. Nevertheless, people were scurrying about in cars, on buses and trolleys, on bicycles, and on foot. They were natives—"born on island," or "B. O. I." The brothers had never seen a place quite like Galveston.

In terms of European colonization, Texas is often thought of as a rather young territory, and in many ways it is. However, European contact with Galveston Island predates that of much of the rest of North America, including the Roach brothers' home state of Pennsylvania. Originally inhabited by the Karankawa, the island was first visited by Cabeza de Vaca, who was shipwrecked on Galveston Island in 1528, just nine years after Hernán Cortés first landed in Mexico to begin his murderous conquest there. However, despite the excellent natural harbor on the island's north side, permanent European settlement of Galveston progressed slowly. In 1785, mapmaker José de Evia named the island for the viceroy of New Spain, Bernardo de Gálvez. Later, the name was anglicized to Galveston (Galvez Town).

The harbor was used as a naval base during Mexico's fight for independence from Spain in the early nineteenth century. Between 1816 and 1821, the infamous pirate Jean Lafitte occupied the island. When John and Bill Roach lived in the area, stories of pirate treasure being buried nearby were circulating, as they still do today. Bill, in particular, was fascinated by the tales.[11]

After the Texas revolution the city of Galveston was first platted as a real estate venture by Michel B. Menard and incorporated in 1839. By 1870 it was one of the nation's leading ports and the largest city in Texas, the first to install public electricity and the home of the state's oldest newspaper, the *Galveston Daily News*. After 1900, however, Galveston's size and influence slipped, due to a changing economy and the devastating 1900 hurricane. To date the nation's worst natural disaster, the hurricane struck the city on September 8–9 with sustained winds of 120 miles per hour and a deadly storm surge that swept a wall of water across the island. Six thousand were killed in Galveston alone. Another four to six thousand were lost elsewhere along the coast. Nearly every structure in the city was destroyed. Galveston was rebuilt, but in many ways it was never the same again.[12]

John and Bill Roach were yet to become aware of this history and the many legends surrounding it, but they were quite cognizant of Galveston's humid, subtropical physical presence as they drove east toward the chancery. Dripping with perspiration, they parked at the northwest corner of Broadway and Fourteenth Street. Before them stood an imposing mansion constructed of native Texas gray-and-pink granite, trimmed in a number of other materials, including white limestone and red sandstone. At the time referred to as "Gresham's Castle" after Colonel Walter Gresham, the original owner who built it in 1886, the imposing structure had been purchased by the Diocese of Galveston in 1923 for use as a chancery and the bishop's residence. Although only one bishop would ever live there, it was already beginning to acquire the new nickname by which it is known today, "Bishop's Palace."

The brothers briefly discussed their plan of action, deciding in the end that John, alone, would try to gain an audience with the bishop. He was more businesslike and adept at argumentation than Bill was. Besides, they thought the sight of just one, rather than two, prospective seminarians asking for a free ride might be easier on the bishop's eyes. So John ventured inside the chancery by himself. He planned not even to mention the presence of a brother waiting outside in the car until he was convinced the bishop might be amenable to the proposal, such as it was.

It seems incredibly optimistic, even quixotic, for the brothers to have ever thought a total stranger might arrive unannounced at the offices of any organization, far less one with the size and complexity of the Catholic Diocese of Galveston, and expect to gain an immediate audience with the head of that organization. However, that was the way John and Bill Roach operated. Things that seemed daunting and unattainable to others often seemed like rather natural, everyday circumstances to the two brothers.

John Roach stepped through the nineteenth-century entryway with electric lights on either side designed to resemble bunches of flowers, past the heavy sliding panels used to seal out storm surges and high winds during hurricanes, and announced himself in the spacious lobby, Gresham's former reception hall. In the car Bill, his clothes soaked with perspiration, watched anxiously as his twin disappeared through the Romanesque doorway, overshadowed by turrets and long, spindly chimneys. Then he turned his gaze to the brilliant white facade of Sacred Heart Cathedral across the street and prayed silently, hoping.[13]

Awaiting a reply to his request for an audience with the bishop, John glanced around the premises. It was difficult not to stare at the myriad details of the mansion, the hand-carved woods—such rarities as rosewood, white mahogany, and satinwood, along with more common American oak and maple—Persian rugs, and stained glass, all once possessions of the original owner, a Confederate veteran of the Civil War, attorney, congressman, and cofounder of the Gulf, Colorado, and Santa Fe Railroad.

What John could not see hidden inside the substantial stone walls was an equally substantial steel frame, a late-nineteenth-century innovation that enabled the house to survive the catastrophic force of the 1900 storm almost unscathed, one of the few structures in Galveston that did. Across the street, an earlier diocesan cathedral, constructed of the same stone masonry as Gresham's Castle but with no interior steel frame, did not survive the storm. The shimmering white church at the same location, whose facade Bill studied as he prayed in the car, was its replacement.

In the lobby a priest approached John and asked him to accompany him to the bishop's offices. John was stunned. The plan was working! He was actually going to meet with the bishop. Simultaneously excited and apprehensive, he followed the priest up the hand-carved staircase, passing a pair of stained glass windows on a landing fashioned like a pulpit. On the second floor, he was led through one ornate room into another. There, behind a large mahogany desk, scrutinizing a stack of papers, sat Christopher Edward Byrne, the fourth bishop of the Diocese of Galveston.

Byrne had a reputation as a formidable character, at times unbending and autocratic. But he was also described as "active [and] easy to approach," a man who was "friends with churchmen of all faiths." His closest personal friends included Protestant ministers, rabbis, and Orthodox priests. Politicians, including more than one Texas governor, all of them Protestant, admired Byrne. Many remembered him as a thoughtful man with a wide, friendly face and a warm sense of humor. He was the first bishop of the diocese to open ministries to Latino/a and African American communities. Byrne also had a profound love for children and a deep regard for the concept of the Good Samaritan. "If we had more love of children and of God," he once said, "we would have greater love for one another."

Most of all, however, Byrne was of Irish heritage, something John Roach hoped would play in his favor. John had no way of knowing at the time that Byrne had a preference for promoting non-native Texans as prospective seminarians. During his tenure he ordained more than two hundred priests, two-thirds of whom were from outside the state.[14]

John Roach and the bishop spoke for several minutes, making small talk at first. Roach was careful to point out his own Irish background, that he had traveled from Pennsylvania to be a missionary, and that he had been enrolled at the seminary in Little Rock. Eventually, notions of faith and vocation entered the conversation, and finally Roach broached the idea of entering St. Mary's Seminary. On hearing that the young man had no means of paying tuition, Byrne was not hopeful. Indeed, at first he told Roach there was no room in the program.

But as the conversation continued the bishop began to warm to Roach. Within a few minutes Byrne reversed his previous statement, telling Roach not to worry about a thing, saying that he would see to it that a place was made for him at the seminary. Smiling broadly, Roach blurted out, "That's good, because there's another one just like me in the car!" Byrne rose from his desk and stepped to the

window overlooking Broadway. Turning back to Roach, he smiled. "Okay! Come
to La Porte [site of the diocesan seminary] and we'll see what we can do. If you
two came all the way in that old car, we'll find room for you!"[15]

St. Mary's Seminary, founded in 1901 by the third bishop of the Galveston
diocese, Nicholas A. Gallagher, acted as more than a seminary. It was a boarding
school for young men and boys—serving as both a fully accredited high school
and a four-year college with an associated six-year seminary program attached.
In fact, the income from the high school program largely financed the college
and seminary, a detail that most certainly made it possible for Bishop Byrne to
so readily offer places to a pair of flat-broke strangers from Pennsylvania at the
height of the Great Depression.

The campus was located on Sylvan Beach, in La Porte, on the mainland some
thirty miles north of Galveston. Sylvan Beach in 1933 was still very picturesque,
located in a natural setting on the western shore of Galveston Bay, a favorite
recreational site for swimming, boating, hunting, and fishing. The petrochemical
industry, so identified with the region today, was in its infancy when the Roach
brothers first arrived in Texas. La Porte, Sylvan Beach, and St. Mary's Seminary
were still in a beautiful pastoral setting that attracted visitors from throughout
Texas and numerous neighboring states. Indeed, the region attained national
prominence beginning in the late 1920s because of regular appearances at the
Sylvan Beach Amusement Park by some of the most acclaimed big bands of all
time, including those led by Rudy Vallee, Phil Harris, and Benny Goodman.[16]

"Sylvan Beach was a bit of a playground," remarked one seminary graduate.
"Not the typical place to find a seminary."[17]

Yet St. Mary's Seminary, described as "a quiet community," was a serious,
scholarly institution with a national reputation whose students had little time for
anything other than school-related activities. During the week, a student's day
typically began at six in the morning and ended at eight-thirty in the evening
with lights out. Each minute was parceled between classes, typically from nine to
three, as well as daily mass, prayer time, study time, recreational activities, and
meals. Weekends afforded free time, but school catalogues of the day more than
imply an ambiance of constant supervision. Students were not allowed off-campus
without permission, nor were they allowed to drink alcohol, use profane language,
or engage in any sort of "rough conduct." Hazing was strictly forbidden.

However, the atmosphere was not all drudgery overseen by stern autocrats.
To the contrary, St. Mary's was a fun, interesting, and challenging institution.
There was football, basketball, handball, tennis, boxing, and baseball, the last

played on what was described as "the best amateur diamond in the state." The property fronted a clean, sandy beach with a 1,200-foot pier, bathhouse, diving board, and numerous rowboats for exploring nearby Morgan's Point, Red Fish Reef, or any other part of the bay. Inland, adjacent to the property, a number of freshwater streams wound through groves and pine forests. It was a peaceful, contemplative area where students could be as physically active or inactive as they desired.[18]

The campus was entirely self-sufficient. Fresh water was pumped from a thousand-foot well into a concrete holding tank. Electricity and steam heat were generated on-site. A farm owned by the diocese just west of La Porte supplied all the food and dairy products consumed at St. Mary's. Kitchen and other domestic chores were performed largely by a group of Dominican sisters.

Of the several buildings on campus, the oldest was a wooden structure from the late nineteenth century. It was once the Sylvan Beach Hotel but was damaged so severely in the 1900 storm that it and the surrounding property were sold to the diocese the following year. After being repaired and extensively renovated, it housed both classrooms and residences.[19] Then in 1908 a new concrete building was constructed for lay students, and the old hotel became the exclusive residence of faculty and seminarians.

By the time the Roach brothers arrived, the old hotel had been moved several hundred feet from the beach and had acquired a concrete sheath of galleries that surrounded the original wooden core. It had also received updated plumbing and heating, but the wood deteriorated visibly during the years the Roach brothers attended St. Mary's and continued to do so afterward. The place was nevertheless idyllic, the invitation from the bishop was sincere and secure, and the future looked bright.

Not long after their enrollment at the seminary, the Roach brothers faced a major problem. It involved Bill specifically, but what affected one brother affected them both. During a routine physical exam to enter the seminary, Bill was diagnosed with diabetes. Bill had been troubled recently with recurring pain in one of his legs. As a result of the diagnosis, he was told the leg might have to be amputated. The diagnosis threatened Bill's acceptance into the seminary—and if Bill was not accepted, John would quit.[20]

Rather than give up though, the brothers met with the college president, Monsignor J. T. Fleming. They begged for another glucose tolerance test for Bill. They argued that the first test had been inaccurate due to a poor diet. Neither brother had been eating properly, especially Bill, a trait that would remain with

him the rest of his life. Both brothers had lost a lot of weight, partially due to lack
of money and partially as a type of religious penance. To demonstrate his weight
loss, Bill ripped open his shirt and pressed the palms of both hands against his
side, drawing the skin tight, grossly exaggerating the outline of his rib cage.

"See, Monsignor," he laughed. "I'm nothing but skin and bone!"[21]

Fleming, like nearly everyone else who encountered the twins, succumbed
to their charm and humor. He agreed to allow a follow-up exam and a second
tolerance test. To prepare, the brothers prayed a novena. Then they went to the
movies to lose themselves in flickering images and light. The subsequent test was
negative for diabetes. The attending physician declared the first test invalid and
told Bill no surgery would be required. Bill was free to enter St. Mary's.

Some in the diocese took this development as the sign of a miracle and a
demonstration of the power of prayer. Others suspected that Bill manipulated
the test results by severely altering his sugar intake beforehand, adding that he
continued to be bothered by symptoms of diabetes, including periodic debilitating
pain in one leg. He definitely walked with a pronounced limp thereafter, a feature
that made him stand out from his brother. Regardless, the incident was unusual
enough for the diocese to document it as a possible example of self-healing and
submit it to the Vatican. Thus, before they had even begun classes, the Roach
brothers were generating much talk. Their reputations preceded them.

"Before I ever met them, there were stories circulating about those two." One
classmate recalled.[22]

There were around twenty-five to twenty-seven seminarians at St. Mary's in
any given year during the 1930s. Within this community the Roach brothers
were remembered as excellent students. In addition to the usual college cur-
riculum—physics, chemistry, languages (especially Latin), biology, mathematics,
and history—seminarians studied two years of philosophy and not less than
four years of theology.[23] Seminarians were always very busy. In addition to their
studies, they all taught in the high school. In fact, it has been observed that the
great success of the high school was due to the hard work of the seminarians.
John Roach taught grammar. Bill taught arithmetic and religion.[24]

There was a great deal of camaraderie, especially at mealtime. The refectory
was a large, open room measuring 50 feet by 140 feet. Faculty and students dined
together, six to a table arranged by age. The seminarians often clustered together,
engaging in heated discussions over which student was the most brilliant. Acting
as young men sometimes do, criticizing everything as a matter of course, many

would present their arguments point by point, outlining the reasons why their choice was the most brilliant. No one ever chose himself, however.

One seminarian proposed a particular candidate, a fellow from Ireland. No one else agreed, chiding the seminarian for his choice. Some said the candidate exhibited "strange quirks." The others' disapproval did not sway the seminarian's opinion, however. "He *is* strange," he admitted. "But he *is* the most brilliant!"

Through it all, the Roach brothers had remained uncharacteristically silent. Bill, in particular, grew bored. Standing, he glanced around the table and announced, "I've got to go!"

"But, Bill," his brother said, "you've always got to go."

"You know," Bill retorted, "when nature calls."

"Well, then, you'd best take *The City of God*. It's got eight hundred pages," John replied.

Everyone at the table burst into laughter at the idea of the great book by Saint Augustine being used as bathroom reading. The surreal spontaneity and irreverence of the exchange was exactly what the other seminarians (and faculty) had come to expect from the brothers.

"We get a great deal of spiritual reading done by taking *The City of God* with us when nature calls!" Bill concluded as he walked away, smiling, clutching something in his hand. Everyone looked. He actually *was* on his way to the bathroom. And he was indeed carrying a copy of Saint Augustine's book. More laughter.[25]

Bill's interest in Saint Augustine was not purely academic. He had grown to greatly admire the North African bishop whose importance to the development of early Christian thought cannot be overstated. Augustine's influence is so profound that both Catholics and Protestants accept him as a universal source of faith and spirituality. The corpus Augustine left is enormous: 113 books and treatises, more than 200 letters, and 500 sermons survive. His monumental *The City of God*, along with *Confessions*, are considered two of the greatest works of western literature, religious or otherwise. Bill's developing spirituality was deeply influenced by the philosophy of Augustine.[26]

First, *Confessions* appealed to Bill, as it has to centuries of readers, because of its frank autobiographical look at a fellow human's battle to overcome the temporal, often meaningless aspects of existence. If we bother to examine ourselves as closely as we should, we can easily relate our own foibles to St. Augustine's experience. Of particularly note is the very moving passage describing the moment Augustine realizes that his life to that point has been rather aimless—a passage amazingly honest, candid, and blunt in his assessment of himself and his licentious pursuit of carnal pleasure. While reading *Confessions,* Bill thought of his own childhood, of the years spent in angry, malicious defiance of circumstances beyond his control. In Augustine he found a kindred spirit, a voice reaching across the centuries, more than sixteen hundred years, guiding him to a deeper sense of self and purpose.

In *The City of God*, Bill found an application of *Confessions* to the history of humankind. Much of Bill's own personal philosophy would derive from the major tenets of *The City of God*, especially that loss of worldly goods is not a bad thing, property is irrelevant, and misfortune can be providential and foster true spiritual development. These sentiments are found throughout the New Testament, including Luke's Gospels.[27] In *The City of God* Augustine also concludes that only grace and goodness exist, that evil is nonexistent and thus cannot be a creation of God. What is perceived as evil is actually the absence of grace and goodness, a loss that occurs when humans, through the gift of free will, make bad choices. Further, between *The City of God* and *Confessions*, Augustine allows that all humans, steeped as they are in their human imperfections, should understand that their past, bad choices and all, can be used as a foundation to build a more productive and meaningful future.

Although some have interpreted Augustine's message as a narrow, pessimistic view of his own world in the last decades of the western Roman Empire, on another level it is really a very universal celebration of optimism. And it was that sense of optimism which Bill Roach took with him, even to the bathroom.[28] *The City of God* was in keeping with Bill's other devotional influences, particularly Mary. He and his brother had long been committed to Mary, the supreme Catholic symbol of spiritual rebirth, life, and hope. Bill's knowledge that his own mother had prayed to the Virgin shortly before she died reminded him that from her death came new life, his own and that of his brother. That fact was never lost on Bill.

The whole concept of Mary is one of consummate optimism tempered by tragedy, the tragedy of the death of her son, Jesus Christ, leading to the hope of spiritual rebirth because of that death. To Bill it resonated perfectly, even if in his case the roles of mother and son had been reversed. The personal tragedy of his mother's death was tempered by his growing determination to make something of the life she gave him, to achieve a sense of personal salvation through self-sacrifice and giving. The same message was at the heart of some of Bill's other great influences: the ancient Irish-Celtic monastic concept of peregrinatio pro Dei amore, Saint Catherine of Siena, Saint Joseph the Carpenter, and most especially Saint Augustine. These inspirations became the catalyst for Bill's rapidly evolving spirituality. But there was something else: he wanted to be a martyr, to go out in a blaze of light, like a meteorite. "He prayed for a dramatic death," said a fellow seminarian, "a dramatic death in the service of his fellow humans."[29]

Bill began fasting perpetually, losing more weight. His fellow seminarians noticed. The faculty noticed. His brother noticed. Water was his staple, that and cigarettes. He was up to two packs a day. But his vitality and positive outlook only increased. He was everywhere, smiling, joking, wagging his finger in various faces, carrying on as he always had, moving rapidly from class to class, partaking in various activities, volunteering off-campus, a bundle of energy. Beneath his flowing black tunic, however, he was becoming thinner and thinner. His limp became more pronounced. His complexion grew pale, taking on the look of smoky-white alabaster. He was becoming an enigma, a friendly, happy-go-lucky, intensely spiritual enigma.[30]

Bishop Byrne visited the seminary frequently. He loved the place, seemingly using it as a retreat, a respite from the intensity of the chancery. He would occupy one of the vacant dorm rooms in the old hotel, making himself quite comfortable, taking his shoes off, and relaxing. His door was always open. Anyone who stopped by was welcomed with a big smile. "Come on in!" He would say, "Let's talk!"

Bishop Byrne liked both Bill and John Roach, who were clearly his favorites at St. Mary's. Whenever Byrne was on campus, Bill Roach would always spot him. "Oh, there's Byrne," he would say excitedly. "He's here at the seminary!" Before long, Bill would knock at the bishop's door. The two men would talk and joke about a variety of things, personal stories, diocesan matters, and world affairs. Eventually, Bill would always turn the subject to his post-seminary dream. He lobbied hard for a missionary assignment, a posting to one of the diocese's more remote parishes, one with a sparsely distributed Catholic community.

"Bishop Byrne, I have a great desire to be a missionary in deep West Texas," Roach would say. And smiling broadly he would add, "I want to be a cowboy more than anything. Oh, a cowboy priest!"[31] But Bill wanted to be more than a "cowboy priest." Byrne recognized that Bill would be a cowboy priest who would set about building churches and converting the population.

In John Roach, the bishop spotted a talent for organization. It was apparent to many at the time that John was already being groomed for an administrative position within the diocese, probably in some capacity in the bishop's administrative offices. He was already working off-campus for Byrne part time.

Compared to John, Bill possessed a deeper interest in the lives of others. He liked being in the field, getting directly involved, working one-on-one with parishioners.[32] "I preferred Bill's company to John's," said one seminarian. "Bill was more sensitive, pastoral. He had a great deal of real human empathy, feeling. John was a very good person too, mind you, very devout. It's just that Bill had this ability to make nearly everyone feel so darned special. But, of course, it was Bill who was special. The rest of us just mirrored his wonderful quality."[33]

The Roach brothers, along with four others, were ordained by Bishop Byrne in St. Mary's Kirwin Memorial Chapel at 9:30 A.M. on May 18, 1939. Three days later, in separate back-to-back services, John and Bill Roach celebrated mass for the first time. The location was the Church of the Nativity of the Blessed Virgin Mary in Media, Pennsylvania. Their father and stepmother were in attendance, and one of the ushers was their long-time friend from the Penn AC, Dan Barrow.

The twins had remained in close contact with their old friend. As seminarians they had been able to see him several times a year when they returned to Pennsylvania for holidays or summer breaks. They were on hand to wish Barrow good luck when he left Pennsylvania to compete in the 1936 Olympics in Berlin, Germany, the games made famous by Adolf Hitler's outrage at the success of African American track-and-field star Jesse Owens. Barrow won a bronze medal in the single-scull rowing event.[34]

The same summer, 1936, Barrow and the Roach brothers worked with Jack Kelly Sr. on Franklin Delano Roosevelt's campaign. Sometimes Kelly's children, Jack Jr. and Grace, who were under ten at the time, would visit campaign headquarters. The children also roamed the banks of the Schuylkill River with the Roach brothers as Barrow trained in his shell, christened "the Jack Kelly Boat." Like his father before him, Jack Jr. would take up rowing and go on to be an Olympic gold medalist. Grace, growing up with no aptitude for athletics, would distinguish herself as an Academy Award–winning actress.

By 1939, the year of Bill and John's ordination, Jack Jr. was twelve years old and Grace was ten. Dan Barrow had moved on from rowing, now working for a large insurance corporation and living in New York City. He told the brothers there was a chance he could be transferred to Texas.

"I don't know" said Bill, in mock seriousness. "There's not a lot of room in Texas!"

"Yeah," agreed John, in equally mock seriousness. "The movies make it look so big."

"Little, bitty, tiny place," Bill said, shaking his head.

"We'll see what we can do," John added, drawing in a deep breath as if he were pondering some major undertaking.

"Yeah," Bill said. "We'll be in touch in case some space opens up down there."

The Roach brothers remained in Pennsylvania for two weeks, renewing old acquaintanceships and generally relaxing after their eight-year odyssey to the priesthood. Sometime in June, however, they received word to return to the diocese. The bishop was ready to issue their assignments.[35]

= 5 =

THE COWBOY PRIEST

Not everyone knew him, but most knew of him. Many would see him, here
and there, in Killeen, Gatesville, Burnet. It was an unusual sight, the old car
rolling to a stop, the driver's side door opening, one Nocona boot hitting the
dusty earth, then another. The emerging figure would then straighten up beside
the vehicle, a long black Roman cassock tumbling over his boot tops. The thin,
almost ethereal frame, barely filling the gown, was topped by a thick crop of
windblown hair. A Roman collar separated the hair and head from the narrow,
bony shoulders. Dragging one foot slightly and grinning broadly, he would
move from the road. Then, after surveying the rolling terrain, he would look
skyward, pull something from his pocket, and place it in a shallow hole he
dug with his boot heel in the rocky ground. After the car pulled away, some
would approach the partially covered object. A few recognized the image, most
did not: a small statue of Saint Joseph. Whatever the case, no one disturbed
the figurine.[1]

Bill Roach was only a few weeks away from his thirty-first birthday when he
arrived in Lampasas, in the heart of the Texas Hill Country, in the summer of
1939 to take charge as pastor of the sprawling St. Mary's parish. Bill's appointment
had caused friction among other diocesan priests with more seniority. To be
assigned to such a position so soon after graduation from the seminary was very
unusual.[2] Not that St. Mary's parish was considered a prize rung on the ladder of

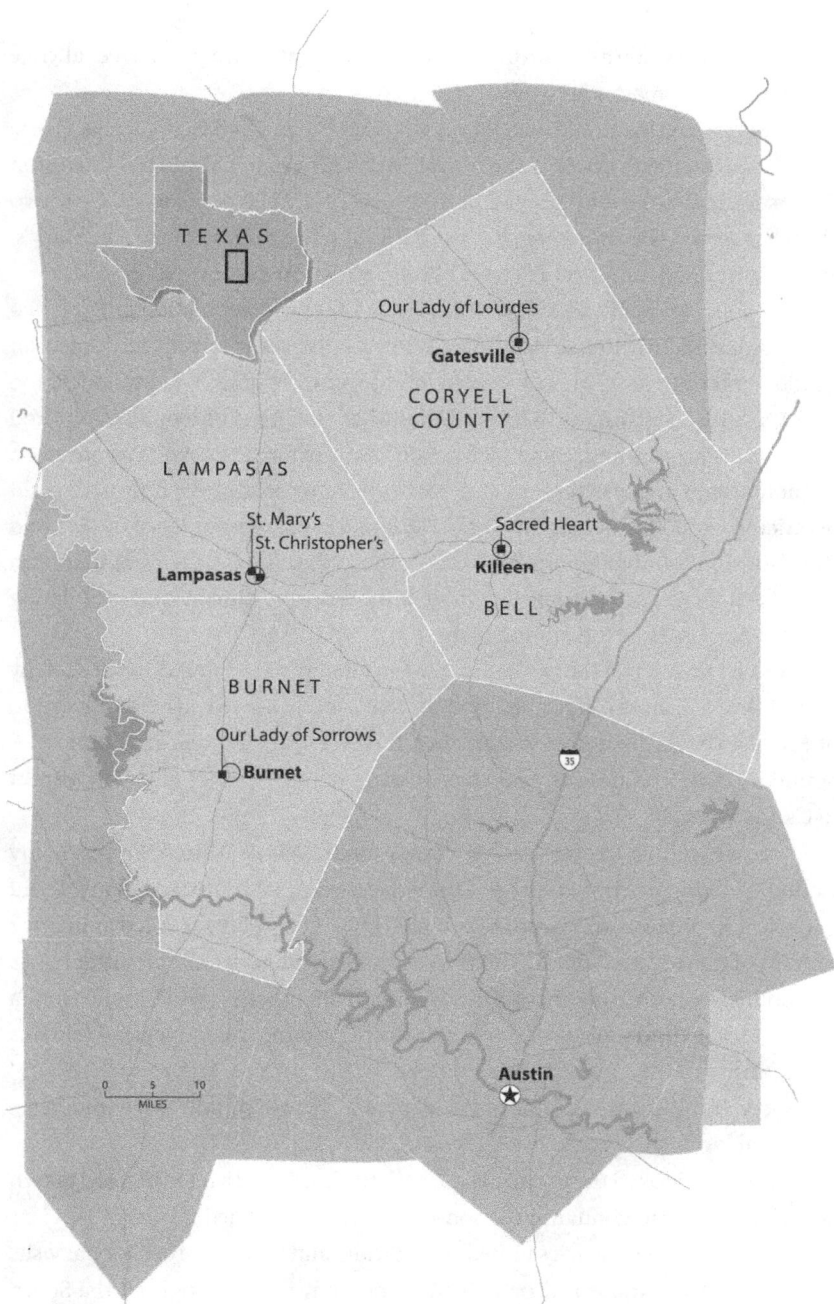

TEXAS

Our Lady of Lourdes
Gatesville

CORYELL
COUNTY

LAMPASAS

St. Mary's
St. Christopher's
Lampasas

Sacred Heart
Killeen

BELL

BURNET

Our Lady of Sorrows
Burnet

35

0   5   10
MILES

Austin

St. Mary's Parish, Texas, showing the locations of five of the churches built by Father Bill Roach, 1939–1945. *Map by Carol Zuber-Mallison.*

diocesan success. It was no ordinary parish and would have proven a challenge to any priest, no matter how much seniority he had.

Encompassing the three counties of Lampasas, Burnet, and Coryell, plus a piece of Bell County, it was not only the largest parish geographically in the Galveston Diocese, but also one of the smallest in terms of Catholic population. Only two churches served the entire area in 1939, including the parish church, St. Mary's, an aging frame structure at Fifth and Broad Streets in Lampasas.[3]

In Spanish colonial and Mexican times, the European population of Texas had been predominantly Roman Catholic. However, the Texas revolution, largely an Anglo-Protestant movement, initiated intense anti-Mexican, and by association anti-Catholic, sentiments. Although the Mexican government had required the thousands of immigrants flowing into Texas before the revolt to convert to Catholicism, it appears that most did so only superficially. Even though eight practicing Catholics signed the Texas Declaration of Independence in 1836 and Sam Houston solidly supported a Texas Catholic diocese, the then-popular term "non-Catholic Catholic" applied to most of the more prominent land speculating revolutionaries, Houston among them.

Mexico's invasion of the new republic in an attempt to reclaim its former colony only stoked the animosity. Statehood, in 1845, and the subsequent US invasion of Mexico the following year, solidified the ever-growing cultural enmity. A boundary of hatred and suspicion has existed ever since, especially with respect to Catholicism.[4]

Upon his return from the Civil War, William Mark Wittenberg, the only Catholic landowner in Lampasas County, experienced much acrimony. It did not help that he was a sheep rancher. At the time, sheep were regarded as inferior bearers of disease and evil by those in the cattle industry. All of Wittenberg's neighbors were cattle ranchers. One evening, Wittenberg arrived home from a business trip to find a group of ranchers gathered around the smoldering remains of his barn.

"Sorry, Mr. Wittenberg," one of the men said. "But we couldn't save your barn. It's a total loss."

Wittenberg looked the group over. "Well, the Lord giveth and the Lord taketh away," he said. "But goddamn the son-of-a-bitch that burned my barn!"[5]

Prior to 1892, missionaries visited sporadically and there were occasional visits from one of the famous railroad chapel cars prominent throughout the South and West in the late nineteenth and early twentieth centuries. Fitted with altars, pews, confessional, office, and priest's lodging, chapel cars served all religious functions, including masses, weddings, and baptisms.[6] By 1880, Wittenberg and his family felt so isolated that they constructed a small chapel on their property, seven miles west of Lometa, the first Catholic place of worship in Lampasas County. The material was hauled by horse-drawn wagon from Round Rock, eighty-one miles southeast of the Wittenberg ranch. Once a month or so, a priest would travel from Temple, seventy-nine miles to the east. Wittenberg would receive advance notice of the impending priestly visit by mail, giving the family time to spread word around the vast territory so that every Catholic within range could attend.[7]

In 1885, a second church was constructed in nearby Lampasas. St. Mary's was a one-story pier-and-beam structure, enclosing perhaps 1,200 square feet. The exterior was sheathed in tier-drop siding. The roof was steeply angled, rising from the four sides to a central peak, like a small pyramid, surmounted by a crucifix. A centrally placed entrance stood directly beneath a small pediment, breaking the line of the front fascia. Another crucifix stood at the apex of the pediment. Two Gothic-style lancet windows with stained glass were located on either side of the door. Three more such windows were mounted above the door. The lancets could not be opened, but five windows on either side of the building could, affording much needed cross-breezes during hot weather. Inside, apart from the church hall itself, the only enclosed room was the sacristy, measuring approximately three feet by six feet.

Regular services did not begin at St. Mary's until 1892, conducted by a handful of priests who roamed the territory by horseback. Most came from Temple, fifty-five miles east of Lampasas, although some ventured from as far as Galveston. These visiting priests often spent the night in the tiny sacristy. Thirty-five years would pass before the first resident priest arrived in Lampasas, only twelve years before Bill Roach's own arrival.[8]

In 1900, a chapter of the Dominican Sisters purchased the building and grounds of the former Centenary College, now abandoned, located on a forty-acre tract one mile north of Lampasas. In October, they opened St. Dominic's Villa, a Catholic boarding school for girls.[9] The campus was pastoral, quiet, with large oak trees and meadows of wild Johnson grass, accentuated by random, impressive growths of Texas prickly pear cactus. The main building resembled an antebellum plantation home, with columns and deep porches. Interior furnishings of plush red fabric filled Victorian-style parlors, and the residences were comfortable.

Students from throughout the United States attended the school, as did a few local girls. Although the student body was largely Roman Catholic, admission was not restricted to Catholics. Girls of many different faiths were represented. One student from Lampasas County was Ida Wittenberg, daughter of William, the man who built a small chapel on the family property near Lometa. She immediately became aware of rumors circulating about the school, rumors that the girls were not students but unwed mothers-to-be, juvenile delinquents, or some other form of social outcast, and that St. Dominic's Villa was, in fact, a reform school. Long after Wittenberg's graduation, the rumors persisted.

Local resentment of the institution escalated in the early 1920s with the rapidly rising power and influence of the Ku Klan Klan.[10] The sisters and students at St. Dominic's Villa began receiving threatening letters. By 1925, so many families had withdrawn their daughters from the school that it was forced to close. The building and grounds were used briefly as a retirement home for aging Dominican nuns, but in 1929 the Dominican order sold the property and withdrew completely from central Texas.[11]

By the time Bill arrived in Lampasas ten years later, the Ku Klux Klan still existed but had lost power as a cohesive political institution. Despite the lack of organization, Klan attitudes remained pervasive, including vigilantism and open hatred of immigrants, African Americans, Jews, Latino/a communities, and Catholics. Hostility toward the last two groups was particularly prevalent at the time. Indeed, animosity toward the Latino/a community, strongly associated with Catholicism, was open and quite visible in the Hill Country when Bill arrived.[12]

Businesses that supported the Ku Klux Klan often identified themselves to members of the "secret empire" by incorporating the letters "KKK" in the company name. For instance, the Koffee Kup Kafe, which operated in a Hill Country town well into the 1990s, was in business during Roach's time. And despite statewide anti-masking laws aimed at the KKK, Klansmen periodically paraded through Lampasas, trying to intimidate groups or individuals they considered unacceptable. Robed men would interrupt Protestant church services and publicly contribute money and offer praise for clergy who espoused Klan ideals. They would also enter Catholic churches, including St. Mary's in Lampasas, to intimidate parishioners. These Klansmen likely thought themselves unrecognizable beneath their flowing white disguises. However, most were easily identified by their boots, or even more telling, their horses and automobiles.[13]

Lampasas County resident Beth King remembered being referred to as "an idol worshiper" because of her Catholic faith. The idea that Catholics worship idols is a centuries-old misconception, rooted in the beliefs of Martin Luther himself. Among other things, Luther referred to the Vatican as sacrilegious because of its use of religious imagery. In the twentieth-century United States, evangelical

Bishop Alma Bridwell White stated that "unless America fought Rome, we shall be swept into paganism," a sentiment echoed by others of her ilk.[14]

Far from being used for idol worship, Catholic religious images have long been teaching tools, especially in the Middle Ages when the vast majority of Christians were illiterate. Each church became a book in stone, glass, and paint, spreading the story of Christianity to people who could neither read nor write. Because European literacy was much more widespread by the sixteenth century, Luther found the imagery no longer relevant and railed against it, especially the money spent to acquire it. Though he may have had a point about lavish expenditures, the accusation of idol worship is a complete misinterpretation of fact.

Beth King and others were also chastised for the liturgical practice of eating fish on Fridays, once a regular part of Catholic life and profoundly misunderstood by beef-eating Hill Country ranchers. Another resident, raised Protestant, remembered friends and acquaintances carefully examining her skull for evidence of growing horns after she converted to Catholicism as an adult. Others, however, remembered no animosity whatsoever toward Catholics in the Hill Country.[15]

Not all Anglo-Saxon Protestant Texans embraced the populist hate-mongering of the Ku Klux Klan, however. On October 2, 1922, Sheriff Bob Buchanan and two deputies attempted to stop a Klan march on the streets of Lorena, about sixty-five miles northwest of Lampasas. Declaring it illegal to parade locally with masks, the sheriff grabbed a burning cross held by a Klansman and was promptly shot under the right arm. A riot ensued, resulting in two men being shot, including the sheriff, and five being stabbed. One victim died. Amazingly, a grand jury ultimately declared that the sheriff "had no right to interfere with something that was none of his business."[16]

In Houston, Mayor Oscar Holcomb refused to bow to the Klan's demand that he fire Catholic city employees. In Galveston, a Jewish rabbi and a Catholic priest successfully blocked a Klan march through the streets. Governor Miriam Ferguson served two separate terms (1925–27, 1933–35). Although publicly anti-Klan, with actions to back up her words, she and her husband were notably anti-Semitic. Governor Dan Moody (1927–31), was very anti-Klan, both publicly and privately. As district attorney for Williamson County, he was the first prosecutor in the United States to win criminal convictions against Klan members.

Despite fervent opposition to the Klan in Texas, much hatred and ignorance persisted. In Houston, a white lawyer who had African American clients was tarred, feathered, and partially scalped by the Grand Goblin of the Klan's western district and several other men. In Dallas, two reporters for the *Dallas Times*

Herald were abducted and taken, blindfolded, to some unknown location to witness the merciless beating of an African American. The victim, who worked at the Adolphus Hotel in downtown Dallas, was accused of some impropriety with a white woman. He was tied to a fence and lashed with a blacksnake whip until he was unconscious and bleeding. The perpetrators then burned the letters "KKK" on his forehead with acid.

The Catholic owner of a laundry business was run out of Waco on threat of violence, both because of his religion and because his business was undercutting a rival laundry owned by a Klansman. To varying effect, the Klan would also boycott businesses owned by Catholics, African Americans, Jews, and anybody not conforming to Klan ideals. When members of the Klan won election to public office they would implement policies designed to marginalize and eliminate their enemies. Their tactics included firing or otherwise removing Catholic and Jewish government employees, particularly those on school boards. All these practices persisted in 1939, the year Father Bill Roach arrived in Hill Country.[17]

Just a few weeks into his tenure at St. Mary's, Bill was working late at night in the tiny rectory next to the church. Through the open window he heard a pickup truck approach and pass. The sound of a vehicle on the street in that sleepy little town so late was unusual enough, but when he heard it turn around and come back, Bill looked up. Through the window he saw a black truck pull slowly to a stop across the street. Only mildly interested at that point, he went back to work on plans for the construction of a new church rectory, the first of many improvements he had already identified as desperately needed in the parish.

Occasionally, he would gaze at the truck. Somebody was sitting in the cab, more than one person. "Kids drinking," he thought to himself. "Or maybe the truck broke down." Bill got up to investigate. Just then, the doors of the truck opened and three figures emerged, dressed in the robes of the Ku Klux Klan. They positioned themselves in front of the vehicle as Roach stepped outside. Roach knew about St. Dominic's Villa. He remembered Arkansas. He also remembered the Klan's particularly vehement anti-Catholic persecutions in his home state of Pennsylvania only ten years before.[18] For several moments Roach and the Klansmen faced each other, neither side moving, neither side speaking. Sensing something hesitant in the manner of the men before him, Bill decided to try something.

Glancing down and gesturing at his cassock, he spoke. "Say fellas. Just because I'm wearing a robe around town doesn't mean everybody has to," he said with a grin.

One of the Klansmen chuckled slightly then broke it off abruptly. Another shot his fellow Klansman a look, then turned back. The third fellow registered no reaction. The four figures stood in the darkness, silently regarding each other for several more moments. Bill decided the standoff was going nowhere.

"Well," he said. "I've got to get back to work. The parish needs a rectory. The parish needs a lot of things."

Roach flicked his cigarette butt to the ground and instinctively reached in his pocket for another smoke. The three hooded figures flinched. Roach halted, his hand halfway out of his pocket. Watching the Klansmen carefully, he withdrew a crumpled pack of cigarettes and a box of matches, placed one of the smokes in his mouth, and lit it. The Klansmen relaxed. Roach took a drag.

"You know where to find me. If you ever want to talk, I'm ready." He then turned and stepped inside. A few minutes later he heard muffled voices, metal doors opening and shutting, and the sound of the truck driving off.

A week later, three men in a black pickup truck pulled up beside Roach as he was walking to the post office. They got out, introduced themselves, and volunteered to help build the new rectory when the time came.

"What church do you men belong to?" Roach asked.

"Baptist."

"Methodist."

"Presbyterian."

Roach smiled. "I've always liked Baptists, Methodists, and Presbyterians!"[19]

Apart from that one incident, and a few minor episodes when he was denied service in some of the smaller, neighboring towns because of his cassock and Roman collar, Bill had few problems in the parish. A firm believer in the philosophy of St. Augustine, he felt, just as Augustine wrote in *City of God*, that evil is nonexistent, that humans through the gift of free will simply make bad choices.[20] Roach hoped to develop the ability to steer humans away from those bad choices. He loved the Texas Hill Country and would come to know it intimately.

From the outset, Bill Roach immersed himself in the Hill Country culture, visiting ranches, country dances, and stock shows. He had always wanted to be a "cowboy priest," traversing the countryside in the manner of Bishop Odin and his "saddle priests." If it would have been the least bit practical, Bill would have learned to ride a horse, abandoning automobiles and the twentieth century altogether.

Roach was intrigued by the history of the region. The name Lampasas was derived from Lampazos de Naranjo, Mexico, the origin of the Franciscan monks who founded missions in the area in the eighteenth century. When the wife of a nineteenth-century settler named Moses Hughes was cured of a serious illness by bathing in one of the many local sulfur springs, the event helped establish

Lampasas as a leading central Texas health resort. The idea of the area's healing powers appealed to Bill. But he was particularly enthralled by oft-mentioned stories of a bloody six-month feud between two families that resulted in three separate gunfights, one occurring right on the town square.[21] To Roach, Lampasas was an authentic Wild West town, right down to shoot-outs on the streets. Despite his aversion to violence, Bill was not beyond being caught up in the romance of it all.

Initially, there was a sense of personal urgency in Bill's activity. His appointment was meant to be temporary, only a few weeks in fact. He had to act fast to accomplish anything, to be a "cowboy priest" converting the West. The previous resident priest had developed a chronic illness that greatly reduced his activity in the parish. In 1939, his condition worsened and he was admitted to St. Francis Hospital in Brenham, Texas, where he stayed until 1943.[22]

Until the summer of 1939, St. Mary's Parish had had limited success with resident priests. Bill was the sixth in twelve years, and his predecessor had been so ill that most of his priestly duties had been covered (sporadically) by the Holy Cross Fathers of Austin.[23] No doubt the parishioners were expecting more of the same, some faceless padre they hardly saw. What they got was quite the opposite.

Throughout his tenure, Bill seemed to be everywhere, sometimes in more than one place at a time, building a mission chapel in Burnet, saying mass in Killeen, visiting families near Sulphur Creek. Indeed, conflicting accounts of his whereabouts at particular moments have become a significant part of the mystique of William F. Roach, a mystique that began to manifest itself in the Texas Hill Country in the summer of 1939 and actually preceded him to Texas City six years later.[24]

There was no mistaking Father Bill. No one else in the Hill Country looked remotely like him. He was quite distinctive: "a slender, chain-smoking, pious priest," given to wearing Nocona boots under his black robe. However, he did not always wear his collar and cassock. He wore denim overalls and a tool belt when he was building, something he did a lot of. His vision included a new parish church in Lampasas and smaller mission chapels sprinkled throughout the parish, in places where parishioners worshiped in private homes, stores, and gas stations because no other facilities existed.[25]

Sometime after Christmas 1939, Roach received a telephone call from George Rhein, a classmate from the seminary in La Porte. A semester behind the Roaches, Rhein had just graduated and been ordained. His grandmother had given him a brand-new Plymouth as an ordination gift. Rhein intended to donate the vehicle to the diocese, but first he wanted to treat himself to a tour of the entire Galveston diocese and, in particular, a holiday visit to Lampasas.

"Yes, George." Roach responded. "Come to Lampasas for your vacation. Better be quick about it, too! [Bishop] Byrne's going to put you to work right away!"

Rhein was hesitant. He had heard stories about the primitive conditions of the parish, especially regarding the rectory, described by the bishop as little more than a hovel.[26]

"Bill," Rhein shouted into the receiver. "Do you have any room out there?"

"George, come on over! I'll show you some real Texas Hill Country living!" Roach responded.[27]

Rhein drove to Lampasas and found that in just six months, Roach had constructed an impressive rectory with plenty of beds. Bill had invited several other seminary friends in addition to Rhein, and the place was packed. Everyone had fun—when Bill Roach was involved, it was difficult not to.[28]

Rhein and the others noticed what an impression Roach was making in the parish. Everyone seemed to know him—whether Catholic or not—and to crack a smile when they saw him. "Howdy, Father Bill!" "Where you headed, Father Bill?" "When's the pope stopping by for a beer, Father Bill?" His humor and optimism were infectious, following him wherever he went. And he went many places. He was always on the move. Of course, he did have close to three thousand square miles of territory to cover, but Rhein never dreamed that anyone was capable of the kinds of things Roach was already accomplishing. Indeed, few thought it possible.[29]

St. Mary's was better attended than it had ever been, with non-Catholics very often attending the services. The same was true at the outlying missions in Burnet, Killeen, and Gatesville and in the chapels at the State School for Boys (Gatesville) and Camp Hood (later Fort Hood), all visited by Father Bill in a seemingly never-ending circuit. Despite such activity, he also found time to oversee missions in Marble Falls, Bertram, and Leander.[30] For this reason, and because Father Bill was so well liked in the region, Bishop Byrne decided before the end of the summer to make the appointment to Lampasas permanent. No one was more pleased than Roach himself. He had confided to a friend that, apart from his brother, he had never really had a family. Now he had all of West Texas.[31]

To minister to his newly adopted family, Father Bill had somehow acquired a couple of vehicles, an old sedan and a bus. The sedan he used for quick trips across the parish and for running errands in and around Lampasas. The bus he used for his very circuitous Sunday journeys to each chapel and mission throughout the parish. In fact, he not only conducted the Sunday services, he collected and transported the faithful as well. It did not matter what faith, not to Roach. If non-Catholics needed transportation, he picked them up as well and drove them to their places of worship.

"Religious affiliation didn't seem to matter to Roach," recalled Beth King. "People mattered. Roach gave a lot of time and money to other denominations. If they were in need he gave it to them." Meanwhile, Joe Wittenberg asserted that Father Bill "endeared himself to everyone, regardless of race, creed, or color."[32]

Roach also lent the parish vehicles to individuals in need; for example, once he let a young Baptist woman borrow the sedan to visit her mother who had been hospitalized in another town.[33] Thus, by creating and maintaining an atmosphere of genuine acceptance and tolerance, punctuated by friendly smiles, good deeds, and down-to-earth humor, Father Bill began winning converts, more converts than anyone expected. Among them was a young Baptist woman, Dana Hollister, and her entire extended family. Dana recalled, "I joined [the Catholic faith] because he [Roach] was so kind and such a great person and such a great priest. Also, I liked the church ceremony, the old Latin mass."[34]

In addition to his other duties, Father Bill taught catechism. He had an affinity for children, and they for him. Even when students were overactive, he had a way with them. One little girl had a very short attention span. Inevitably, she would start to roam about the class, giggling and squirming. Roach would grab her and hold on to her as he continued the class, calling her "wiggle-bug" and laughing almost as much as she was. In addition, Father Bill made it a point to visit sick children in their homes or at the hospital, and as always, he did so regardless of church affiliation.[35]

Roach's long, arduous Sunday drives throughout the massive parish usually began the day before at Kirk Buttrill's ranch near Lometa, seventeen miles northwest of Lampasas. Kirk Buttrill was a Methodist, but he and Roach grew close over the years. Intrigued by ranch life, Roach thought Buttrill's place was the quintessential spread—a real slice of Texas. For his part, Buttrill was only too happy to have his guest tag along as he made his rounds and did chores throughout the property, Roach usually lending a hand eagerly.

Father Bill liked to spend the night at the ranch and say mass first thing Sunday morning at Good Shepherd Church in town before continuing on to his other stops. After Sunday mass, Ida Buttrill would prepare a large breakfast, much to Father Bill's pleasure. Sometimes neighbors and other parishioners would drop by. Roach liked that as well. Buttrill's wife was Catholic, a fact that seemed to have no adverse effect on family harmony. Ida Wittenberg Buttrill had attended

St. Dominic's Villa. Her grandparents were William Mark and Augusta Wittenberg, the first Anglo-Catholic settlers in the area, who built a small Catholic chapel on their property near Lometa. Various sources indicate either he or Augusta bequeathed money for the construction of the Good Shepherd Church, to provide Lometa with a permanent church.[36]

The Buttrills' daughter Beth remembered Roach as easygoing, very approachable, and someone who made her feel immensely comfortable. "He was always open to his surroundings and would meet people easily. He was especially intrigued by Texas ranchers."[37]

Meanwhile, Roach found Texas Hill Country ranchers resilient, resourceful, and fiercely independent. Not far from Lometa, in fact, the Farmers' Alliance Number One had formed a grassroots populist agrarian organization in the late nineteenth century. Most of all, Roach enjoyed the quick-witted, self-effacing humor of Hill Country residents, particularly ranchers.[38]

Spending time at the Buttrill ranch may have been Roach's only truly personal indulgence, apart from smoking. He was developing a reputation for living a life of self-sacrifice and austerity. Over the next few months, his rectory developed a Spartan look, devoid of nearly all personal items and often lacking even basic necessities, including food.[39]

"He didn't think of himself," parishioner Joe Wittenberg recalled. "He rarely spent money on himself." "He would give everything away. It didn't matter who it was, if someone needed something he had, he gave it away. If you gave him money and you didn't specify that he was to use the money for himself, to buy a pair of shoes or something, he'd give it all away. Sometimes he'd give it away even if you specified."[40]

In book 1 of *City of God*, Saint Augustine extols the virtues of losing one's possessions, saying among other things, that possessions only hinder one's journey to a higher spiritual plane. Roach accepted the concept literally and remained true to it throughout his life. Such behavior solidified an ever-growing mystique surrounding Bill Roach.[41]

"It was penance," said a colleague. "He hardly slept, too. It was all penance, in the manner of the ancient early Christian Coptic [Egyptian] desert monks, the ones all of those early Irish monks revered. The 'green martyrdom' the Irish monks called it, achieving Heaven through self-sacrifice, sometimes extreme self-sacrifice."[42]

There is evidence, however, that Father Bill was not universally accepted. Cryptic references to problems appear in an otherwise glowing newspaper article about Roach that appeared in the *Lampasas Record* in 1945. "[Roach is] cognizant of the perplexities that sometimes annoyed him. When he is sure an offense is intended, he at once begins to analyze, being deeply versed in psychology and possessed of a keenly analytic mind. He soon has the solution and is sorry for the one who sought to offend. Then, all is forgotten." The article did not mention any specifics, but this passage well describes the approach Roach took when he was confronted by the three Klansmen.

The same article noted Roach's outgoing manner. "He loved people. His residence was at all times open to guests, and there were many. No matter what he was doing, he stopped to visit." The article also claimed that Roach stood apart from others because of his energy and focus. "Once he decides to do a thing, he accomplishes it with bewildering rapidity."[43]

This statement certainly refers to Roach's parish-building campaign, unprecedented in the area and still described to this day as an amazing feat of logistics, organization, and sheer perseverance. Accounts list the construction of at least five churches in six years, perhaps more.[44] "He built those churches pretty much with his own hands," recalled Sister Mary William Montegut. "Maybe not all the construction, but a lot of it. It was more penance. More of his 'green martyrdom.'"[45]

6

"BUILDER OF CHURCHES"

In the early months of 1940, Father Bill Roach was in the midst of planning a new church for Lampasas. The aging frame building at Fifth and Broad Streets was by then nearly fifty-five years old and in bad shape. Built sixteen years before the area became a parish, the original St. Mary's was never intended as a permanent structure, merely as a mission chapel.[1] It was certainly never designed to function as the parish headquarters. But it was still a usable space, unlike facilities in other parts of the parish.

In the outlying communities Catholics were holding services in homes, stores, and even barns. Lack of facilities caused numerous problems. Among other things, whenever Father Bill ventured away from St. Mary's, he had to pack everything needed for mass and bring it with him. Sometimes, in the rush from place to place, he would forget something. He once arrived in Killeen, twenty-nine miles east of Lampasas, without a cincture, the thick cord used to secure the flowing white linen alb of the priest's vestments. He looked frantically for some sort of replacement but found nothing. Time was running out, so he simply removed the belt from his pants and cinctured the alb with it. Moments into the service, however, after having just addressed the congregation with the salutation, "Dominus vobiscum," Roach turned back to the altar, only to feel his pants fall to his ankles. Unperturbed and without missing a beat, he merely stepped out of the pants, kicked them to one side, and continued saying mass, the alb and other vestments covering him sufficiently.[2]

The situation was more serious in Burnet, twenty-two miles south of Lampasas, in neighboring Burnet County.[3] The first mass ever performed in Burnet, indeed in the entire county, had taken place just one year before Roach's arrival, at a private home on Texas State Highway 29. The Catholic community in Burnet was an oddly amorphous entity. There were only a handful of permanent Catholic residents. The majority of the faithful consisted of Latino/a migrant farmworkers who were often traveling away from home on a seemingly never-ending and circuitous route from one farm to the next in search of work. When they were in Burnet, their homes were often nothing more than tents or wooden lean-tos standing just west of town, in the vicinity of old Fort Croghan.[4] Catholic campers and other visitors to the newly erected Buchanan Dam Reservoir, opened in 1937 a few miles farther west of Burnet, and boys from the newly installed National Youth Administration Camp at nearby Ink's Dam contributed to the fluctuating Catholic numbers in the area.[5]

The local Lion's Club had been allowing the use of its hall for Catholic services, but anti-Catholic pressure had resulted in the sudden withdrawal of that venue.[6] Catholics were then forced to use yet another private home for a while. Eventually, a movie theater, the Burtex, was made available on Sunday mornings. There were problems with that arrangement as well, however. The theater was not always cleaned up following the Saturday-night movie. Communion had to be administered on the stage in front of the big screen. Confessions were heard in a side aisle with the priest, often Roach's assistant Father Frederick A. Schmidt, sitting on a suitcase behind some makeshift blind.[7]

It was more than time for a real church, and Roach knew it. Indeed Roach's predecessor, Father LeBlanc, had already identified the need for a permanent church in Burnet and had received permission from Bishop Byrne to build one. With LeBlanc's illness and subsequent hospitalization, it fell to Roach to carry out the plan.[8] He set aside work on the new church building in Lampasas and began scouting possible locations for a Catholic church in Burnet, the first such structure in all of Burnet County.

The road from Lampasas to Burnet makes a gradual and picturesque descent from the highland hills to Mesquite Creek, then climbs a low, brilliant white limestone ridge, passing within sight of old Dobyville.[9] Little evidence of this town remains, only a nearby cemetery dating from the 1850s. Past the cemetery, on the south side of the ridge, the road begins another descent, taking the traveler down to Burnet and the Colorado River bottoms.

During the short drive, Roach had time to think about Burnet, along with the other regions of the parish. Gazing at the scenery from behind the steering wheel, watching stands of ancient oak trees give way to open, rolling ranchland, sprinkled here and there with groupings of evergreen cedar, he decided the only solution was to carry out Father LeBlanc's plan. He would build a permanent church in Burnet, something designed to bring the fragmented Catholic community together.

West of Burnet, in proximity to the tents and shotgun houses of the desperately poor Latino/a Catholics of the town, Roach spotted a piece of property on the south side of State Highway 29 (Buchanan Drive), not far from a local landmark called Lookout Top Mountain.[10] The plot appeared unused, untended, abandoned. Parking his sedan, described by some as "a jalopy," Roach got out and tromped among outcroppings of pink granite, Texas sage, lantana, wild grape, chinaberry, wild peach, pecan, and live oak. Producing a small statue of St. Joseph from his pocket, Roach scooped out a shallow trench, placed the statue in the earth, and went off in search of the property owner.[11]

Roach discovered the property was owned by Thula Cole Altman, a non-Catholic. Armed with absolutely nothing, not even money, Roach approached Altman with the audacious proposal that she donate the land for the project. She agreed immediately, a tribute to Roach's personality and his ever-increasing ability to "wriggle things out of people."[12] The deed was transferred on August 7, 1940.[13] Funding for the construction was another matter, however.

To generate publicity for fundraising, Roach approached the University of Notre Dame School of Architecture in South Bend, Indiana, the oldest Catholic school of architecture in America.[14] He proposed a student competition called "A Stone Church in a Country Setting." The winning entry was then submitted to the Houston architectural firm of T. G. McHale, which produced blueprints and models from that entry free of charge. All this activity did indeed call attention to Roach's Hill Country church project. Donations began arriving, but they were not enough.[15]

Father Bill approached the Catholic Extension Society, a group literally dedicated to "extending" the reach of the Catholic Church in mission territories like St. Mary's Parish. The Extension Society donated a thousand dollars toward building the proposed church in Burnet and completing the new church in Lampasas, among other projects.[16] Roach then launched a speaking tour to raise additional money, traveling to major Texas cities such as Austin, San Antonio, and Houston. He even took his project to the Eastern Seaboard, visiting his home state of Pennsylvania, as well as Boston and New York City. While in New York in 1940, Father Bill caught up with two very important people in his life, his twin brother, John, and rowing champion Dan Barrow.

Barrow, the Roach brothers' close friend from their Schuylkill River days, had become a special agent for Old Fidelity and Casualty Insurance Company (later Continental) and was living in New York City. A member of the New York Athletic Club, he still rowed occasionally, but not competitively. His last major race, and win, had been in a double scull a few years earlier at the Canadian Henley. His time was now taken up by work and preparations for his impending marriage later in the year.[17]

John Roach was working on a master of social work degree at Fordham University. Immediately following his ordination, while Bill was settling in Lampasas, John served as assistant pastor of the parish of St. Mary in Houston. But the assignment was short-lived. The Diocese of Galveston sent John to graduate school to study social work, first at the Catholic University of America in Washington, DC, then at Fordham, for his master's degree.[18]

Bill stayed with John in New York. Apart from his speaking engagements, Bill spent a lot of time with John and Dan, just having fun and catching up, especially with John. The brothers, rarely separated before ordination, had seen little of each other since. The transition had not been easy for either of them.

While at Fordham, John volunteered at a private community outreach center in Harlem called Friendship House. Whether this work was a degree requirement or simply an extracurricular activity is not known. Nevertheless, almost as soon as Bill arrived at the Fordham University's Rose Hill campus in the Bronx, John took him on the short subway ride to Friendship House so that he could "meet the gang."[19]

Located at 34 West 135th Street, half a block from the intersection of Lenox Avenue, Friendship House consisted of a converted house and three rented storefronts. The complex contained a library, a room full of free clothes for those in need; another room filled with food staples, also free; and a recreation area for children under the age of twelve. There were also spaces for after-school programs and adult study groups, as well as an area where people of different ethnic backgrounds—particularly Anglos and African Americans—could mingle and get to know one another.

Friendship House was founded by a woman of noble birth, Baroness Catherine de Hueck, a refugee of the Bolshevik revolution in Russia. She had escaped from her native land through Finland, then made her way to Toronto via England.

In 1930, in thanks for having survived her ordeal, de Hueck rejected worldly possessions and moved into the heart of Toronto's slums. Emulating the lives of Saint Francis of Assisi and the early Christian Irish monks whose white and green martyrdoms so influenced Bill Roach, she established a place where poor and disadvantaged people might congregate and receive help in improving their lives. Severely persecuted for her interracial tolerance, however, de Hueck was forced to close the Toronto house in 1936. In response, the priests of St. Mark's Parish in New York—backed first by Cardinal Patrick Hayes then by his successor, Cardinal Francis Spellman—asked de Hueck to found a similar institution in Harlem, one that would continue her work of combating racism through interaction and understanding. Friendship House opened in 1938.[20]

Bill Roach was quite aware of the growing social activism within various American religious denominations, including Roman Catholicism, before his arrival at Friendship House. What he saw at Friendship House reinforced this attitude. Throughout the 1930s, as the Great Depression worsened and Franklin Delano Roosevelt's New Deal sought to combat it, a perceptibly liberal, sometimes even radical, shift occurred in both Protestant and Catholic communities. The liberalization of American Catholics, in particular, can be seen in the 1936 national election, when 78 percent of Catholics voted for Roosevelt. Recall that the Roach brothers helped Jack Kelly Sr. campaign for Roosevelt's reelection.[21]

Friendship House, grounded in the idea of promoting racial equality through empathetic community interaction, was an excellent example of what some referred to as a new kind of Catholic apostolate.[22] There were other examples as well, such as Dorothy Day and Peter Maurin, missionaries, speakers, and publishers of the *Catholic Worker*. A movement of the mind was underway in clerical America, and the Roach brothers would become a part of it, championing the rights of poor and working-class citizens.[23]

Like his brother, Bill Roach fit in well at Friendship House, visiting and helping out on several different occasions over the next few years. He would continue to visit his brother and volunteer at Friendship House, usually during vacations, until 1943, when John received his master's degree in social work and returned to Texas.[24] Bill certainly must have made careful note of Catherine de Hueck's innate ability to persuade people to do things. Traveling throughout the country, de Hueck delivered speeches and called for help, bringing in a steady supply of goods as well as volunteers from near and far. Everything in the organization was donated, and everyone working there was a volunteer. Some traveled great distances to resettle in Harlem, all due to the exceptional charisma of de Hueck.

Friendship House was a vast sociological experiment, and at the time it was successful.

Bill Roach encountered a vast, multicultural cross section of people at Friendship House, among them Belle Mullin and Larry Lee. Mullin had moved to Harlem from her home state of Wisconsin after hearing de Hueck speak. Lee, a native New Yorker, was a graduate student at Fordham. Already friends with John Roach, Lee would become a friend of Bill's as well.[25] Thomas Merton was also there, not yet the legendary spiritual leader and world-famous author he was to become, but already charismatic and compelling. These individuals were typical of the volunteers at Friendship House: idealistic, hard-working, and ready for change.[26]

Merton, in particular, was a most interesting character. He seemed to have much in common with the Roach brothers, including a rather raucous youth followed by a religious epiphany. Born in France to artist parents, Merton had attempted an education at Cambridge University in England but was expelled for failing to study. He had also fathered an illegitimate child, a daughter, later killed in a German air raid during World War II. Because of his notorious behavior, the British government suggested to Merton, some say strongly suggested, that he leave England and never come back.

Merton moved to New York City and enrolled at Columbia University as an art student. Although he was more mature academically in his new home, actually studying and producing work, close friends state that Merton still possessed a wild, loud, and unpredictable personality, drinking heavily, partying, and chasing woman, lots of women.[27] Merton also maintained a very complex love-hate relationship with American culture. Throughout his life he was utterly enthralled with American jazz and blues music, particularly Louis Armstrong, Bessie Smith, Jelly Roll Morton, Billie Holliday, Pee Wee Russell, and Eddie Condon. On the other hand, Merton despised racism and what he perceived as disparity in the treatment of the poor and disadvantaged in America.

In 1938, the same year he earned a bachelor of arts degree from Columbia, Merton underwent a particularly intense religious experience, converting to Catholicism and shunning his vices. It was probably during this period that he began volunteering at institutions like Friendship House. The following year Merton earned a master of arts degree, also from Columbia. His thesis dealt with the English Romantic artist and poet William Blake. In retrospect, given Merton's later life as a deeply religious activist, writer, and mystic, one can see how he might be intrigued by Blake, for Blake was all of those things.

By the time Merton crossed paths with the Roach brothers at Friendship House, he was teaching at Columbia University Extension and at St. Bonaventure College. Within a very short time he would join the Abbey of Gethsemani monastic community in Kentucky, Cistercians of the Strict Observance (the Trappists), and take the name Father Louis. But that was in the future. At Friendship House he was still Tommy.[28]

All too soon, Bill Roach's speaking tour was over and he was back in Texas. Despite the tour, he still did not have enough money to complete his projects. But he proceeded anyway. Father Bill was never one to let little things like logistics stand in his way. On his return to Lampasas, Roach contracted a Burnet stone masonry company, and construction began in the late months of 1940, just in time for winter.[29]

Bad weather and lack of funds dogged the project. By spring 1941, the foundation, nothing more than a severely uneven flagstone floor, and the structure's skeletal frame were all that stood on the site. Many feared the project would fail. Indeed, some never thought such an undertaking was possible in the first place. But not Father Bill. He never wavered, at least not publicly.[30]

A few more donations arrived, principally from the Society for the Propagation of the Faith and from a number of local benefactors who wished to remain anonymous. Those who could not donate money, and even some who could, volunteered to help build the structure. In the end, Father Bill did most of the carpentry.[31]

The church, a truncated basilica-style floor plan with no transept, rough-hewn limestone exterior walls, limestone buttresses, and a simple, open bell tower straddling the apex of the steeply pitched roof, was blessed by Bishop Byrne on June 11, 1941. On that day, Byrne said, "The great simplicity of the building, being just as Our Lord would have it since all materials are nature's own, is rugged and beautiful." Then commenting about Bill Roach's perseverance, Byrne added, "Only the grace of God could have carried him through this ordeal."[32]

Torrential rains severely hampered construction throughout the winter and spring. But on the day of Byrne's blessing, the bad weather ceased.[33] Much finish work remained. There was no heat or water, and there were no confessionals. Confession was heard in the tiny sacristy with the priest, often Father Schmidt, again sitting on a suitcase behind an improvised screen, just as he had done at the movie theater in town. The church was frigid during the first winter, until a large oil heater was installed in the center aisle. For three years it noisily belched smoky warmth until a more efficient gas-fired unit replaced it. But at least the space was open and ready for worship.

Byrne, alluding to Father Bill's plan for the new church to serve as a catalyst to solidify the fragmented Catholic community of Burnet, told those assembled for the blessing, "Catholics will come, now that you have a church." He was right. Within weeks regular attendance grew from two families to forty-two, most of them having previously traveled to Lampasas, Llano, and elsewhere to attend mass. And as expected, worshippers from the National Youth Administration Boys Camp at Ink's Dam and Catholic visitors to the Buchanan Dam Reservoir also joined local resident Catholics at their new church, Our Mother of Sorrows. Roach loved the name. For him it was the perfect choice, evocative of the intense struggles entailed in the planning and execution of the building.[34]

Back in Lampasas, Roach returned to his initial project, a replacement for the dilapidated St. Mary's church. In fact, he had never forgotten about the venture, even as he worked steadily on the construction of Our Mother of Sorrows. Just a few weeks before the blessing of the church in Burnet, he identified a suitable location for the new Lampasas church. The one-and-a-half-acre property, north of town on the east side of what was then referred to as Texas State Highway 66 (now US Highway 281) near Burleson Creek, belonged to G. W. and Margie Lee Green. On May 27, 1941, less than a month before the blessing of Our Mother of Sorrows, the Diocese of Galveston purchased the land for eight hundred dollars.[35]

Construction started immediately, even before the Burnet church was finished. The floor plan followed the traditional cruciform basilica style, oriented strictly east-west, with a transept crossing the main nave and affording more square footage. The concept dates to the ancient Romans. The north wing of the transept would serve as a recreation center. The south wing would house the rectory. On the south corner of the limestone western facade stood a stubby limestone bell tower. A short stairway led to a single doorway, flanked by narrow lancet windows. Above the door, a Gothic-style rose window was installed. Above that, a pitched roof covered the length of the building and the two wings of the transept.

Father Bill used native limestone and other local materials in the church construction. Part of the motivation for choosing such materials was certainly economic.[36] Much of the material and labor was donated. As was the case in Burnet, Roach himself worked long hours on the project. He was often seen, sometimes well into the night, uncharacteristically dressed in a soiled undershirt and jeans or coveralls, with a weathered tool belt strapped to his waist. For Roach, the result was a synthesis of the Roman Catholic Church's past and future, of its Mediterranean roots and its new footing in a new land.

Completed sometime in the fall, the new St. Mary's Catholic Church was blessed by Bishop Byrne on Tuesday, December 16, 1941. The temperature was a cool fifty-one degrees. Local newspapers were full of war headlines. The Japanese attack on the US naval base at Pearl Harbor had occurred just nine days earlier. The day before the dedication of St. Mary's, the federal government officially acknowledged the complete loss of the battleship USS *Arizona* in that attack. Meanwhile, Soviet troops defeated three German infantry divisions, the first such loss for the Nazi regime. In Dallas, a Javanese dance troupe performing at Southern Methodist University was detained by Inspector of Detectives Will Fritz due to an apparent misunderstanding of the difference between Java and Japan. The headlines overshadowed the bishop's visit to Lampasas, but the event was stunning nonetheless. It was the second dedication of a Roach-built church within six months, a phenomenal achievement considering the obstacles. But Father Bill was not finished. Lampasas needed another church, and factors other than sparse materials, lack of money, and a thinning labor force would influence its construction.[37]

The early 1940s was a time of strict segregation in the Texas Hill Country and the United States as a whole. Fresh from his experience at Harlem's Friendship House, Roach was working to eradicate those kinds of barriers in his parish. Although separate communities of Anglos and African Americans existed, the more pronounced racial tensions were between Anglos and the Latino/a community in and around Lampasas.

Such tensions were not unique to the Hill Country, however. They were integral to the culture of Texas and the Southwest. Even professional Texas historians including Walter Prescott Webb, Eugene C. Barker, and T. R. Fehrenbach largely misrepresented and vilified Latino/a Texas settlers, called Tejanos, as dangerous pro-Mexico, anti-Texas, anti-Anglo, anti-US, and anti-capitalist agitators. These views found their way into the Texas educational system, presented as fact in state-mandated history textbooks as late as the 1960s, regardless of the reality that Tejanos predated Anglos in Texas and played a major role in the pro-Texas, pro-US, and pro-capitalist development of the entire region.[38] And, of course, all of this ignored the displacement, subjugation, and marginalization of the indigenous populations of Texas.

Tejanos, particularly Mexican citizens and Texans of Mexican ancestry, were even cast as subhuman. Five years before Father Bill Roach arrived in Lampasas, a legendary former Texas Ranger, discussing his career during an interview with reporters, was asked how many men he had killed. "Twenty-three men," he answered. "Not counting Mexicans."[39] The distinction made between "men" and "Mexicans" cannot be overlooked. This attitude was pervasive among Texas Anglos in the early twentieth century, and to some extent still exists today.

"When Father Roach arrived there was a terrible race problem between Anglos and the Latino community," parishioner Joe Wittenberg commented.[40]

Roach paid no attention to such divisions. When he got behind the wheel of his bus, he not only transported members of any and all faiths, he also turned a blind eye to color and ethnicity. The interior of his bus became a multicultural and multilingual mix of people. It was a Friendship House on wheels, but not without a measure of grumbling. A Latina parishioner stated, "A lot of my people didn't like that! A lot of white people didn't like that!"[41] That did not stop Roach. Many parishioners, especially those from the Latino/a community, had no cars, and there were a lot of elderly and sick people who had tremendous difficulty getting around. Roach helped them all.

The Spanish-speaking Latino/a community in Lampasas had no church. They were using an all-too-familiar alternative: a private home, located on East Fifth Street not far from Sulphur Creek. At some point Roach conceived the idea of building a permanent church specifically for this community. He visited Latino/a parishioners in their homes and took a very active part in local meetings of the Society of the Sacred Heart and the Sociedades Guadalupanas.[42]

"I liked that just fine [Roach's involvement]," said one resident. "It made me feel more interested in the project. The other priests, the ones before Father Roach, didn't seem to have time for us. Father Roach was a good friend of the Mexican people."[43]

Roach proposed staging events like the traditional Mexican *jamaica* to raise money for the church-building campaign. Jamaicas are fall festivals featuring music, food, and games. Such fiestas had long histories in neighboring towns but never in Lampasas, not until Father Roach arrived.[44]

The local Guadalupanas and other organizations began working, donating time and materials to the planned jamaica. Sopapillas, flan, and tamales, lots of tamales, were made to sell at the event. Roach and others secured lumber for booths. Musicians volunteered their time. In the end, the jamaica raised nearly eight hundred dollars, a lot of money in the early 1940s, but not enough to build a church.

Repeating his earlier strategy, Roach secured more funding from the Catholic Extension Society and was able to get much of the construction material and labor donated. An unforeseen obstacle, however, was the sudden and substantial shortage of material and labor in the opening months of US involvement in World War II, a situation that would not ease until after the war ended. Somehow Roach and the Latino/a community prevailed. A piece of property was acquired on East Fourth Street, on the west bank of Sulphur Creek, next to the bridge, and construction began in 1942 on the Church of St. Christopher, named for the patron saint of travelers.

Finished in the same year, the Church of St. Christopher was stylistically similar to Roach's first two churches: a basilica floor plan with a transept and rough limestone exterior. But this new church featured an arched entryway, scalloped facade, and multilevel open bell tower, attributes reminiscent of some of the Spanish missions of San Antonio, particularly Mission San Antonio de Valero (the Alamo, 1718), Mission San Francisco de la Espada (1731), and Mission San Juan (1731).[45]

In the same year, 1942, Father Bill, who was becoming known as the "builder of churches,"[46] began work on his fourth church, fifty-three miles northeast of Lampasas, in Gatesville. Located just west of town, on US Highway 84, Our Lady of Lourdes would become the first Catholic church in Coryell County. Previously, Catholics either traveled to Lampasas or used the chapel at the nearby Texas State School for Boys. Roach made regular visits to the children housed at the Texas State School for Boys, a reform school for minors convicted of felony crimes.

Bishop Byrne blessed Our Lady of Lourdes on February 11, 1943, on a cold, overcast day. Once again, war dominated the newspaper headlines. Dwight D. Eisenhower had been promoted to the rank of four-star general, German Field Marshall Irwin Rommel was being pushed back in North Africa, and the Japanese were facing defeat in New Guinea.[47]

A few months after the blessing of Our Lady of Lourdes, in late May, Larry Lee, the Friendship House volunteer, paid a visit to Father Bill Roach in Lampasas. Lee had graduated from Fordham University the year before with a master's degree in social work. Particularly influenced by Bill Roach, and perhaps following the example of another Friendship House colleague, Thomas Merton, Lee had decided to enter the priesthood. But rather than choosing monastic life, as Thomas Merton had done, Lee moved to La Marque, Texas, and enrolled in St. Mary's Seminary, the Roach brothers' alma mater. He wanted to be a parish priest, in Texas, out amongst the people, just like Father Bill.

Lee arrived in Lampasas by bus. Three things impressed him about his stay in the Texas Hill Country: that a breakfast of steak and eggs cost only fifty cents, the incredible display of stars in the night sky, and the energy of Bill Roach. "Being in the seminary, I had not eaten well in a long time," Lee said. "Those breakfasts were a real treat. And the stars! I was just a city kid, raised in New York. I had never seen such stars! I was particularly awestruck! But Father Bill, he was everywhere, and doing everything. And it seemed like he was doing it all at once. Our drives around the parish, all of the activity, everything he was involved in, it made my head spin! And [Roach was] laughing all the time. He was such a jolly man, with a deep abiding spirit. It was obvious he was a huge influence on many, many people."[48]

When Lee arrived, he found Father Bill planning his fifth church in four years.[49] The location was twenty-eight miles east of Lampasas, in Killeen, where Roach once lost his pants during mass. "A dusty little farm town, a sleepy market and railroad settlement near the center of the state," Killeen had been established forty-two years earlier as a depot for the Gulf, Colorado, and Santa Fe Railroad and named for Frank P. Killeen, a railroad officer. By the time Roach started actively planning the construction of a church there, Killeen's population was approximately one thousand, and growing fast. In 1942 the US government established a new army training facility, Camp Hood, just a few miles northwest of town. The construction of this base caused a tremendous influx of both armed services personnel along with civilian engineers, laborers, and assorted government employees to the area. Among the influx of new residents there were enough Catholic families that Roach wrote yet another in an ever-lengthening series of letters to Bishop Byrne, asking permission to establish and build another mission church in St. Mary's parish.[50]

During his visit, Lee traveled around the vast parish with Roach. Sometimes they used the bus, but most of the time they rode in Roach's rattletrap sedan.[51] The road from Lampasas to Killeen is flanked by rocky ridges and hills. These hills are particularly pronounced east of Copperas Cove. On the north side of the road between Copperas Cove and Killeen, the remnants of an old stagecoach station, grain store, and post office could still be seen. Dating from 1878, the buildings once composed a stopover called Ogletree.[52] Such places were special to Roach, forever fascinated by the frontier days of Texas.

On the western approach to Killeen, south of the railroad tracks running parallel to Highway 190, Father Bill pulled over and climbed out of the car.[53] Lee watched as Roach walked a few paces from the car, his stride slightly off-balance. With a decidedly precocious grin, Roach surveyed the dusty terrain, accented here and there by ocotillo, sotol, and prickly pear. He pulled a small statue of Saint Joseph from his pocket, carved a shallow trough in the earth with the heel of his boot, and dropped the figurine in. After partially covering the statue, Roach returned to the car. "Works every time," he said, referring to his use of images of the patron saint of fathers, families, and workers to acquire properties to build his churches.[54]

The practice is old, dating back at least to the time of St. Teresa of Ávila (1515–82), a nun who encouraged members of her reformed Carmelite community to bury images of Saint Joseph as a sign of devotion.[55] For Roach, a deep abiding devotion was the key to success, and thus far it certainly had worked for him. Killeen would prove no different. Somehow, the property was obtained.

Within a few weeks, financed in part by the Catholic Extension Society but mostly from local donations, construction began on Sacred Heart Church in Killeen. Like Roach's other churches, Sacred Heart was built of limestone with a basilica-style floor plan.[56] Bishop Byrne blessed the new building on December 5, 1943. Again, the newspapers were full of war news: Franklin D. Roosevelt, Winston Churchill, and Joseph Stalin announced plans to release a report of their conference in Tehran, Iran. Allied troops were pushing north to Rome, the Soviet army was retaking the Ukraine, and 85,000 were reportedly killed in Berlin air raids.[57]

That year also brought positive developments on a personal front. Dan Barrow was transferred to Texas, first to Abilene then to Dallas, where he stayed until after the close of the war. These cities were, respectively, 150 and 170 miles from Lampasas, so Father Bill and his childhood friend were able to visit occasionally. Meanwhile, John Roach was conferred a master of science degree in social work and returned to Texas. He arrived while work was still underway on Sacred Heart and accompanied Byrne to Killeen for the blessing. Shortly thereafter John became the bishop's assistant.

Despite being in the same state together once again, finding time for visits was difficult for the brothers. Their schedules were too tight. The blessing in Killeen afforded a rare moment together. That was to change, however. In 1945, Father Bill Roach received word that he would be transferred from St. Mary's Parish in Lampasas to another St. Mary's Parish, this one in Texas City, just a few minutes north of Galveston, not far from the cathedral, the bishop, and his brother John. The reassignment was to take effect at the end of June.

Such moves were, and still are, a reality for diocesan priests, who can live a rather transient lifestyle. Roach knew this, but he did not like the idea of leaving his beloved Lampasas, even if the move brought him physically closer to his brother. Lampasas and the Texas Hill Country had become his home, like no place before. His parishioners, and indeed nearly everyone in the area, had become a surrogate family to him. He was not eager to part with that family, nor were they eager for him to leave.[58]

"Father Roach will long stand out clearly against the historic background of illustrious padres," the local newspaper stated. The article lauded Roach for his sense of humor; his penchant for helping anyone in need, regardless of religious affiliation; and his hand in boosting the local economy by inviting the National Catholic Community Service (NCCS) to the area. "It [NCCS] not only boomed the business of the town, it aided those of modest means in garnering a little money to mend a leaking roof, add a coat of paint, or just have a little money. And the salaries were invaluable."[59]

Nevertheless, by July 1, Roach was on the western shore of Galveston Bay, walking the streets of the booming port town of Texas City, a vastly different place from Lampasas and the Texas Hill Country.[60]

=7=
BOOMTOWN

The population of Texas City would more than triple between 1940 and the summer of 1945, when Father Bill Roach arrived there.[1] That growth would be significant to Roach's subsequent activities there. At the time, the city was experiencing unprecedented development, due in large part to World War II, but the roots of Texas City's boom can be traced back much further.

Located on the west shore of Galveston Bay, only a few miles from Galveston's central business district, the area that would become the site of Texas City had long been attractive to humans. Native Americans, principally the Karankawa, inhabited the locale long before the arrival of European settlers. They were formidable warriors, brutally protective of their home territory. But were also welcoming and very helpful to many of the first Europeans to visit in the region.

Indeed, the first documented Europeans to reach Galveston Bay, Cabeza de Vaca's party, were not only helped by the Karankawa but also lived with the tribe for several years. Initially, European contact with the Karankawa and other coastal Native American bands was sporadic, allowing these groups to live rather autonomously for nearly three centuries. By the nineteenth century, however, Spanish, French, and American settlement collided violently with the Native population. The slave trader and pirate Jean Lafitte killed a large force of Karankawa warriors who had amassed to avenge the kidnapping of a village woman in 1819. Within a few years, volunteer militias, or "ranger" companies, formed by settler Stephen F. Austin began murdering Karankawas. A quarter century later, a force led by Texas rancher Juan Nepomuceno Cortina deliberately killed the last remaining Karankawa. Since 1858, the Karankawa have been considered extinct as a separate people.[2]

By the early nineteenth century, Texas and Galveston Bay were Spanish possessions, but Galveston Island was still under the control of Jean Lafitte. When a cohort of Lafitte's, Jim Campbell, gave up the pirate life to farm and raise a family, he settled on the mainland just north of the island, building a modest house overlooking a sluggish stream that emptied into the bay. Campbell became the first permanent European resident of the future site of Texas City. The stream still bears his name, Campbell's Bayou.

Following the Civil War (1861–65), the US government built a lighthouse not far from Campbell's Bayou, at a site on the west shore of Galveston Bay called Shoal's Point. Shoal's Point, so-named because of an extensive oyster reef extending from the shore far out into the bay, and its new lighthouse soon attracted settlers. By 1878, fifty families had settled there, opened a post office, and built a school.[3]

In 1891 or 1892, Benjamin, Henry, and Jacob Myers, brothers from Minnesota, happened to go on a duck-hunting expedition near the western shore of Galveston Bay.[4] The hunt became secondary when the brothers, all involved in the shipping industry, began to speculate about the feasibility of building a major port near Shoal's Point. The brothers enlisted several other Minnesota investors and started acquiring property, about ten thousand acres of it. Soon they had constructed docks and a rail connection to the major lines nearby. They named the location Texas City and went into business.

Initially, business was slow. Then the notorious 1900 hurricane devastated the area, causing substantial damage to Texas City and its fledgling port. It took four years to rebuild the port, causing serious financial reversals for investors. Initially on its reopening in 1904, business was disappointing. Only twelve ships were serviced that year. Thereafter, however, port activity steadily increased. By 1910 more than two hundred ships per year were docking at Texas City.

Part of the impetus for the port's growth was the establishment of the Texas City Refining Company in 1908, not long after the discovery of a massive oil reserve at Spindletop in East Texas. This oilfield and other similar discoveries would soon make Texas a major player in the rapidly growing petrochemical industry. The founding of Texas City Refining was innovative, advancing the emerging concept of refining at the point of shipment rather than in the field. From that point on, Texas City would become increasingly attractive to oil refineries and related chemical companies. On September 16, 1911, with a population of 1,619, Texas City incorporated. William P. Tarpey, a former Texas state representative, was elected the first mayor.[5]

In 1913, Texas City had a brief stint as a military town. Ostensibly to protect US interests during the Mexican Revolution, raging just across the border, the US Army Second Division established a base at Texas City. Several thousand troops and the nation's first aero squadron were soon stationed there, at first creating shortages, then bringing prosperity. That prosperity was destroyed in 1915 when another devastating hurricane swept through Galveston Bay. The port was damaged again, and the army, having lost nine soldiers in the storm, relocated to San Antonio, never to return.

In 1921, the Texas City Terminal Railway Company assumed control of the port. Organized in 1905, the company was jointly owned by three railroads: the Atchison, Topeka, and Santa Fe Railroad; the Missouri-Kansas-Texas Railroad; and the Missouri-Pacific Railroad. Under the leadership of Texas City Terminal Railway president Hugh B. Moore, a large number of varied industries developed in Texas City, including Stone Oil Company, Knox Process Corporation (engaged in gasoline-cracking), Texas City Sugar Refinery, two cotton compressors, a fig-preserving plant, a grain elevator, and an assortment of warehouse enterprises.[6]

By 1930, the sugar refinery had closed, a victim of superior competition and the Great Depression. The closing was a temporary blow to the local economy, but the following year Republic Oil Company opened a new refinery near the docks. Then Mexican Petroleum Company, a Louisiana-based subsidiary of Standard Oil of Indiana (one of seven companies created by the forced breakup in 1911 of John D. Rockefeller's monopoly, Standard Oil), began exploring the Galveston Bay area for a place to build a refinery. The port of Houston was also making overtures to Mexican Petroleum, as were other bay-area cities.

In 1933, an advance team from Mexican Petroleum began scouting Texas City. The team included Max Montegut and Al Laiche, both of whom had young daughters who would grow up to become nuns and colleagues of Father Bill Roach. Their favorable report—and much behind-the-scenes manipulation on the part of Texas City Terminal Railway's Hugh Moore—ultimately resulted in Mexican Petroleum establishing its operation in Texas City. Montegut and Laiche began work in a shack hurriedly assembled in the middle of an open field. The move was so momentous that, once it was complete, the company changed its name to Pan American Refining Corporation. Today, we know it as Amoco Oil Company.[7]

While the rest of the nation struggled with the economic catastrophe of the Great Depression, Texas City became a boomtown, replete with the advantages and disadvantages of such. Hundreds of people poured into the city from all over the country and from outside the United States as well. New heavy construction created 1,400 jobs and attracted an influx of workers in support industries, including engineers, pipefitters, and welders, among others.

New railroad lines were constructed and the port was enlarged. Within a few years, the population almost doubled. Lack of housing became a problem. Trailers and other temporary units had to suffice until permanent homes could be built, bringing even more construction crews and related workers into the city, exacerbating the problem. Schools were overcrowded and qualified teachers in short supply. In fact, some students not only skipped grades because of overcrowding but also were promoted to high school early because their school was destroyed in a 1943 hurricane.[8]

Compared to workers nationwide during the Great Depression, the people of Texas City were living reasonably comfortable lives despite the associated aggravations. Max Montegut and Al Laiche were making only forty dollars a month, slightly less than the average per-capita income, but they were glad to have jobs at a time when unemployment seemed permanently stuck in the double digits, reaching as high as 24.9 percent in 1933.[9]

When the Japanese attacked American army and naval installations in the Philippines and at Pearl Harbor, Hawaii, on December 7, 1941, the United States was thrust into World War II. Texas City, at the time the fourth largest port on the Gulf Coast, was already poised to become a major center for war production. Over the next three years, as its population increased exponentially, Texas City witnessed its greatest industrial growth.[10]

In 1942, the only tin smelter in North America began production in Texas City. In the same year, the federal government purchased the old sugar refinery then leased it to Monsanto Chemical Company for the purpose of manufacturing styrene, a critical element in synthetic rubber. Union Carbide and Carbon Company was already producing petrochemical products in Texas City. Indeed, by the time Father Bill Roach arrived in July 1945, very near the end of the war, seven petrochemical plants were in operation. They, along with the many oil refineries and other burgeoning industries, surrounded the dock area (by then servicing more than two thousand ships annually) and dominated all life in Texas City.[11]

Roach's new parish was dramatically different from the one he left in the Texas Hill Country. The livelihood and community focus of the parishioners of St. Mary in Texas City revolved around urban twentieth-century industrial technology, in marked contrast to the rural, agrarian world of St. Mary's in Lampasas. The scenery was different too, with docks, railroads, and towering bundles of oil- and chemical-stained pipes and storage vessels in place of open, rolling, austere spaces filled with limestone hills, arroyos, and rivers. On still days in Texas City the air became choked with thick, acrid odors.

At night, flames from natural gas burn-off spewed from towering orifices, bathing the town in a surreal, dancing glow of orange lights. Of course, Father Bill was not totally unfamiliar with the west side of Galveston Bay. He had spent six years as a seminarian at Sylvan Beach in La Porte, just north of Texas City. But the area had changed radically since his ordination in 1939.

Nevertheless, Roach seemed to thrive in Texas City. For one thing, his new parish was very much smaller geographically. Instead of having to travel great distances by car, often over roads that left much to be desired, Roach found he could walk almost everywhere in Texas City. That alone freed up his time tremendously. In addition, he was no longer consumed with the seemingly endless task of building churches. Roach quickly understood that he could get involved in Texas City community life in ways he could only have dreamed of in Lampasas. It would become apparent that his first week in Texas City, marked by marathon visits to every parishioner to drum up business at the Communion rail, was only an overture to things to come. Soon, he seemed to be everywhere, at all hours of the day and night.

The Catholic presence in Texas City was less than a half-century old when Roach arrived. Reverend E. A. Kelley performed the first mass there in 1900, before there was a church. Initially, services were conducted in private homes such as the residence of John A. Siebert. By 1909, other homes were added, including future mayor William Tarpey's place at 132 Eighth Avenue North and Jack Quinn's house, not far away at the intersection of Eighth Avenue North and Fourth Street. Sometimes the International Longshoremen's Association hall and other public venues were used.[12]

In 1911 a permanent church building was constructed. The simple frame structure, measuring only twenty-two feet by sixty feet, was blessed and dedicated by Bishop Nicholas Gallagher, Bishop Byrne's predecessor.[13] Priests from the Order of Oblate Fathers traveled sporadically from Houston to say mass in the new church. In wintertime, parishioners warmed themselves beside a solitary wood-burning stove and knelt at wooden sawhorses that doubled as pew railings. The church was destroyed in the 1915 storm. A similar wood-frame structure was quickly built to replace it.[14]

On November 24, 1921, St. Mary of the Miraculous Medal became a parish with its own resident pastor, Reverend Michael J. Leahy. The following year a rectory was constructed. In 1929, however, the residency was moved to nearby Dickenson, renamed the Mainland Parish, and St. Mary was downgraded to an ancillary mission.[15] By the time Roach arrived in Texas City in 1945, the prevailing belief was that St. Mary had never been a parish and had never had a resident priest. Indeed, there was much excitement about Roach's arrival because for many he was the first resident priest in Texas City. That notion persists today, no doubt due to the fact that in 1945 approximately 80 percent of the populace had arrived in Texas City after 1929 and therefore had no memory of the earlier parish.

In 1934, when Bill and his brother were seminarians, Father Thomas A. Carney became pastor of the Mainland Parish, based at the Shrine of the True Cross Church in Dickenson. He had previously been pastor of St. Mary's in Lampasas, Bill Roach's first post after his ordination. Carney was in Lampasas for only a little more than a year before he was transferred to Dickenson. Plagued by chronic illnesses all of his career, he was nonetheless a magnetic presence with a powerful, booming voice. He was such a good speaker that he hosted a regular weekly radio program and was called upon to host numerous public functions. It was Carney who announced that Father Bill Roach would become resident pastor of St. Mary in Texas City, telling parishioners that "a saint is coming into your midst."[16]

In 1943, yet another hurricane struck Texas City. It struck without warning because the military kept impending storms secret during World War II. The city, totally unprepared—with no food or water stores, no windows boarded, no evacuation plan—sustained severe damage, particularly in the dock area, the downtown district, and the poorer neighborhoods between the two. Trailers, still a mainstay of Texas City housing, proved the most vulnerable. But even large, substantial structures were destroyed, including the Southern Hotel and Wolvin Junior High School, affecting most of the city's students. Some industrial plants were damaged as well, especially portions under construction. And the second St. Mary of the Miraculous Medal Church was knocked completely off its foundation and wrecked beyond repair.[17]

The Mainland Parish was determined to rebuild the mission church at Texas City because the congregation had grown considerably during the war. In 1939, only four years earlier, the Sunday collection had been twelve dollars. When the hurricane hit in 1943, the collection was in the hundreds and growing. In fact, serious consideration was being given to establishing St. Mary as a new, separate parish once the church was rebuilt.[18]

Houston architect Maurice J. Sullivan designed the new church. Reinforced with steel and sheathed in stone, it would be larger and more hurricane resistant than its two predecessors. But therein lay a problem: because of the war, building materials were scarce and labor in short supply. In particular, the government controlled the allocation of steel. Consequently, construction dragged on interminably. Roach had encountered the same problem, at almost the same time, when he was trying to build Our Mother of Sorrows in Burnet.

Despite these logistical problems, the church was completed in 1945, but the bell tower was much shorter than originally designed. The federal government would not release enough steel to build the tower to its intended height. Moreover, there was a restriction on the height of nonessential towers during the war. On March 18, 1945, Bishop Byrne dedicated the new church, St. Mary of the Miraculous Medal, so-named because a priest of the Order of St. Vincent DePaul, who once served the church in its mission days, had referred to it as such. A lot of timber was substituted for steel (particularly the trusses and beams), the sheathing was largely hollow tile and stucco, and the floor was asphalt tile on concrete. There was no heating or air-conditioning, although the building was constructed to allow for installation of these facilities later.[19]

The congregation did not mind, however. The new church seated 450, it was elegant, it was finished, and it was theirs. Three-and-a-half months later, Father Bill Roach was installed as resident priest, and once again St. Mary of the Miraculous Medal became a parish in its own right. This time, the elevation to parish would prove permanent.[20]

— 8 —

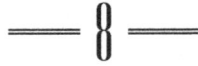

"A SAINT IS COMING INTO YOUR MIDST"

When Father Bill Roach's appointment was announced, Maxine Montegut was skeptical, not at all impressed by the talk of some "saint" descending on Texas City. "A saint?" the teenager thought to herself, scoffing. "I'm not too interested." If indeed such a person truly existed—of which Montegut was not convinced—a saint would undoubtedly be too aloof, too unapproachable, and definitely too out of touch with the real world to be relevant to her. Nonetheless, there she was, kneeling in church, waiting for the ten o'clock mass to begin and give her a first glimpse of the promised "saint." It was a hot morning, July 1, 1945.

Montegut was not even sure why she was there. Mass had become for her nothing more than a habit, something she did because she was supposed to do it. She never even thought to ask herself why she was still going to church. The whole process had become a dull ride to nowhere. She could not even remember the subject of the previous week's sermon. She knelt there, daydreaming, pretending to pray.

Then, suddenly, there he was, the new priest, moving toward the altar, an ethereal sight, not really walking, seemingly gliding, his feet concealed beneath the flowing mass of his vestments. He was thin, strikingly so. His face and hands seemed luminous, appearing both to absorb and reflect light. Everyone rose for the start of mass.

Unexpectedly, the priest paused in front of the altar. He turned in Montegut's direction, as if searching for someone or something. Then he looked directly at

Montegut. Unnerved, she straightened. Yet, as her gaze met his, a kindly, playful glint sparkled in his eyes. Just as quickly, he turned back, genuflected before the altar, and proceeded with the mass.[1]

Montegut could not wait to describe the experience to her friend Betty Laiche. She caught up with Betty that night at Dick Meskill's house, a popular hangout for Texas City Catholics of all ages. Meskill's parents, Richard and Cora Tarpey Meskill, were prominent in both the church and the community, and Dick was part of Maxine Montegut's rather extensive circle of friends (both she and Betty Laiche were very attractive and very popular).[2]

Montegut cornered Laiche and started talking about her experience that morning, about how something had happened, something strange and beautiful. She spoke of an instant connection to this new priest, not a physical experience but something otherworldly, something spiritual. "Like a bolt of lightning," she said.

"Oh, go on," Laiche replied.

"No, really!" Montegut said. "I think I've seen a saint."

Betty Laiche was not so sure. Like Montegut, she had attended mass that day, but she had witnessed Roach's very first mass in Texas City, at six in the morning. Because she worked seven days a week at a local defense contractor, that was the only possible time for her. Her experience with the new priest was vastly different from her friend's. In fact, she had been a bit annoyed because Roach spent most of his short sermon lamenting that he was "sorry to leave the wonderful people of Lampasas and the churches he'd built in West Texas" and how disappointed he was to arrive in Texas City to find so few parishioners going to Communion. "This will change!" Roach said, visibly irritated.

"Not many people went to Communion at ten o'clock either," Montegut recalled. "And he said the same thing to us, 'This will change!' But I was very impressed with the homily. He didn't say anything about West Texas."

"Well, I wonder what sort of pastor he's going to be," Laiche said.[3]

Suddenly, there was a commotion on the front porch of the Meskill home. The sound of loud, boisterous laughter and heavy footsteps, punctuated by sharp, rapid smacks on the screen door filled the house. The screen door opened and in lurched Father Bill Roach with his arm wrapped around what appeared to be an exact duplicate of himself, his brother Father John. Both wore long black cassocks and clutched lit cigarettes. They looked like mirror images of each other, right down to the broad grins and howls of laughter.

"It's the Roaches," one of the priests announced. "But hold the bug spray!" the other said. "We don't carry germs."

"Not me anyway. I'm not so sure about my brother."

"Only the Blessed Virgin Mary would know about that."

In the next instant, both made the sign of the cross to each other, then turned and blessed the house and everyone present.[4]

Immediately, everyone in the house, even the skeptical Betty Laiche, crowded around the two priests. They were magnetic, instantly so, especially Father Bill. The true purpose of the visit was to generate more participants in the following Sunday's Holy Communion. Bill Roach was determined to visit every parishioner over the next few days. John Roach had driven in from Galveston to see Bill and decided to join him, especially since he already knew the Meskills.[5]

For the next hour or so, the brothers carried on like some comedy team, filling the house with hilarious, self-effacing stories and cigarette smoke. Few had ever seen two people smoke so much, especially Father Bill. Few had ever seen priests carry on so, cutting up, joking, making fun of each other, and constantly interspersing it all with frequent references to Mary, the Blessed Virgin.

Betty Laiche didn't think priests like those two existed. Priests to her, in her eighteen year-old reality, were old, too old and sedate to be of any interest to her. These priests seemed so alive and fun to be with. She immediately felt comfortable with them, especially Father Bill. He had a way of making everyone in the room feel special. "They were very magnetic, very attractive, and very spiritual," Laiche said later.[6] But Laiche, like many others, perceived their spirituality as being so genuine, so matter-of-fact, and so unobtrusive as to make their humanness and sense of humanity more alive. Laiche felt different, completely different, around them. They reminded her of Father Chuck O'Malley, the easygoing, self-deprecating character Bing Crosby played in the 1944 film classic *Going My Way*.[7] She was beginning to understand what her friend Maxine was talking about.

Most of the brothers' stories centered on their seminary days, telling of kitchen raids, ice-cream runs, and practical jokes played on nearly everyone, including professors and even the bishop. Although they both, particularly Father Bill, had adopted Texas colloquialisms like "ya'll," their accents were distinctly northeastern. Few thought much about that though. Given the heightened fears of attack in the wartime United States, a foreign accent could spell trouble for the speaker. But due to the prosperity of the local oil, gas, and chemical industries that had attracted most of the city's residents, Texas City had become such a melting pot of different people and cultures by 1945 that regional American accents were prevalent.[8]

"Father Roach," someone called out at one point. Both priests turned.

"Which Roach?" they said in unison, laughing.

"In case you haven't noticed, there are a couple of us invading your peaceful home." Everyone laughed.

"Please, just call me Father Bill. And him, Father John."

"We never liked that 'Roach' business anyway."

"Too formal."

"Too insectoid."

"Insectoid? Is that a word?"

"Only the Blessed Virgin Mary would know about that."

More laughter. Amidst the laughter, the brothers very solemnly turned to each other and made the sign of the cross. That is the way the visit went—genuine, open fun accentuated by the brothers' obvious deep devotion to their faith and especially to the Blessed Virgin.[9]

Then, just as suddenly and noisily as they had arrived, the priests left, tromping off down the street, joking and slapping each other on the back as they headed toward the next unsuspecting parishioner's house. From the sidewalk, Father Bill invited the Meskills and their guests to attend the Wednesday-night devotion at the church. "It'll be fun," he shouted, tugging on his brother. By then, no one doubted that anything involving Father Bill could possibly be less than fun.

The church was packed for the Wednesday devotion, a weekly prayer service traditionally dedicated to St. Joseph, the steady center of the Holy Family. As patron saint of the universal church, immigrants, and working people, among other things, St. Joseph was, of course, one of Father Bill's favorite saints. The size of the crowd was a testament to the fact that the new pastor had worked hard to visit as many parishioners as possible. Father Bill had personally invited each one to the devotion. Everyone was special to Roach, and everyone present was responding to the power of his energy and charisma.

Maxine Montegut and Betty Laiche were there. Montegut, of course, was already persuaded of Roach's special nature; she was convinced from the moment she saw him the previous Sunday. Laiche had softened her initial skepticism following her encounter with the Roach brothers at the Meskill house. By the end of the Wednesday devotion, any lingering misgivings had clearly faded. Like her friend Maxine, Betty felt she "had been touched by an angel."

After the devotion, the two girls decided to speak directly to Roach. They had not really done so the previous Sunday night at the Meskills' house. Timidity, an unusual trait for the two teenagers, had held them back. As they rushed to the front of the church, however, they found to their disappointment that the entire congregation had the same idea. Parishioners surrounded Roach, eager to shake his hand and speak with him, enclosing him in a human cocoon.[10]

The girls glumly walked outside and sat down on the curb of the narrow street that separated the church from the Third Avenue Villa Apartments across the way. Father Bill's temporary rectory was in the corner apartment. Montegut and Laiche deliberately chose the spot, hoping Roach would eventually finish with the other parishioners then walk past them. After waiting several minutes, they heard the sound of footsteps.

"Hi," Roach said as he approached, the ever-present cigarette glowing in one hand. "Ever thought about becoming saints?"

"Saints?" Both girls answered in unison, straightening up, startled by Roach's rather sudden appearance and strangely direct question. "Well, not really."

Father Bill smiled and kept walking, plumes of smoke trailing behind him. Before the girls could react, he had already crossed the street and ducked inside his makeshift rectory. The girls followed, not really understanding why, and nervously knocked on the priest's door.

"Aw! Miss Laiche. Miss 'Money-gew,'" he said, smiling.

"Father Roach?" Montegut replied softly.

"Father Roach?" he asked, swinging the door wide open and turning to sit behind his desk. "What did I tell everyone the other night? Call me Father Bill. Now, come in. I'll give you the grand tour. This is this room," he said mockingly, gesturing around him. "And that's that room, which is about all there is to this place. Any questions?"

The girls looked around. It was a tiny apartment, a living space that doubled as an office. Papers were stacked everywhere and books, open and closed, occupied shelves and other surfaces. A lone picture hung on the wall, a reproduction of a painting depicting a boy carving the image of the Virgin Mary. A cloud of cigarette smoke lingered overhead.

A small kitchenette stood just off the living room–office area. What was supposed to be a bedroom was filled with more paper and books. There appeared to be no place to sleep.

Montegut picked up a book, a biography of St. Catherine of Siena. When she opened it, money fell out.

"Father Bill?" she asked, picking up the bills.

"Yes, St. Cath. . . ."

"No, Father," Montegut said, holding up the money.

"Oh, that. Donations," he said. "I guess I forgot about it. We don't have a safe or anything. I just put it here and there until it's needed."

Montegut and Laiche both picked up other books. They found more money. Nearly every book, almost all about saints, had one or two bills stashed in it.

"Feel free to grab a Coke or something from the icebox," Roach said as he worked at his desk.

They went to the refrigerator, but the only thing they found was a pitcher of water, no food whatsoever and certainly no Cokes or other soft drinks.

"Oh, I'm sorry," Roach said grabbing a dollar from yet another book. "You ladies run up to the corner and get some ice cream. We'll eat and talk about saints."

Upon their return from the icehouse, the two eighteen-year-old women joined Father Bill for an evening of ice cream, laughter, and explorations into the nature of spirituality. When they expressed interest in some of his books, Roach let them borrow whatever they wanted. He was completely open and comfortable and made them feel the same way. Frankly, the girls were impressed that Roach even spoke to them at all, that he was so friendly and approachable, so human and yet so visibly spiritual, almost otherworldly. No priest had ever paid much attention to them, treated them as fellow humans. Clearly Father Bill was something quite apart from other members of the clergy they had encountered.

"In that moment, because of him, my whole life was transformed," Montegut said years later. "I did not just want to increase my faith. I wanted to give myself to it. I decided to become a nun that very day." Her friend Betty would arrive at the same decision. Thus, having barely finished their first year of college, Montegut and Laiche came to realize what they truly wanted to do for the rest of their lives: enter the convent. For the time being, however, they agreed to keep their mutual decision to themselves. They would not tell Father Bill, or anyone else, until the following summer.[11]

On Sunday, Roach's second in Texas City, the church was filled for mass—every mass—including the earliest mass at six o'clock, the one Betty Laiche attended. Maxine Montegut went to the ten o'clock service. The parishioners packed in the pews were all talking about one thing, the new pastor. He was the reason they were there. Father Bill had accomplished a lot in a week.

Everyone heard the heavy sound of rustling fabric coming from the side aisle. Swoosh, swoosh came the sound. All heads turned. It was Roach. He had emerged from his apartment/rectory just moments before and stridden rapidly across the narrow street to the front of the church, pausing at the door just long enough to take one last drag from his cigarette.

Inside, he practiced what would become his trademark entrance, a rapid stroll down the side aisle, smiling broadly, briefly chatting with parishioners, playfully tousling the hair of a child, or knocking the cap from some boy's head, until he reached a niche with an auxiliary altar and a statue of the Blessed Virgin Mary. If he was late, as he often was, he would rush past the statue, waving a hand and saying, "I'll talk to you later."

If he had time, however, Roach always stopped there, kneeling before the shrine and praying, sometimes for an extended period. Afterward, he would rise and linger, arranging and rearranging the haphazard collection of votive candles that usually covered the surface of the small side altar. Candles also occupied much of the floor space around the altar, and he spent as much time with them. During this activity, Roach would casually survey the congregation. Some thought he did so to see who was praying and who was not. Others suspected he was simply curious about the faces in the pews. The priest would then disappear into the sacristy to don his vestments and prepare for the start of mass.[12]

The final test came during Communion. The previous week, annoyed at the poor turnout for the Eucharist, Roach had openly proclaimed that matters would change. So, when he turned to face the congregation to distribute the sacrament on that second Sunday, Roach was pleased to see the rail was packed two and three deep.[13] Everyone at the ten o'clock mass, and indeed everyone at every mass throughout the day, took Communion.[14] Father Bill was visibly pleased. His work that week, his visits to each and every parishioner, had paid off. But he was not finished. In fact, he had barely begun.

After mass, he characteristically positioned himself at the front door of the church, cigarette in hand, to greet the congregation. Soon, as always, he was surrounded by well-wishers.

"This priest! This priest!" they were saying. His heart may have still lingered in Lampasas, but as far as Texas City was concerned, Father Bill had arrived.[15]

— 9 —

THE MYSTIC AND THE MONASTERY

Father Bill Roach had not been at his new post in Texas City for more than a week when his brother John enlisted his help. The superior of a convent of Dominican nuns in Detroit, Michigan, Mother Imelda of the Monastery of the Blessed Sacrament, had written Bishop Byrne about the possibility of establishing a new community of nuns somewhere in the Galveston Diocese.

This practice is not unusual. Whenever monastic populations increase and outgrow their living space, it is interpreted as God wishing the community to establish a sister convent in another location.[1] Typically, such new monasteries are founded somewhere far away from the existing community and in a place without a similar institution. This is the way such communities spread and flourish. In this particular instance, however, there was an additional dynamic.

The request from Detroit was driven by mystical visions that a member of the Detroit community, a novice named Sister Diane, had received. Diane's visions, which Mother Imelda believed were coming directly from God, featured a star, the letters "C" and "E," and wisteria. Wisteria grew abundantly on the grounds of the Detroit convent. Its presence at any proposed new location would signal a physical connection between it and the Detroit house.

Sister Diane and Mother Imelda thought the star represented Texas, the Lone Star State, as well as the official seal of the Diocese of Galveston, which contained a single star. These symbols were reinforced by the two letters, which happened be the first two initials of the bishop, Christopher Edward Byrne. There was other imagery as well, but only the star, the two letters, and the wisteria were recorded.[2]

Although mystical visions have played a major part in church history, in modern Roman Catholicism such happenings are viewed with a great deal of skepticism. As a member of the church administration, the bishop had to distance himself from claims of mystical visions, assuming the role of devil's advocate while at the same time remaining close enough to monitor developments. Father John Roach, by then a close personal assistant and advisor to the bishop, was instructed to follow up on the letter from Detroit.[3]

Father John's investigation was favorable. He found the stories of the visions from Detroit credible and sincere. Besides, he opined, the visions were really secondary to the fact that a religious community needed to found a new chapter. Who was he to say otherwise? John consulted his brother, who agreed. The decision was made to help the Dominican nuns establish a new community in Texas.

John and Bill began working together on the project. It was a perfect reason to allow them to spend a few more hours together. They started with a search for properties on the market that might be suitable for the quite specific needs of these nuns from Detroit. They were Second Order Dominican nuns, followers of Saint Dominic (Dominic de Guzman, 1170–1221). But they were also *moniales*, or cloistered nuns, completely removed from everyday society. A *moniale* is a nun in the strictest sense of the word. Although the terms "nuns" and "sisters" are frequently interchanged, as if they were synonyms, in fact, the words refer to very different concepts. Sisters profess "simple vows" and directly interact with the material world, usually as teachers if they are members of the Dominican Order. Moniales are cloistered nuns who profess "solemn vows" and have no contact with the material world, except in cases involving health and other issues that cannot be resolved except through very limited contact with the outside. They are a wholly contemplative society, "living a hidden life of study and humble labor, pondering and living the word of God in imitation of Mary," steeped in prayer and meditation.[4] Economically, such communities sustain themselves through the sale of handmade vestments, unconsecrated hosts, and related materials used during mass and other Roman Catholic services.

The concept of cloistered nuns dates to Saint Dominic, a Castilian Spaniard who founded the Order of Preachers (Dominicans) as well as the first female monastic community, near Prouille, in southern France. In large part, cloistering was about safety, designed to protect a group of local women against the threat of marauding bandits, who were numerous at the time. Eventually, Dominic persuaded the pope to enact a rule that became canon law, providing for automatic excommunication of anyone who entered the cloister of a moniale community. At a time when all of western Europe was Roman Catholic, including even bandits, excommunication meant a one-way ticket to hell. Although not always effective, the rule became a powerful deterrent to almost all individuals who might otherwise have found such a community easy pickings. The nuns, however, were required to remain completely separated from the material world. They could receive visitors, but only with a substantial barrier, like a heavy iron screen, between them. From the time of Saint Dominic forward, cloistered monasteries were constructed to near fortress-like specifications.[5]

Furthermore, mystical visions have been a major part of the story of Saint Dominic. A thirteenth-century prior of the Dominican order wrote that during her pregnancy, Dominic's mother had a vision that she would give birth to a dog bearing a flaming torch in its mouth. She asked a monk about its meaning. He told her the child she carried would set the world on fire with his words. To this day, the dog and the torch have been central to Dominican imagery. According to some, the word "Dominican" is a play on the Latin, *Domini canes* (dogs of the Lord).[6]

The Roach brothers scouted properties on Mondays, their one day off each week. Although Father John could have performed the task on any day of the week as part of his diocesan duties, Father Bill was too consumed with his parish, day and night, to spare any other day.[7]

By this time Father John was based in Houston, living downtown at an office-residence in the Electric Building. He remained a close confidant of Bishop Byrne's, traveling to Galveston often to function as Byrne's secretary, chauffeur, and all-around right-hand man. At the same time, he had become increasingly involved in organizing the dozens of separate and disparate diocesan charities into one cohesive unit. The result was the first chapter of Catholic Charities (a national foundation) established in Texas.

John, like his brother, was good at raising money and materials for any purpose. But whereas Bill preferred to mix with poor and working-class people, John was very comfortable rubbing elbows with the most powerful figures of the day in Houston. By 1945, he was on a first-name basis with the likes of Dr. Ernst "Billy" Bertner, who was instrumental in establishing the Texas Medical Center; Oscar Holcomb, eleven-time mayor of Houston; and oil wildcatter Glen McCarthy, the inspiration for Edna Ferber's novel *Giant* and the 1956 film adaptation, directed by George Stevens. McCarthy's fictionalized literary character, Jett Rink, was played by James Dean in the movie.

Father John phoned real estate agents during the week, then met his brother
the following Monday to view the prospective properties in person. July 2, the
day after Father Bill's first mass at St. Mary of the Miraculous Medal, was the first
such scouting trip. They repeated the exercise on the following Monday, July 9.

Bishop Byrne had initially wanted the new monastery to be established close to
the cathedral in Galveston. However, although wisteria is common in Texas, none
was found on nearby real estate. In addition, the closer properties were located
in densely populated urban areas of Houston. Wanting a change from Detroit,
the new cloistered community desired a more remote setting.

Surprisingly, within two weeks, the brothers had found a hundred-acre, densely
wooded property in deep East Texas, on a rural farm-to-market road called
Lotus Lane just outside of Lufkin. There was a two-story wood frame house
with a wraparound porch and a few outbuildings on the property. The structures
were rundown, but they were certainly habitable. Most of all, though, it was the
remoteness of the place that appealed to the Roach brothers.[8] Something was
missing, however.

"You know, there isn't any wisteria," Father Bill said to the real estate agent.
Initially joining the search for a property as means to spend more time with
his brother, Bill had quickly developed a deep interest in Sister Diane's mystical
visions, pumping John for more information about them. They appealed to his
own deep-rooted sense of the spiritual world, and he became convinced that the
new monastery property should match perfectly every aspect of Diane's imagery.

"Oh yes, there is!" the agent replied. He led the brothers through a thicket of
pine trees to the rear of the lot. The whole area was covered in wisteria. Later,
Father Bill would say, "When I saw that, my knees started shaking."[9]

Soon, Father John was on the road to Michigan. On July 16, he collected Mother
Imelda and Sister Diane at the Monastery of the Blessed Sacrament, not far from
the cathedral downtown, and drove them by car to Texas to view the property.[10]
On their approval, a contract was signed, earnest money was placed in escrow,
and plans for a portion of the Detroit community to relocate to East Texas were
quickly implemented. In fact, the Detroit nuns had been making serious plans for
that eventuality as early as the fall of 1944, so focused was their determination.[11]

On Tuesday, July 24, the first group of nuns left Detroit for Texas, followed
three days later by several moving vans. More departed on August 4 and
August 12. A month later, on September 18, the final group began their journey
south. In all, eighteen nuns left Detroit, eleven of them novices, including
Sister Diane. Although the prioress, Mother Imelda, and two of the founding

members of the Detroit community made the move to Texas, the majority of the new monastery's inhabitants were under age twenty-five. In fact, only one novice remained in Detroit, and the majority of the nuns who remained there were over the age of forty.[12]

The new inhabitants had barely arrived and started to settle into a routine when local anti-Catholic feelings began to surface. There was a small Catholic church in Lufkin, serving an equally small Catholic community. Another such church and community existed in neighboring Nacogdoches, to the north. However, the vast majority of the surrounding population was Protestant, largely Southern Baptist.

Some who saw the predominantly white habits worn by the nuns thought they were Ku Klux Klan women, an irony since the Klan, among other things, was rabidly anti-Catholic. Others refused to interact at all with the community, thinking them cultish and strange. Considering the self-sufficient nature of cloistered life, these would normally have been only minor concerns. In those early days, however, the nuns did need provisions, requiring some interaction with those living around them. Once established, they would be able to work the farmland and grow their own food, but when they arrived they had nothing. Some local grocers refused to sell to them. Not all grocers were like that, of course, but there was enough resistance to make life uncomfortable.

The nuns regarded all these developments as penance and moved forward as best they could. Fortunately, Father Bill and his brother made weekly trips in a borrowed truck filled with fresh fruit, vegetables, and in particular, doughnuts, all donated from one or more of their sources for such things. Then the former owner of the property tried to back out of the sale. Staunchly Protestant and quite openly anti-Catholic, he had not realized the farm was being purchased by a group of Dominican nuns from Detroit. Raised in a South that in some respects was still fighting the Civil War, he was both anti-Catholic and anti-North. It did not matter that some of the nuns, such as Mother Imelda, were actually from Canada. All he knew was that a bunch of "Yankee Catholics" had settled on his land and he wanted them gone. He had been working through a real estate agent and did not realize the identity of the buyer until the time came to close the sale.

Eventually, the owner reversed his decision. There are two different stories about what happened. One story has Father John retaining a diocesan lawyer, who filed a breach of contract suit for "specific performance." "Specific performance," one of two choices in such cases, involves the court forcing the breaching party to follow through with its legal obligation—which is what the nuns needed most. They had little interest in seeking "money damages" as compensation.[13] The other story involves the wife of the seller, herself a Catholic from Nacogdoches, persuading her husband to honor the deal. As the story goes, he agreed to do so only if his wife promised never again to attend a Catholic church service. She agreed, and for the rest of her life she attended her husband's Protestant church.[14] Although the first story seems the more plausible, it might be that the latter also has some truth. What was important for the nuns, however, was that they were allowed to stay.

On November 9, 1945, the Dominican Monastery of the Holy Infant Jesus was formally erected and blessed by Bishop Byrne. Among those in attendance were Father Bill and Father John. The brothers continued to make regular pilgrimages to Lufkin with large quantities of fresh produce, fruit, and other perishable items to sustain the community. Anything the nuns did not consume during the week, and there was a lot of it, they canned and stored. One Monday, the brothers delivered a large refrigerator. On another visit they brought a washing machine. On several occasions they brought seminarians from La Porte to clear land, build work sheds, and make repairs. For nearly two years, the brothers kept the monastery fed and reasonably operational. It was at least a three-hour drive from Houston to Lufkin in those days. The Roach brothers usually stayed for lunch after saying mass and hearing confessions. It would be late, often after dark, when they returned to Houston and Texas City, respectively.[15]

Early on, Father Bill became deeply influenced by Sister Diane. Her visions, mysticism, and a quality described as "extraordinary spiritual grace" were attributes he aspired to, mostly to help others aspire to the same transcendence.[16] In the coming months Roach would listen carefully to Sister Diane. In turn, through Father Bill, her words would begin to be heard with growing frequency in Texas City, most often as part of Sunday sermons delivered at St. Mary of the Miraculous Medal.[17]

=10=

"A GUARDIAN ANGEL VISITED ON THE CITY"

Early in 1946, longshoremen began reporting that railroad boxcars loaded with hundred-pound bags of potentially explosive ammonium nitrate fertilizer were arriving at the Texas City Terminal Railway Company so hot as to make them hard to handle, reportedly as hot as 200 degrees Fahrenheit.[1] The railway's vice president, W. H. "Swede" Sandberg, was notified right away. In late December 1945, Sandberg had arranged to have the fertilizer moved through Texas City from at least three manufacturing plants in Nebraska and Iowa for transatlantic shipment to the French Supply Council, an entity formed to restart, among other things, farming and food production in postwar France.

Problems appeared with the arrival of the very first shipments in January. It was suspected the bags of fertilizer were already hot when loaded at the point of origin, particularly at one plant in Nebraska, due in part to the waterproofing on the bags.[2] Ammonium nitrate fertilizer must be granular in order to be easily spread over open fields. If the fertilizer gets wet, it cakes, sometimes becoming almost as hard as stone if the conditions are right. To keep the fertilizer dry, it was packed for transportation in a multi-ply composite bag consisting of several layers of paper sandwiching at least one layer of asphalt.

Longshoremen were finding many bags burst open on arrival in Texas City, with fertilizer strewn about the interior of the boxcars. The ammonium nitrate coming into contact with the exposed layer of asphalt generated a lot of heat. This excessive heat caused the unbroken bags to become dry and brittle, so that they broke open easily when unloaded.

Sandberg contracted a professional photographer to document the condition in which the bags of fertilizer were arriving in Texas City. Then, on February 12, 1946, Sandberg mailed the photographs along with his findings to the Military Chemical Works in Coplant, Nebraska, the source of the problem shipments. In response to the letter and photographs, Floyd Steed, a representative of Military Chemical Works, traveled to Texas City. He met with Sandberg, who explained the situation in detail. The two men also observed the fertilizer being unloaded from the boxcars, noting the excessive heat and broken bags. Sandberg knew that Military Chemical Works had been under federal contract to produce military ordnance during the war, and also that ammonium nitrate was an ingredient in the manufacture of certain explosives. He asked Steed whether ammonium nitrate on its own was explosive. "No," Steed answered.

After Steed's visit, the incidents of broken fertilizer bags and overheated boxcars subsided for a while. In late spring, however, overheated shipments, with multiple broken and brittle bags of fertilizer, again started arriving in Texas City. Apart from a handful of people who were directly involved, no one in or around Texas City had the slightest idea that massive quantities of ammonium nitrate, thousands of tons at a time, were being handled nearby. Not even the mayor knew.[3]

However, Dick Benedict knew. As the local union agent and timekeeper for the International Longshoremen's Association, he was aware of everything happening on and around the docks. It was his job to acquire gangs of longshoremen for whatever work materialized and to keep careful logs of precisely how long each individual in each gang worked. He would submit the hours to management and follow up with workers to make sure they were paid accordingly. The reconciliation of time logged with pay had been a contentious issue before Benedict cofounded a Texas City chapter of the union in 1935. Benedict spoke with Father Bill frequently and at length about the docks and the numerous labor issues that arose there.[4]

These discussions with Dick Benedict were only a small part of Roach's schedule. Father Bill's routine began early. On Sundays he said two masses, at 6:30 and 9:00 A.M. When he first arrived in Texas City the second mass had been at 10 A.M., but Roach moved it an hour earlier to allow him more time to visit parishioners. On weekdays, mass was at 6:45 A.M. (later changed to 7:00 A.M.). Each Wednesday evening there was a novena at 7:30 P.M. Confessions were heard from 7:00 to 9:00 P.M. on Saturday nights.

Roach wrote his own Sunday sermons and homilies. He really labored over them, being more comfortable with speaking face-to-face than writing. His schedule might suggest a lot of downtime, but he was always on the move, ranging back and forth across Texas City, visiting families and those who were elderly or sick. As the only person occupying the St. Mary church, he was responsible for maintaining the property and all other business related to the physical structure.

On Mondays, Roach's day off, he would drive to Houston to visit his brother John. The itinerary might be lunch and a round of golf or a run to restock the Monastery of the Holy Infant Jesus in Lufkin. Sometimes he would stop in La Porte on the way and invite one or two of the seminarians to join him and his brother for the day. Larry Lee and Dick Meskill often accepted.[5]

Father Bill and the seminarians usually arrived at Father John's downtown residence-office during the lunch hour, when every parking place on the street was taken. Larry Lee remembered being anxious that they might not find a spot and might miss Father John altogether. But Father Bill would always recite the *Hail Mary*, drive around the block once, and suddenly a spot would open up. Lee recalls that happening more than once. Father Bill would merely laugh and park the car. They were never late.[6]

Frequently, the Roach brothers would borrow a pickup truck, load it with fresh vegetables and fruit bought at roadside stands, and spend a half day or so at the Lufkin monastery. Seminarians from La Porte, Lee and Meskill among them, would be genially conscripted into helping with fence repairs and other jobs around the property.[7]

On Sundays, after reciting mass in Texas City, Father Bill would drive to the home of Richard and Cora Meskill for biscuits and coffee. The Meskills had a long history of hosting the local clergy, and Father Bill had an open invitation to drop by the house anytime. Richard was the postmaster of Texas City. Cora was the daughter of William Tarpey, the first mayor of Texas City, and the sister of Ruhl J. "Pete" Tarpey. Their son Dick was one of the seminarians who would sometimes accompany Father Bill to Houston and Lufkin on Mondays. Recall also that it was at the Meskill home where Maxine Montegut and Betty Laiche first met the Roach brothers.[8]

After visiting with the Meskills, Roach would walk down to 132 Eighth Avenue North, not far away, to visit Pete Tarpey, whom he had befriended almost immediately on arriving in Texas City. The youngest son of William Tarpey and a parishioner of Father Bill's, Pete Tarpey was very active in labor organizing but chronic alcoholism hampered his effectiveness as well as his ability to keep a job.

When Roach first met him, Tarpey was delivering food to longshoremen and other dock workers as a livelihood, but he lost that job as well. Tarpey was responsible for sparking Roach's interest in labor issues in Texas City. In part because of his family name, but mostly due to his own deep concern for working conditions in his city, Tarpey was in close contact with most of the local union leadership. It was through Tarpey that Father Bill first met Dick Benedict, the aforementioned representative of the International Longshoremen's Association.[9]

Benedict lived at the corner of Texas Avenue and Bay Street North, about a thousand feet from Galveston Bay. He moved there specifically so that he could keep an eye on the shipping channel and the docks. When an arriving ship passed Snake Island, he had just enough time to walk to the docks and oversee union work there. Benedict's house became a regular Sunday stop for Father Bill, part of the circuit that included the Meskills' and Pete Tarpey's homes. But Roach visited Benedict at other times during the week as well, often accompanied by Tarpey. On workdays they would sometimes find Benedict at home, waiting for the next ship to pass Snake Island. If a ship arrived, Roach and Tarpey would go to the docks with Benedict. On other occasions they would roam the docks without Benedict, being careful not to interfere or get in the way. They simply observed the working conditions, mostly for Roach's benefit. He was trying to understand the many issues important to both labor and management.[10]

Roach kept incredibly odd and long hours. He often made unexpected late-night telephone calls to parishioners and non-parishioners alike. He would also appear suddenly at their homes or places of business. When not doing that, he roamed the streets on foot, sometimes all night long. He visited with homeless people, drunks, vagrants, sailors on leave, prostitutes, and other creatures of the night who frequented the area just south of Texas Avenue, toward the Bay Street side, between downtown and the docks. The area was known locally as "sailors retreat," a notorious part of town that was sometimes a dangerous place to be, especially at night.[11] Also located south of Texas Avenue, between sailors retreat and the docks, was the poorest neighborhood in Texas City.

Father Bill would arrive with trays of coffee and doughnuts from the Uneeda Café on Texas Avenue. He also scrounged more substantial food from whatever nearby café or diner had scraps and leftovers that were about to be tossed out. Roach distributed the food to the homeless, quite a few of them because of the housing shortage. Roach also gave away some of the parishioners' donations he had stashed inside the many books in his apartment-rectory. He would always stuff a few bills in his pockets before leaving for sailors retreat.

Father Bill would find a place to sit with the coffee and doughnuts at or near sailors retreat and wait for whomever wished to chat and sip coffee for a while. Roach was so likable, self-effacing, and full of jokes that he was readily accepted by the regulars, particularly the homeless and the prostitutes. He never seemed to want anything from them. He was just there, always smiling. It was his way, a nonconfrontational approach to changing the direction of people's lives. Some changed. Most did not. Those who did change Roach referred to as "caught fish," a play on the passage in the Gospel of Matthew: "Come after me, and I will make you fishers of men."[12]

One of the night creatures who became a "caught fish" was Eddie, a young merchant marine and sometime dockworker. His drug and alcohol abuse, along with nights carousing near Texas Avenue, had destroyed his marriage and left him unemployed and homeless. After a few sessions sitting with Roach, drinking coffee and breaking bread acquired from some unknown café, Eddie started talking about making a change, cleaning up his life, and getting back on track. But he did not know how to start, or where. Understanding his dilemma, Roach gently nudged Eddie every time he saw him. Eddie eventually committed to getting sober, with Roach's help. Father Bill also helped Eddie find a permanent job on the docks and found him a small apartment across the street from St. Mary.[13]

Once, when asked why he spent so much time with the people of sailors retreat, Roach asked, smiling, "Wasn't Jesus homeless?"[14]

Roach would often drop in on Dick Benedict, who lived only a few blocks away from sailors retreat, either before or after his late-night excursions. Sometimes Roach arrived at one or two in the morning, but Benedict never seemed to mind. Roach was welcomed everywhere, a good trait for someone with very little concept of time. In fact, Roach spent so much time touring the city—visiting the sick, helping the homeless, and sitting in on city commissioners' meetings, among other things—he would often have to rush back to St. Mary for mass, confessions, or other church duties. Parishioners awaiting his arrival would eventually spot him dashing along the side aisle of the church before disappearing into the confessional or through the door of the sacristy to prepare for mass.[15]

Not long after Father Bill's reassignment to Texas City, parishioner Katherine Hunter experienced the frustration of trying to find him. Her mother was near death at one of the local clinics and was asking for the Sacrament of Last Rites. Hunter went to the church, then to Father Bill's apartment across the street, but he was not at either place. She drove to the Meskills' home. They had not seen him since the morning. The Tarpeys had not seen him all day. She drove to other homes and past a few of the town's cafés, looking for Roach walking along one of the streets, or at least for his car. He was nowhere to be found, and all the while Hunter's mother was dying.

Hunter finally went back to St. Mary. She rushed inside the absolutely empty church. Desperately, she raised her arms before the statue of the Virgin Mary and cried out, "Father, please. Where are you?"

"I'm right here," came a voice from behind her.

Hunter turned to see the smiling face of Father Bill, standing only a few feet away. She never heard him approach, and she was certain no one had been in the church when she entered. She rushed to the clinic with Father Bill, who administered the Last Rites and remained with the family until the dying woman had passed. From that day forward, Hunter regarded Father Bill as a guardian angel visited upon the city.[16]

One Sunday morning, Father Bill noticed Pete Tarpey was not at mass. Later, on his regular daily circuit of the city, Roach found Tarpey at his kitchen table, drinking and looking the worse for wear. Roach simply sat down at the table with his friend and started talking with him as if nothing were out of the ordinary. They sat together in the kitchen until early afternoon, then moved into the living room. Hours passed. Eventually, the sun set and darkness fell. Father Bill kept talking. Pete kept drinking. At one point early in the evening, Pete finally said he was going to bed to sleep off his drunk. Roach had not left Pete's side all day. He helped his wobbly friend climb the stairs and locate his room. Once they were inside the room and the door closed, however, neither man emerged for another thirty-six hours.

On the morning after the following day, the door to Pete Tarpey's room swung open and out he strode, stone cold sober. Behind him was Father Bill, tired but laughing and joking as usual. No one ever knew what transpired in that room, but from that day forward Pete Tarpey never touched another drink. For many years, his friends and family had tried unsuccessfully to help Tarpey get sober, and they had largely given up hope that Tarpey could ever change. Seemingly, Father Bill had worked another miracle.[17]

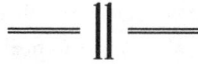

=II=
CRACKS IN THE SKY

On the night of September 12, 1945, the turbine engine of the tanker *Black Mountain* exploded, injuring three crew members and causing the ship to run aground a short distance from the Texas City docks. Loaded with fuel oil and 180-octane gasoline, the tanker, owned by Gulf Oil, completely blocked the shipping lane linking the Ports of Houston, Texas City, and Galveston—one of the busiest waterways in the nation. Two of the injured sailors were released from Marine Hospital in Galveston within a week, but the third was hospitalized longer.[1]

The incident, occurring only ten days after the formal surrender of Japan and the end of World War II, signaled the emergence of an unexpected systemic flaw caused by the cessation of hostilities. Since 1941 the US Coast Guard had done precisely what its name suggests: guard the coast. Among other things, it extensively monitored maritime shipments to and from ports and industries, especially those involved in war production. In particular, the Coast Guard exerted strong security and safety oversight over interstate shipments of unstable, combustible materials, such as munitions and their components. Once the war ended, the diligent Coast Guard monitoring evaporated, with little if any regulation to replace it. As one government study stated decades later, safety regulation was left to "a consensus of expert judgments for the three parties with direct interest in the problem, namely the shippers, the carriers, and their suppliers."[2]

Lack of interstate and maritime safety oversight of industrial shipments would become a major issue in the months and years following the explosion on the *Black Mountain*.[3] Because the issue directly affected his parishioners, many of whom worked on the docks and in the vast network of surrounding industries, Father Bill became involved in the issue almost from the day of his arrival on July 1. First, he began educating himself about the realities of Texas City. He became a regular at the old two-story community building on Sixth Street that housed city offices, a small jail, the public library, an auditorium, and a meeting room.[4] He attended meetings of city departments as well as the Chamber of Commerce, speaking with anyone willing to spend a few minutes with him. He made it abundantly clear his only agenda was to understand both sides of any given issue. He was, at this early stage of his research, only an observer.[5]

The more Father Bill found out, the more he realized working conditions, specifically general safety, was not the only concern of his parishioners nor of the other residents of Texas City. Apart from safety issues, wages, working conditions, public heath, and the very infrastructure of the whole town needed immediate attention. It did not take long for Roach to identify some of the major players in the discussion, particularly with regard to labor. Pete Tarpey (a Catholic) and Dick Benedict (a Protestant), both of whom quickly became close friends and confidants of Roach's, were among his earliest contacts. As events unfolded in Texas City over the next several months, Father Bill came to understand he was going to need all the help he could get to fully understand the inner workings of Texas City.[6]

On September 28, 1945, Texas City petroleum workers belonging to Local 449 of the Oil Workers International union joined a nationwide strike and walked off their jobs. The move immediately affected local refineries, including three of the largest in the nation—Pan American Refining Corporation, American Liberty Pipe Line Company, and Republic Oil Refining Company. Because of their dependence on refinery products, other local companies would feel secondary effects of the strike, as did Monsanto, Carbide and Carbon, and the Tin Processing Company, all located near the docks.

The strikers were seeking better wages and a reduction of the workweek from forty-eight hours to forty. Federal attempts to freeze wages and prices during the war were mostly successful in preventing inflation and cost-of-living spikes. Some aspects of the controls had mixed results, however, despite the efforts of all the federal agencies created to combat the problem.

Prices, production, and procurement were controlled by the War Production Board (WPB). But it had little if any power to enforce its policies, particularly with regard to procurement. Military contracts had long been the realm of the army and navy, and both refused to hand over to the WPB the job of issuing contracts. Thus, throughout the war, the army and navy handled their own contracts, always favoring the largest corporations. The result was a 100 percent increase in profits for the thirty-three biggest US corporations by the end of the war. In contrast, wages, though incrementally increasing, always lagged behind corporate profits and, more importantly, the cost of living.

In July 1942, the National War Labor Board capped wage growth at 15 percent annually, based on cost-of-living increases between January 1941 and May 1942. By the end of the war, however, the cost of living was increasing much faster than during that seventeen-month baseline, outpacing wages. Additionally, some aspects of price controls failed to regulate much of anything, especially food costs. One problem was congressional legislation that undermined farm price limits set by the Office of Price Administration, causing escalating grocery bills.[7] Moreover, while tax reduction incentives were heaped on corporations to fuel war production, individual tax rates increased substantially.[8] On top of that, workers were required to purchase war bonds by payroll deduction. Of course, in return the workers received an interest-earning savings account, but it was payable only after the war ended.

By the end of the war citizens were ready for a change, starting with a forty-hour workweek. The longer workweek may have served to sustain large-scale production for the war effort, workers thought, but it seemed unnecessary nearly a month after the Japanese surrender and suspension of government contracts. Father Bill would learn a lot from the oil workers' strike.

The National Association of Manufacturers released a statement warning that a sudden increase in wages would lead to inflation and unemployment. On the other side, labor leaders viewed the specter of unemployment as an oft-used management ploy, sometimes referred to as "restructuring." It was a not-so-vailed threat that strikes and higher wages would result in fewer positions being available. Workers believed that companies lamenting the prospect of paying higher wages were less concerned with the overall economy than with their own profit margins.

Labor had the backing of President Harry Truman. Stating publicly that business must either raise wages or lower prices, the president sent a twenty-one-point domestic program to Congress just days after the formal surrender of Japan and the end of World War II. Among the items Truman proposed was an immediate increase to the minimum wage, tax reform for individuals, and federal housing aid. Congress vowed to give Truman nothing. An increasingly anti-labor and anti-union Congress was instead focused on dismantling as much of President Franklin Roosevelt's New Deal as possible.[9]

There was more than one reason Congress and a growing number of state governments had begun to embrace business and reject labor by 1945. For one, big business was funneling a great deal of funding to electoral candidates. Secondly, after the Japanese attack on Pearl Harbor, labor leaders had announced no-strike pledges. But pledges are not laws, and there were thousands of labor strikes during the war, some of them crippling.

To Congress and many Americans, the worst was the coal strike of 1943–44. In May 1943, with the war well under way, John L. Lewis, head of the United Mine Workers, demanded a pay increase of two dollars a day for union members because the cost of living had outpaced government-controlled wages. When company owners refused, two million mine workers walked out and coal production ceased. Work resumed within a few weeks on assurances of raises from mine owners, but as negotiations faltered in June, the strike resumed. The cycle was repeated a number of times until November 1, when coal miners struck and refused to return to work until their demands were met.

Not only did homes go unheated that winter, but war production slowed substantially, especially steel manufacturing, and coal-dependent railroads were forced to cut schedules radically. The strike dragged on into 1944, ultimately resulting in a union victory. Workers got their raise, but that event, and the image of John L. Lewis in particular, did a lot of damage to the hard-fought gains of labor in the twentieth century. As the oil workers' strike got underway in Texas City, a growing desire to create sweeping anti-labor, anti-strike regulations was gaining ground on the state and federal levels.[10]

On October 5, despite his affinity for labor, President Truman ordered the US Navy to seize all oil refineries affected by the strike, nationwide. Such a move was possible because after the coal strike of 1943–44, Congress broadened the president's power to use the military to keep plants open and operational during a strike.[11] Even though the war had ended, the law remained in effect.

On the same day as the president's order, Pan American Refining Corporation placed a full-page advertisement in the *Texas City Sun*, stating its position. Among the points Pan American made were that oil workers' wages were already among the highest being paid, union strikes were illegal, union members were being duped, and finally the "present dispute is a test of whether all industry will take the unsound and inflationary path or the sound way to a secure situation for all." For all these reasons, the corporation called on union members to break the strike and work independently.[12] A week later, the *Texas City Sun* reported that the refineries were "back in operation under US Navy control."[13]

In the midst of this labor unrest, there was a housing shortage in Texas City and across the nation. Millions of discharged military members combined with years of rationing of construction materials were the root causes, yet another aftereffect of the war. Gradual relaxation of rationing had initiated a lot of new construction in Texas City—houses, department stores, and a Methodist school, among other things—but it was not enough. Compounding the problem in Texas City were outdated zoning laws. Improper zoning leads to odd structural combinations, such as car dealerships wedged between homes, or bars adjacent to churches. In October, Mayor E. A. Johnson and the four city commissioners began work on new zoning laws. Meanwhile, to ease the housing crisis, Texas City citizens were asked to consider renting a portion of their homes to people in need of housing.[14]

On Tuesday, October 30, Bill and John Roach convened a meeting of the Catholic Men's Club. They had asked a colleague, Father Thomas O'Rourke of St. Thomas College in Houston, to speak about labor in Texas City. Echoing statements by President Truman, O'Rourke said, among other things, "Labor wants a wage above the starvation level, and to bring forward a standard of living."[15]

Father Bill's self-initiated education about labor-management issues was eye-opening, particularly with respect to the complexities involved. The more he learned, the more he realized wages and working hours were only the topmost of multiple layers of concerns, some deep-seated and years in the making. All of this was new to Roach—who had not encountered anything remotely similar in Lampasas—but he kept digging and reveling in his discoveries.

One of those layers of concern involved job classification, which on the surface might seem rather incidental. In fact, the vocabulary of job classification includes the term "work incidental," a perpetual proposal of management.[16] Work incidental allowed that if workers needed to conduct work outside of their job description in order to perform their regular duties, then that extra work was "incidental to the job" and thus did not require additional compensation. This concept seems rather logical and reasonable, but Roach soon discovered that it was a long-standing technique of management to erode union-defined job descriptions. If allowed to progress, work incidental would expand to the point of eliminating job descriptions altogether and creating more responsibilities for those remaining in the workforce. It has been an age-old corporate cost-cutting measure. "Consolidation" is another of the names it goes by.

Of course, on the surface, loss of job security is at the heart of the issue. However, heaping more duties on overworked employees becomes a safety concern as well. Father Bill could not help but notice how nearly every labor issue eventually pointed back to safety.[17]

Father Bill also became immersed in the effect of the oil strike on the local community. Texas City, a small but vibrant municipality, was economically dependent on all of the many large industries located just beyond its city limits. They provided most of the jobs in that part of Galveston Bay, and since most of the industries were interrelated, a strike involving the refineries had ripple effects on nearly every other type of business in the area.

A strike, especially a long strike like that of the oil workers, not only caused economic hardship for the affected industries and striking workers (the minimal union strike pay did not stretch very far), but hit every other local business as well. Grocery stores, service stations, cafés, restaurants, movie theaters, drugstores, icehouses, and other commercial trades lost income. Roach observed how quickly the strike generated animosity and frayed nerves on multiple levels.[18]

Father Bill had the unique ability to empathize with elements of all sides, making him quite effective at smoothing over a lot of the nastiness of that strike and of many other disagreements to come. He was not always a welcomed figure in negotiations, but no one ever doubted his sincere desire to find common ground.[19] That distinguished him from most (not all) other Texas City residents.

Strike tensions seemed to ease slightly when the Tin Processing Company near the docks adopted a forty-hour workweek and agreed to a 15 percent wage increase on November 23. Father Bill was a guest attendee when local Texas City oil workers' union members met in the auditorium at city hall to discuss negotiations with the three refineries. The glimmer of hope for an end to the strike ended on November 27, when Pan American workers rejected a 15 percent pay increase, apparently without a forty-hour workweek.[20]

Following the union vote, Pan American's general manager, P. J. Sweeney, stated publicly that oil workers who had not attended the union meeting could expect to begin working a forty-hour week when they returned to their jobs. Any Pan American employee who had attended the meeting and participated in the negative vote would however continue working the full forty-eight hours a week.[21]

In early December, oil workers at eleven Sinclair refineries nationwide accepted their company's offer. Shortly thereafter, the US Navy relinquished control over those operations and workers resumed their duties. Although Sinclair was only one of a great many refineries, clearly some progress was being made.[22]

Then, on December 4, an accidental fire caused half a million dollars worth of damage at the Monsanto chemical plant, located adjacent to the north slip of the Texas City wharf. A cold front colliding with the warm Texas Gulf Coast air produced heavy storms and a sudden drop in temperature, which cracked a porcelain pipeline filled with ethyl benzene in the plant's alkylation unit. Lightning then ignited the benzene. Although plant first responders and Texas City firefighters brought the blaze under control in two hours, the damage was extensive enough to close the facility for repairs. Partial operations were restored by March 26, 1946, but not until June 14 did the plant return to full capacity. The facility in Texas City was at the time one of only two locations nationwide producing styrene, an ingredient in the manufacture of synthetic rubber. In a matter of two hours US styrene production was cut in half.[23]

Just twenty-three days after the Monsanto fire and fourteen weeks after the *Black Mountain* incident, there was another sign of the inherent danger on the docks. At 4:10 A.M. on December 27, there was an engine room explosion on board the Swedish tanker *Sveaborg*, moored at the Texas City docks. The blast crushed the ship's superstructure and ripped a jagged hole fifteen feet wide below the port side water line. The tanker sank to the bottom of the slip in seconds. Three crew members were killed outright, twelve others were injured, and nine were missing, including a cook, a cabin boy, and a watchman. The blast damaged houses and other structures several hundred feet away. Texas City watchman J. P. Cartwright, making his rounds nearby, was blown through the air, suffering a gash and bruises.[24]

The tanker had been loading gasoline when the explosion occurred. Chief H. J. Baumgarten of the Texas City Fire Department reported that the gasoline was being pumped out of the tanker in advance of attempting to raise it. Baumgarten and his crew of volunteer firefighters had assisted in both the Monsanto fire and the *Black Mountain* explosion. By January 22, recovery teams were still cutting into the wrecked tanker. Eight of the nine missing crew had been located, all dead. The ninth, presumed dead, was never found. The cause of the explosion, if known, was never made public.[25]

Meanwhile, oil workers voted to reject Pan American's latest offer, which included an 18 percent pay raise. On January 25, three days after the vote, Pan American claimed that the oil workers had misunderstood their offer. Regardless of whether there actually had been a misunderstanding, on January 29 the union voted to accept the offer of an 18 percent increase along with a forty-hour workweek. The navy moved out of Pan American, and the oil workers stepped into their old positions. Workers at the other Texas City refineries, including American Liberty and Republic, followed suit. Even Monsanto and other interests not directly involved in oil refining adopted the 18 percent increase and forty-hour week as well. The oil workers' strike was over in Texas City, but the danger they faced was not.[26]

On February 7, 1946, an oil barge exploded, burned, and sank in the shipping lane near Pasadena, forty miles north of Texas City. Two days later, two workers were killed in an explosion at the General American Tank Storage Terminal at the Port of Houston Authority, just across the channel from Pasadena. Eleven weeks later, on April 29, a storage tank exploded at American Liberty Pipe Line Company in Galena Park, adjacent to the Port of Houston Authority. On May 8, a fatal explosion occurred at Houston Refining Company in Houston, forty-five miles from Texas City.[27]

While these and other calamities played out, a series of epidemics heightened public health concerns. Throughout the summer of 1945, polio swept the Texas Gulf Coast, hitting Houston particularly hard. In December, flu struck. Memories of the devastating flu pandemic of 1918–20, at the close of another world war, were still fresh in the minds of those who lived through it. A disease that had caused the deaths of an estimated five hundred million people worldwide was not to be taken lightly.

In March 1946, rabies replaced the flu as the central public health concern in the Galveston Bay area. The outbreak had begun the previous year in Galveston, but now had spread to Texas City and Houston. Like the polio epidemic, rabies severely affected Houston. On March 12, fifteen persons were treated for rabies symptoms in one day. By June, 245 rabid dogs had been identified in that city.[28]

Also in March, a Texas state health officer warned of the potential for a rise in typhus cases due to lack of waste control, particularly municipal garbage disposal. The unsanitary conditions also accounted for the mounting cases of rabies and polio throughout the southeastern part of the state, the officer stated. Though the area dodged the danger of typhus, Chagas disease (similar to African sleeping sickness) broke out in Corpus Christi and San Antonio. Then typhoid fever struck Houston at the end of April, coinciding with a 63 percent increase in major crime and a 100 percent increase in murders in the city.[29]

═ 12 ═

"THE BATTLE"

On February 26, during a meeting of the oil workers union in Texas City, a group calling itself the Independent Federation of Pan American Refinery Employees attempted to initiate a union vote to make itself the official liaison between labor and management. The Independent Federation subsequently applied to the National Labor Relations Board for authorization to replace the oil workers union. Such a move would have effectively destroyed the existing union shop in Texas City.

In response to suspicions that the Independent Federation was actually a front created by Pan American Refining Corporation, the National Labor Relations Board initiated an investigation and demanded a full disclosure from Pan American. At a subsequent union meeting, monitored by the National Labor Relations Board, a vote was taken to address Pan American's attempt to undermine official union business. Indeed, during the meeting the Independent Federation of Oil Workers was unmasked as a front for the corporation. The vote succeeded in thwarting the attempt by Pan American to take over the local union chapter.[1]

Also in February, Texas City announced the creation of two new full-time city positions: fire marshal and superintendent of garbage.[2] Until that point, the Texas City Fire Department was composed entirely of volunteers. Even its chief, Henry Baumgarten, was only a part-time employee.[3] His full-time job was as purchasing agent for the Texas City Terminal Railway. The city's rapid growth before and during the war had made a volunteer force insufficient to deal with the threat of fire and maintain community safety. The garbage situation was even worse.

There had never been any form of regular garbage collection in Texas City, any official location for garbage disposal, nor any plan for burying or otherwise treating refuse. Generally, city residents had been hauling their garbage out to the dike and dumping it somewhere—anywhere—along its length. The Texas City dike, accessed from Eighth Avenue North and Bay Street, had been constructed as a breakwater between Galveston Bay and the harbor in 1914. Six years later, it was extended five miles into the bay. Promoted as "the world's longest fishing pier," by 1946, it was overflowing with rotting garbage.[4]

The Texas City Chamber of Commerce petitioned the city commissioners to outlaw dumping on the dike. Describing "flies and hordes of rats," the petitioners also proposed establishing another location for collecting and burying the city's garbage in order to combat the problem of disease.[5] Disease was indeed a growing problem in the winter of 1946. An outbreak of flu struck the city particularly hard beginning in December. Cases of polio, sleeping sickness (Chagas disease), and rabies had already been confirmed and were on the rise.[6]

Swarms of rats ranged over the length of the dike. Infamous carriers of rabies and the plague, they spread a host of other diseases as well. For instance, the insect that transmits Chagas disease feeds on both rats and humans. Naturally, the dike was also full of flies, which at the time were mistakenly thought to spread polio. Flies are, of course, a public health risk, but the major risk factors for polio—lack of sanitation and improper disposal of human fecal waste—were also prevalent in Texas City.

The storm sewer system in Texas City was rudimentary at best and nonexistent at worst, owing largely to the devastating 1943 hurricane, the same storm that so severely damaged St. Mary of the Miraculous Medal. For a community located at sea level, drainage was essential—but there was none.[7] Even worse, disposal of the city's raw sewage was fast becoming a significant, serious health problem, particularly with respect to polio. Wastewater from every sink, lavatory, urinal, and toilet was being drained directly into the bay, as had been the practice since before the founding of the city. By 1946, with a city population approaching eighteen thousand, a procedure that might have worked fifty years earlier was a disaster in the making. The Texas Game, Fish, and Oyster Commission eventually intervened on September 3, 1946, declaring Texas City in violation of state law for causing the widespread death of marine life in Galveston Bay. The commission ordered Texas City to install a sewage treatment plant. Ten days later, the Texas City health officer resigned. In the meantime, residents were swimming, fishing, and crabbing in bay water laden with raw sewage and disease.[8]

On March 19, a consortium of Texas City religious, business, and veterans' organizations staged a protest during that week's meeting of the city commissioners. Declaring the dike "a menace," they demanded the development of a proper plan for handling garbage and the immediate implementation of covered garbage cans. Father Bill Roach participated in that protest, and so did the local League of Women Voters, which caught city officials' attention because an election was scheduled for the next month.

Against the backdrop of disease, rats, and raw sewage, electoral campaigns were underway for the mayor, city commissioners, and a host of other city positions. The main issue, not surprisingly, was sanitation. The incumbent mayor, E. A. Johnson, had gained approval for sewer repairs and had established the full-time, paid positions of superintendent of garbage and fire marshal. Johnson also led the successful drive to establish a city charter, which allowed Texas City to create its own statutes and other regulations. A municipality without a city charter—as Texas City had been until February 1946—is bound by Texas State common law alone. Establishing a city charter was a big move in the right direction for any municipality wishing to expand.

Despite his achievements, Johnson's reelection appeared to face an uphill battle. In addition to the issue of sanitation, Johnson also governed a community endlessly at odds with the massive industries bordering its city limits. Thus, it was not helpful to his campaign when it was revealed that he was also the superintendent of Stone Oil Company—a perceived, if not actual conflict of interest. As soon as the local newspaper, the *Texas City Sun*, ran the story, Johnson announced his resignation from the oil company. But the move was seen as hollow. To drum up support, less than two weeks before the election, Johnson promised the dike would be cleaned up and that the cost would be covered from a 25 percent tax surplus he said remained in the city treasury. He further declared the surplus was large enough that taxes would be reduced after the election. On April 2, Johnson and the city commissioners passed a resolution outlawing dumping on the dike. Yet none of the promises, declarations, and actions worked.[9]

On April 5, Curtis Trahan was elected the ninth mayor of Texas City by a three-to-one margin, on a platform of improving sanitation, safety, and public parks. On taking office, Trahan discovered the tax surplus announced by the former mayor was nonexistent. It was all a lie. The city had no money. Four days after the election, Trahan and the newly elected city commissioners took office. One of the first things they did was raise property taxes to generate operating cash for Texas City.[10] That shortfall fueled a movement that would occupy much of the city's business for the next twelve months—the annexation of all the adjacent industries—which some residents called "the battle."[11]

Father Bill, Pete Tarpey, and Dick Benedict initiated the battle.[12] Another participant was Max Montegut, the father of Maxine Montegut and a St. Mary's parishioner, who had won election to the school board. He was also part of the industrial complex at issue, being a longtime employee of Pan American Refining Corporation. He had been part of the advance team that established Pan American's Texas City location in the 1930s, when the company's name was still Mexico Oil. Nevertheless, Montegut understood that the school system, such as it was, needed cash and that the potential tax base of the neighboring industries would go a long way toward rectifying the biggest problem with local education—lack of space.

The children of Texas City were being forced to skip over multiple grades each year because there were not enough desks, classrooms, or buildings to accommodate the increasing student population produced by such a rapidly growing city. Complicating an already challenging situation, Wolvin High School and other schools still needed major repairs to damage caused by the 1943 hurricane, three years earlier.[13] Even before the first school board meeting, Montegut understood that the schools were so underfunded the district could barely make payroll. He was aware of all these issues because his own children were part of the educational meat grinder of Texas City. His daughter, Maxine, had skipped several grades and ultimately graduated from high school at age fifteen. So had her best friend, Betty Laiche, whose father also worked for Pan American. Both Maxine and Betty were in college when Max Montegut was elected to the school board. To Montegut, the new mayor and city commissioners, Roach, Tarpey, and Benedict, the answer to financing needed public services, including the schools, was to annex the industries and assess appropriate taxes.

As expected, there was pushback from the industries, led by Carbide and Carbon, Monsanto, and Pan American.[14] Their main argument against annexation was that taxation would discourage other industries from locating in Texas City. Roach countered that taxation had not prevented other municipalities, including Baltimore and Philadelphia, from attracting industry. Indeed, Roach contended that Texas City industries, which he called the "steel band," in veiled reference to the Iron Curtain, were themselves discouraging businesses from locating in the area by allowing Texas City Terminal Railway to control the only access to the dock area and charge exorbitant fees to reach it.[15]

The only easement of any kind to the wharf area was by rail, wholly owned by the Texas City Terminal Railway Company, which controlled a quarter square mile of docks, warehouses, freight yards, and rail lines. To break this monopoly, Mayor Trahan, with the guidance of the city commissioners, was able to have the Texas State Department of Highways construct a public road from Sixth Street South to the north slip of the harbor. There, the road made a 90-degree turn south, past the main slip, to reach the south slip, where it terminated. For the first time, trucks and other road vehicles had free public access to the Texas City docks. Locals called it Dock Road. Roach's steel band had been penetrated.[16] The industries were not invincible. Texas City had won the first skirmish in the battle but annexation still seemed a long way off.

On May 17, Texas City officials declared a health emergency. A city-appointed commission had been wrestling with the problem of garbage collection and disposal to no avail. Cleanup of the dike was publicly acknowledged as impossible. Streets were in disrepair, storm drainage was nonexistent, weeds were left uncut—and no public money was available to address these issues. Corpus Christi and San Antonio had already issued health emergency declarations in an attempt to contain the spread of polio and other diseases. Houston, forty-five miles north of Texas City, would soon do the same.[17]

In June, the mayor and city commissioners of Texas City passed a fifteen-point plan to clean up both the city and the dike. A new commission was appointed to oversee the plan. In July, the city likewise initiated a plan to address flooding and proper drainage. Despite a complete lack of operating cash, the city passed a budget of $297,531. The money would have to be borrowed. Two weeks later, the commission voted to adopt a system of open-ditch drainage throughout Texas City.

The mayor and city commissioners also took steps to address fire safety. They reviewed and revised local fire codes, and due to the growing frequency of explosions and fires along the ship channel, including the Monsanto fire and the sinking of the *Sveaborg* the previous December, they purchased a fire boat to protect the waterfront. Initially, local industries had agreed to share the cost of buying and maintaining the fire boat, but they backed out of the arrangement in August, just after the city took possession. Unable to shoulder the cost on its own, the city was forced to sell the fire boat. The whole transaction, from start to finish, only took a few weeks. Texas City owned the fire boat a few days and then it was gone.

Eight months later, the need for such firefighting equipment to protect the very industries rejecting the deal would become critically self-evident.[18]

Meanwhile, inside the steel band, super-heated boxcars filled with ammonium nitrate fertilizer had started arriving again on the docks at the Port of Texas City. The situation had improved since earlier in the year, when the issue had become alarming and Texas City Terminal Railway Company Vice President W. H. Sandberg had intervened, but shipments were still intermittently arriving dangerously hot. By June, overheated boxcars were again a regular occurrence. On June 26, 1946, Sandberg wrote a letter to Roy J. Calkins of the Military Chemical Works in Nebraska. Again, he included photographs and detailed the substandard conditions in which ammonium nitrate fertilizer was arriving.

Sandberg also placed a number of phone calls to Arthur Clark, the Galveston manager of J. D. Latta Company, the shipping agent for the ammonium nitrate. During one call, Sandberg spoke also directly with the owner, J. D. Latta. Sandberg asked Latta the same question he had asked Floyd Steed of Military Chemical Works earlier in the year: was ammonium nitrate an explosive? Like Floyd Steed, Latta also replied, "No." He added as reassurance that the Federal Bureau of Explosives required a special red placard be placed on any explosive material transported by train or by any other means. The absence of such labeling indicated that ammonium nitrate was not an explosive. After these exchanges in June 1946, the condition of fertilizer shipments passing over the Texas City Terminal Railway improved.[19] It appeared Sandberg's efforts had finally worked.

Early in the summer of 1946, Father Bill became reacquainted with two early Texas City admirers. Maxine Montegut and Betty Laiche were home after their second year in college. Roach had seen Laiche the previous fall, when she visited her family during the Thanksgiving holiday, though he did not recognize her at first. When she approached him after Thanksgiving mass he took her for a visitor or a new parishioner. Stylishly dressed in a suit and a small fur pillbox hat with a short veil falling partially across her face, she was unrecognizable. When he finally realized who she was, he jokingly dropped to one knee, genuflecting and saying, "Pardon me, madam!" as if he were in the presence of royalty.[20] Months later, when she returned again, he did recognize her. He had not seen Montegut, "Miss *Money*-gew," as he called her, since the previous summer. Maxine Montegut had returned to her regular summer job at Southport Transit Company, a trucking company on Texas Avenue, where she worked in the office as a secretary. Montegut described Southport Transit as "a dangerous place to work," because of its location. That part of Texas Avenue, between First Avenue and Texas Avenue, was very close to sailors retreat.[21] Populated with merchant marines on leave, prostitutes, and outlaws, sailors retreat was a place where fights broke out day and night, some involving weapons. It was the same area Father Bill cruised at night, "fishing for souls." He witnessed a fight or two, always intervening. Fortunately Montegut never witnessed such events. She just went to work, did her job, and left at the end of each day.[22]

Montegut and her best friend Betty, both popular and attractive, divided their time between day jobs and above-average social lives. Both were unattached, so boys were a regular feature of their lives, and the two nineteen-year-olds enjoyed the attention. One young fellow Maxine noticed from a distance worked for a ship channel barge company. His company had offices in the same building as Southport Transit, so she would spot him strolling through the building to get his daily assignment or on some other business. He was tall, blond, and Hollywood handsome. "He looked just like an angel . . . this very beautiful young man," Maxine said.[23]

"Who is *that*?" she asked a coworker.

"That's Eddie," was the answer. "He's a drug addict and divorced. He lives in that old hotel across the street. He's just no good."

"What a shame," Maxine thought. "He's so beautiful."

So she was taken aback at mass that Sunday to see Eddie in one of the front pews at St. Mary. She was so surprised at the sight that she asked Father Bill about it afterward. "He's turned to God," Roach answered.

This was the same Eddie whom Father Bill encountered on his nocturnal sojourns through sailors retreat. Within the span of a few weeks, Father Bill had made such a profound impression on Eddie that he had changed his life considerably, with Roach's help. He started attending mass daily at St. Mary and moved from his hotel in sailors retreat to an apartment across the street from the church. He chose the apartment specifically so that he could see the St. Mary sanctuary light at night. He was even seriously considering entering the seminary. After he finished work, he assisted Roach however he could around the church.[24]

Maxine and Betty also visited Father Bill whenever they could. Since he was rarely at his apartment across the street from St. Mary, they started attending Wednesday-night novenas and visiting with him afterward, as they had done the previous summer. Alternatively, they would join other worshippers from the novena at the Lucas Café for coffee and doughnuts afterward.

If they happened to catch Father Bill at home, he would typically repeat his pattern from a year before. Digging a couple of dollars out of one of the many books lying about, he would send them to the store for ice cream. The three of them would then spend hours eating ice cream and talking about saints and the value of leading a selfless life.

Immediately, Roach resurrected the challenge he had posed to the two teenagers earlier—that of becoming saints. Interestingly, Maxine and Betty had been thinking along the same lines, even to the point of considering joining a religious order. As college roommates they frequently discussed the prospect together, and although they were not sure how to proceed, they believed Father Bill could help.

Roach started taking the two young women to visit various convents in Southeast Texas. His brother John was the chaplain of the Villa de Matel, home of the Sisters of Charity of the Incarnate Word in Houston, so that was one of the first stops they made during their search. Then they visited the Ursuline convent in Galveston, which had founded the Ursuline Academy, one of the first parochial schools in Texas. They also visited the Sisters of Charity in Galveston, who had established St. Mary's Hospital there. Invariably, Roach would dismiss each location as "too nice," "too established," or simply "not right" for Maxine and Betty. "You need something where you really have to dig in the dirt," he said.[25] Eventually, the trio made the drive to Lufkin and the rugged, struggling, and completely cloistered Dominican Monastery of the Holy Infant Jesus. In hindsight, it was clear Roach had Lufkin in mind from the start. He merely presented the other convents as sharp contrasts to religious life in the Lufkin community.

Under Father Bill's influence, on August 8, Maxine Montegut and Betty Laiche left the secular world behind them and entered the monastery in Lufkin as novitiates. They became Sister Mary William and Sister Mary Catherine, respectively. Both young friends chose their new names very carefully and in honor of Father Bill. "William" is an obvious reference to Roach. "Catherine" is an allusion to St. Catherine de Ricci, one of Father Bill's favorite saints. "Mary," apart from being a common choice for religious women worldwide, was certainly the most important and influential saint to Father Bill Roach.

Back in Texas City, Maxine's and Betty's choice of a cloistered life in Lufkin was not universally acclaimed. Their mothers both privately harbored resentment, one saying Roach "drove them into the convent."[26] The popular young women also left a line of perplexed boys behind. One, overheard speaking to a group of friends, said derisively, "What a waste of womanhood."[27] For their parts, Maxine and Betty never felt that way and always thought they made the right choice. They asserted they felt a true calling to religious life, never felt the slightest pressure from anyone, and never regretted a day of their lives in the monastery. Maxine described her experience thus: "I entered the convent in 1946 through the influence of Father Bill Roach, not directly, but through his sanctity," said Maxine Montegut. "That always impressed—greatly impressed [me]—his holiness. At his first mass in Texas City on July 1, 1945, my whole life was transformed and I decided that I wanted to become a nun and find a very fervent monastery. Father Bill helped me and a year later I entered, here at Lufkin, and I've been very happy."[28]

If Roach was aware of ill feelings over his part in steering Maxine and Betty toward the path they chose, he never made it known. Certainly, it never caused him to question his actions. Indeed, he was instrumental in guiding other young parishioners, both male and female, to religious lives. Yet Maxine and Betty remained special to Roach, and he to them. Of course, the Lufkin monastery was one of Father Bill's most beloved places on Earth. He continued to visit often with his brother, bringing supplies, hearing confessions, and consulting with Sister Diane, the community's young mystic.

However, on August 8, as he was driving Maxine and Betty to Lufkin to join the community there, Father Bill said a curious thing. At some point Maxine brought up the subject of Eddie.

"Eddie is going to be killed in an explosion driving a truck," he said bluntly and without explanation.[29]

═ 13 ═

"I FEEL LIKE I'M SITTING ON A KEG OF DYNAMITE"

In the first week of October 1946, the International Longshoremen's Association struck nationwide. The implications were enormous. Every port and nearly every mode of transporting goods throughout the United States would be affected. Texas City, as the fourth largest US port in terms of tonnage handled, would be hit especially hard.[1] Coming so close to the November midterm elections, the strike had political implications as well. With anti-union and anti-strike fervor on the rise across America, many candidates seeking election or reelection, especially Republicans, ran on an anti-labor platform. Both sides, labor and management, had legitimate arguments about union use of strikes to gain the upper hand in collective bargaining.

Republicans generally favored management and Democrats, labor, but both parties questioned the benefits of what seemed to be an endless stream of strikes and lost work hours. In the thirteen months since the Japanese surrender and the close of World War II, nearly 2.5 million workdays had been lost to between 100 and 150 separate strikes.[2] Even the Democratic President Harry S. Truman, usually sympathetic to labor, had signed executive orders to have the US military seize businesses closed due to strikes and reopen them under government control. That had happened in Texas City during the oil workers' strike the year before. Truman even once harbored a plan—though never implemented or even made public—to draft striking workers into the army.[3] This was the atmosphere in which the International Longshoremen's Association called their strike. As the strike got underway, Truman stated publicly that he supported "good wages and low prices," tacitly siding with labor.[4]

Influenced by the successful demands of other unions earlier in the year, the longshoremen were demanding an 18.5-cent-per-hour raise and a forty-hour workweek. Nearly every union that went on strike from spring 1946 on wanted the same.[5] And such a wage increase was badly needed, despite statements to the contrary from company management and certain politicians. The inflation rate was 8.33 percent in 1946, and rising sharply. Within a few months it would reach 14.36 percent.[6] Workers could no longer live on wartime-level wages. Truman understood this and said so publicly.

Texas City braced for another long period of tension and violence. Past longshoremen's strikes had resulted in solitary assaults, group fights, and full-scale battles. Police, Texas Rangers, and even the National Guard had been variously ordered to intervene. But the strike of October 1946 was uncharacteristically peaceful, "the first non-violent strike they ever had in Texas City," according to Dick Benedict.[7] The new mayor, Curtis Trahan, was credited with using an unusually diplomatic approach to cooling tensions. Father Bill Roach and Pete Tarpey also acted as liaisons between the local union representative, Dick Benedict, and management, in this case the Texas City Terminal Railway Company.[8]

On October 31, it was announced that a nationwide agreement had been reached with the longshoremen's union. Among other demands, the pay increase and forty-hour workweek were agreed to. But the strike, lasting most of the month, was reportedly the costliest to that date.[9] That fact added even more fuel to anti-union sentiments. In the midterm elections just a few days later, Republicans won twenty-five governor's races and regained a majority in both chambers of the US Congress for the first time since 1931. That majority was quite large enough to override any veto by President Truman.

Since 1938, Texas politics had become increasingly dominated by ultraconservative corporate interests. Far-right lobbying groups such as the Texas Regulars and Christian Americans worked to secure laws protecting the corporate interests of the wealthy in Texas and throughout the South. With heavy patronage from approximately two dozen millionaires, they fought against legislation that would levy taxes on the rich, promote labor, and seek to regulate business in any way.[10]

In Texas, they worked closely with governor, and later senator, Wilbert Lee "Pappy" O'Daniel to craft anti-union legislation. They also joined forces with Major William Ruggles, editor of the *Dallas Morning News*, to push legislation for open shop workplaces, where employees were not required to join a union. The first regulations curtailing unions became law in 1947, and these laws were strengthened in 1951 and again in 1955. Thus began a marked decline in workers' rights in Texas.

In their periodicals, the Texas Regulars and Christian Americans also worked to undermine unions through race-baiting. Without actually mentioning unions, these groups attempted to stir racial hatred by pitting whites and African Americans against each other. Although segregation existed, free association between races was commonplace in unions. The hate-mongering of the Texas Regulars and Christian Americans helped to inflame violent incidents.

President Truman, alarmed by a series of racially motivated murders of African Americans in 1946, proposed legislation that would make lynching a federal crime and would also outlaw state poll taxes, a common strategy to suppress African American voting. Governor Beauford H. Jester, another Texas ally of the Christian Americans and the Texas Regulars, publicly condemned the move as an affront to states' rights. Leaders of the oil industry in Texas supported Jester's states' rights position, not out of any interest one way or the other in Truman, poll taxes, or lynching, but from a desire to loosen federal control over massive oil reserves off the coasts of Texas and Louisiana that they sought to exploit.

The same day as the longshoreman's strike ended, the US Office of Price Administration, abruptly removed all the wartime price controls on commodities, causing a sudden spike in the cost of food and other necessities. On November 10, Truman rolled back a portion of the Office of Price Administration deregulation, announcing that rents, rice, and sugar would still be subject to government price controls. Rent control was welcome news for workers struggling to make ends meet, despite recent wage increases. This was especially true in Texas City, where the ongoing severe housing shortage would have sent rents skyrocketing. Rising food prices were bad enough, but if rents had increased, the wage increases won by several unions in the previous months would have been completely cancelled out. Moreover, not everyone in the labor force had received pay raises. Most workers in Texas City still subsisted on prewar wages.[11]

On Armistice Day (now called Veterans Day), November 11, 1946, a dedication ceremony took place in Texas City to honor local citizens who had died in war, including World War II. High winds and driving rain reduced attendance and cast a pall over the event. Nevertheless a procession of officials and invited guests solemnly wound through the streets of Texas City, starting at the American Legion Hall at Third Avenue North and Third Street North, moving south to

Texas Avenue, then west to Sixth Street, and finally north to city hall. There, a seven-foot stone stela had been erected with a bronze plaque containing the names of the war dead. Nearby, several scheduled speakers offered their thoughts about the moment. Father Roach was one of those invited to speak.[12]

Roach's remarks, less than two typed pages long, talked as much about the future, particularly the city's economic and political future, as about the past. "The world is mad with lust and hangs bleeding to death upon the cross—a cross forged in hell, with nails of greed, hate, dishonesty, and prejudice," Roach intoned, standing in the rain. "Let the spirit for which this monument was erected be an example of devotion to the ideals that have made here a great nation . . . the hope of the oppressed and poor, the refuge of the weak."[13] Roach was certainly less interested in the physical object erected in front of city hall than in its deeper meaning, or what he believed that deeper meaning to be. Every one of his words directly highlighted the struggles of the poor and working-class citizens of Texas City. Still, Roach was always more about deeds than words.

As the Christmas season unfolded, Roach concentrated on managing the parish-wide food drive for the hungry of Texas City. He had initiated this drive the year before with great success, and 1946 was a repeat success. Most of the food went to the black and Latino/a families living in appalling conditions south of Texas Avenue, adjacent to sailors retreat. There was a separate Catholic church, Our Lady of the Snows, in the neighborhood. Although located within the parish boundaries of St. Mary, it operated independently as a mission of the Oblate Fathers (Oblates of Mary Immaculate) serving Spanish speakers.[14]

This was the same situation as Roach had experienced in Lampasas, and he was just as uneasy with it because of the minimal contact with the church it offered to the faithful. An Oblate priest visited once a week to say mass and hear confessions, then left. During the week, no Catholic representative existed (officially) in the neighborhood. Latino/a communities were traditionally self-reliant, but because they tended to be economically depressed and suppressed, the church was part of their support system. Father Bill understood that the local Latino/a community was populated with mostly lower-income families who saw the church as a second home. In Texas City, however, they were locked out of that home most of the time. Therefore, Father Bill visited the neighborhood as often as possible, as he had done in Lampasas.

The Catholic Church in the United States had begun establishing what were called "national parishes" in the early twentieth century in response to a great influx of immigrants from southern and eastern Europe. These parishes operated in the native languages of the immigrants, not as a means of segregation, but to help them feel comfortable as they acclimated to their new homes.

In Texas, the Diocese of Galveston adopted a similar approach to meet the needs of immigrants, most of whom were Spanish speakers. Unlike their counterparts arriving from Europe, however, many of these Texas immigrants continued to maintain very close ties to their native countries in Mexico and Central and South America. The situation could become very complex in terms of ethno-Catholic identity within a single parish. Although mostly Spanish-speaking, parishioners were from countries as diverse as Mexico, Honduras, and Venezuela, to name a few. Even Mexico alone is incredibly diverse culturally—a parishioner from Yucatan is culturally rather different from one from Jalisco.[15] By the mid-twentieth century, as the social ministry of the Catholic Church changed from helping communities only when needed to an organized network of aid available at all times, it began to close these national parishes and assimilate all parishioners together.

Roach spent a lot of time with African American and Spanish-speaking residents in the area south of Texas Avenue, Catholic or otherwise. He was a regular visitor. When Curtis Trahan was elected mayor, Roach found a solid political ally on the issue of neighborhood uplift. During the mayoral race, Trahan received 100 percent of the black vote and 80 percent of the Latino/a vote. His returns were weakest with white voters, especially those from what he called "the silk stocking district"—white-owned businesses along Sixth Avenue North and Texas Avenue. Trahan, like Roach, was committed to improving living conditions south of Texas Avenue. The mayor and city commissioners had already initiated plans for parks, proper drainage, and sewer systems (most of the homes south of Texas Avenue only had outhouses), but lack of money was still a major obstacle. Annexation of the industrial area and an upper middle-class bedroom community called the Heights would supply an expanded tax base to raise the needed revenue.[16]

During this time, two related headlines appeared in the *Texas City Sun*. On December 24, the oil workers' local union filed suits totaling nearly three million dollars against Pan American Oil, Republic Oil, and American Liberty Oil. The suits alleged the three companies were required to pay union workers retroactively for uncompensated portal-to-portal hours. Portal-to-portal pay refers to an interpretation of the minimum wage clause of the Fair Labor Standards Act of 1938 that declares "all preliminary and postliminary activities done for the employer's benefit are compensable."[17] Such time might include the period spent traveling from the plant entrance to the worksite or donning required clothing. Between 1945 and 1947, unions filed numerous suits like this one to recover back pay. On

December 26, a representative of the National Association of Manufacturers warned that higher wages would lead to inflation and unemployment. Those words rang hollow because the inflation rate was already rising, and the US cost of living was the highest since 1920—largely because of skyrocketing food prices.[18]

Then, in the last days of 1946, longshoremen in Texas City again started complaining about boxcars loaded with extremely hot bags of ammonium nitrate fertilizer arriving from Iowa and Nebraska.[19] The situation would only worsen.

After Christmas, Bill and John Roach traveled by train for a short holiday visit to Pennsylvania to see their family. On the way back to Texas, Bill told his brother that he was resigned to dying young. Perhaps, like Jesus, he foresaw his own death.[20]

New Year 1947 arrived with gusto. The coldest temperatures on record descended on Galveston Bay, falling to twenty-two degrees in Texas City. The cold weather exacerbated flu and other deadly seasonal diseases, which were again on the rise. Oil workers and pipefitters struck and walked away from their jobs at Republic Oil and Monsanto, respectively. Boilermakers also struck in Texas City. In Houston, developer Frank Sharp pulled a pistol on striking workers at one of his jobsites and opened fire. Fortunately, no one was injured. Sharp later pled guilty to carrying an unlicensed concealed weapon and paid a hundred-dollar fine.

When the Eightieth US Congress convened, the Republican majority immediately introduced anti-strike and forced arbitration legislation. Senator Joseph H. Ball of Minnesota proposed a bill that would outlaw collective bargaining nationwide. Meanwhile, the House Un-American Activities Committee demanded that only US citizens be allowed to lead trade unions and that closed (all-union) shops be outlawed.[21] To temper these moves, President Truman proposed the establishment of a labor congress consisting of representatives from every union. During testimony in favor of this proposal, New York City Mayor Fiorello La Guardia was interrupted by Senator Ball, who charged La Guardia and the president with trying to create "a monopoly." "I call it cooperation," La Guardia responded.[22]

As spring approached and the weather warmed, so did the battle to annex the industries surrounding Texas City. Discussions at public meetings of the mayor and city commissioners brought sharply divided opinions, usually along socioeconomic lines. Typically, poor and working-class residents supported the proposal, while business owners and industry representatives opposed it.

The fact that the proposed annexation included the Heights, where owners of businesses in the anti-Trahan silk stocking district made their homes, increased the divide. Trahan and the city commissioners believed it was time for the industries and the residents of the Heights who profited by the city's existence to contribute to the larger well-being of the city that helped supply their livelihoods.

Father Bill attended those meetings and sometimes spoke at them. His tone was always thoughtful and respectful. Initially, he tried in his remarks to create a middle ground that both sides might agree to. But as the weeks wore on and meeting after meeting produced little progress, it became more and more evident that he was in full support of annexation.

Roach sometimes facilitated evening meetings at St. Mary. These meetings usually focused on parish issues, but often they included discussions about helping the poor, labor concerns, and the proposed annexation. During one meeting devoted to a proposal to offer substantial help to families south of Texas Avenue living in extreme poverty, Roach became uncharacteristically annoyed at the wall of silence coming from the assembly regarding the idea. Flustered, he turned to the crucifix, shook his head, and walked out of the church.[23]

Simultaneously, Roach was acting as an unofficial mediator in a labor dispute at Monsanto. Monsanto, headquartered in St. Louis, had established itself in the dock area of Texas City during World War II. The US government had paid the cost of Monsanto's expansion into the abandoned sugar refinery in Texas City as a war incentive and retained ownership of the plant throughout the war, using it to produce styrene used in the manufacture of synthetic rubber.

In August 1946, Monsanto bought the location from the government and began a substantial expansion to make a styrene derivative called polystyrene, a clear solid thermoplastic still widely used today. Construction crews working on the expansion had complained of being paid substandard wages. When their complaints went unanswered, they stopped work and walked off the job. At that point Father Bill began his mediation efforts. To ease the rapidly growing tensions, Roach became the face and voice of both sides in the negotiations. He took union proposals to Monsanto representatives and relayed responses, if any, back to labor officials. Roach tried hard to remain neutral, but occasionally his working-class sympathies would peek through the veneer, usually in a humorous way.

Once, on transmitting a response from management to a group of union workers, Roach began comically imitating one of the Monsanto officials. Reacting to a suggestion that he was anti-labor and ignoring the needs of workers, the official stated emphatically that he was, indeed, in favor of workers. To illustrate his support, he produced a pack of cigarettes from his pocket, saying, "See. I smoke union-made cigarettes." Roach immediately pointed out to the Monsanto official that all cigarettes were union-made. The union members listening to the story roared with laughter.[24]

On February 21, 15 people were killed and 158 injured in a perchloric acid explosion at the O'Connor Electro-Plating Corporation in Los Angeles. In a March 2 comment on the accident, Marie Luppold, director of nursing at Houston's Methodist Hospital, warned, "A big tragedy would catch Houston short of nurses if Houston were struck by a tragedy like the recent explosion in Los Angeles." Just two days later, a work crew making repairs on the oil tanker *Lyons Creek* ignited an explosion that tore the vessel in two and sent it to the bottom of the Houston Ship Channel Turning Basin north of Texas City. Seven were injured. In public testimony on March 10, it was revealed that one of the onboard fuel tanks had been declared "not safe" by a chemist. A "steam blanket" was applied (steam pumped directly into the ship belowdecks, a common and usually effective method to avoid fire and explosions) to stabilize the tank and make it suitable for a "gas-free" certification. The procedure did not work.[25]

On the same day as testimony was being taken in the *Lyons Creek* investigation, Mayor Trahan and the four Texas City commissioners formally proposed the city annex the local industries and the Heights. A final vote was scheduled for one month later, on April 10, to allow time for arguments on both sides of the issue to be presented. Within two weeks, those opposed to annexation had filed formal declarations.

By this time the Catholic liturgical season of Lent was underway at St. Mary, as it was throughout the Roman Catholic world. Lent, a succession of solemn religious events culminating in Easter Sunday, is a time of self-sacrifice and good deeds, among other things. It is also a time to reflect on, do penance for, and atone for one's sins. "Lent" comes from the Latin *lencten* or *lenctentid*, meaning "spring" and "springtide," respectively. It is a time of rebirth, in this case, spiritual rebirth.[26]

Throughout Lent, Roach's homilies (remarks delivered after a reading from Scripture) during mass focused on the Lenten theme of charitable works, particularly as applied to the ongoing labor-management battles in Texas City. On February 23, the first Sunday after Ash Wednesday, the homily focused on Jesus's statement, borrowed from his cousin John the Baptist, "Unless you do penance you shall likewise perish."[27]

Another of Roach's homilies was titled "Human Relations in a Christian Social Order." It included this Bible passage: "I will come to you in judgement, and will be a speedy witness against ... those that oppress the hireling [laborer] in his wages" (Malachi 3:5). The homily continued:

Capital and labor are now at war about their future relations, and a bewildered nation patiently and anxiously waits and suffers. Employers are ill at ease because they cannot control the forces that disturb and tend to destroy their industrial relations. They will never find the remedy until they put aside human pride and bend low enough to enter the workshop of Christ, the carpenter of Nazareth.

Workmen are fearful of the future and the stability of their jobs and the protection of their homes and families. They too, will never attain their goal until they learn to live and work in the spirit of Nazareth and the laws of God.

[The Church] points out the moral abuses in both industrial capitalism and labor . . . [and] emblazons the precept of economic justice as a great rainbow in the sky—a rainbow of hope to the poor, the oppressed, and the downtrodden everywhere.[28]

A third homily, "Human Relations in a Christian Social Order Are Cooperation Not Conflict," expanded on the same theme: "The social revolution is a very present reality," Roach stated. "The revolution is a popular movement for the revindication and the attainment of full human rights, for all people. It is a concerted effort to reestablish the primacy of the human person, in a world dominated by selfish, cynical, and proud men."[29] The title of this homily, particularly use of the word "cooperation," is reminiscent of Mayor La Guardia's response to Senator Ball during hearings about the formation of a labor congress in early March 1947.

Whenever his schedule permitted, Roach visited the monastery in Lufkin. In addition to his regular priestly duties, he made a point of spending time with Maxine and Betty, now Sister Mary William and Sister Mary Catherine, respectively. He also spent a lot of time with the mystic Sister Diane, listening carefully to her pronouncements and descriptions of mystical visions. During one of these visits, some time between the second and third Sundays of Lent, she told Father Bill of a recent vision in which she saw blood flowing in the streets of Texas City. Father Bill was shaken.

The following Sunday, March 16, was Laetare Sunday. Traditionally Laetare Sunday, meaning "to rejoice," is set aside as a moment of relaxation of the strict rules of observance during Lent, particularly with respect to fasting. Roach had prepared a homily focusing on this day of relaxation. However, driven by Sister Diane's disturbing new vision, he abandoned the homily almost as soon as he started it. Facing the congregation, he began with the word "rejoice" followed by a long pause as he looked down at the typed pages before him. Then raising his head he asked, "Rejoice? What do we have to rejoice about? If we don't get closer to God, the streets will be ankle deep in blood! We should make this Lent as if it were our last, because for some it will be the last!"[30]

Katherine Hunter, listening from a pew nearby, thought Father Bill seemed agitated. "He was a little cross with us," she would later say. Bernice Smith, another member of the congregation, responded to a question about what she thought of the homily with, "I believed it!"[31] Four days after Roach's Laetare Sunday homily, a petroleum fire caused substantial damage to a large oil tank farm near Houston. No injuries were reported.[32]

Near the end of March, parishioner Vincent Schmidt found Father Bill sitting on the back steps of St. Mary. It was something Roach did frequently between mass, confessions, and visiting parishioners. Schmidt greeted Father Bill and sat down beside him. They chatted for a while about nothing in particular. Then he and Roach noticed a few small insects scurrying around on the ground.

"What do you call those?" Roach asked.

"Well, I don't know much about one bug from another," Schmidt replied.

"But you know a Roach when you see one, don't you?" Roach asked, laughing.[33]

A day or two later, parishioners Lawrence and Bernice Smith were driving past St. Mary when they spotted Roach sitting on the steps to the church's entrance, facing south, toward the industrial area at the docks. This time, though, he was in a pensive mood.

It was a warm, humid night and the air was thick, heavy with salt. A slight breeze rustled the leaves of nearby palm trees. Roach was bathed in an eerie, flickering yellow-orange light from the ever-present multitude of flaming hydrocarbon gas flares sprinkled throughout the nearby oil refineries. Even though it was eight o'clock at night, the whole church was lit, as if by a floodlight. Roach sat, motionless, staring blankly at the flames.

The Smiths pulled in front of Roach and stopped, momentarily breaking his concentration.

"What are you doing sitting out on the church porch, Father?" they asked.

"I feel like I'm sitting on a keg of dynamite," Roach responded, nodding toward the industries.[34]

On Tuesday, April 8, Roach published an op-ed, "Texas City Absorbs Industry or Industry Absorbs Texas City," in the *Texas City Sun*. The piece promoted annexation of the neighboring industries and reminded readers that the city government would vote on the proposed ordinance in two days. Roach also made no attempt to conceal which side he supported. He described the coming vote as "the most momentous decision in history affecting the future of Texas City," adding that annexation would be "for the common good of the majority and not for the end of a small, selfish minority." Roach also mentioned benefits such as reduced phone and utility rates and a sufficient revenue stream for the city to repair and upgrade its infrastructure.

The principal argument against annexation—that increased taxation would impede industrial growth—Roach continued, came from the affected industries. To counter that argument, Roach pointed out that the industries themselves had dictated such high prices for new businesses to locate near to the docks that they alone had driven away growth. As he reminded readers, it was only when a city commissioner arranged for the construction of a free public road leading to the docks that it become possible for new industries to avoid "'Jesse James' prices to come through the 'steel band' which surrounds the city."[35]

Two days later, on Thursday, April 10, the mayor and city commissioners convened the meeting to hear arguments for and against annexation then take a vote. Timing was critical. City Commissioner Bill Voiles, in favor of annexation, had received information that the nearby city of La Marque was making its own move to annex all the industries. However, La Marque was hindered by the fact it had no city charter. Rather than simply vote on whether to move forward with annexation, La Marque had to file a formal legal motion before a judge, who would make the decision. Texas City had created a charter. Charters give city governments in Texas a lot of power to make decisions for the greater good of the community at large, including powers of eminent domain and annexation. Technically, the city didn't need anyone's permission to annex territory, as long as it was not part of another incorporated municipality. So Texas City could proceed more expeditiously.[36]

Approximately fifty residents attended the meeting. Mayor Trahan opened by appointing a commission to investigate the overcrowded and substandard living conditions in the black and Latino/a neighborhoods of Texas City. He then read the annexation ordinance and opened the floor for discussion. Commissioner W. P. Ludwig immediately called for an adjournment "for further study" a motion that was overruled by the mayor. Discussion proceeded with the city commissioners in turn presenting their views on the pros and cons of the annexation ordinance. Commissioners W. P. Ludwig and L. C. DeWalt were clearly against the proposal. Commissioners James Matthews and Bill Voiles were in favor. The mayor facilitated as a neutral party.

E. B. Ware, a resident of the Heights, presented a petition opposing annexation, signed by 132 people. He asked what Texas City could do for the Heights. Trahan answered that the city would start garbage pickup in two days, begin construction on parks and recreation areas in forty-five days, and reduce utility bills immediately. Henry J. Mikeska, president of the Texas City Terminal Railway, also spoke against annexation. Among other things, he stated that the move would bring indiscriminate taxation, causing the industries either to fail or move to some other location.

Father Bill Roach spoke in favor of annexation: "A healthy social environment will make men happy and they will produce more," he said, adding that it was the duty of industry to aid such institutions as schools. In answer to Mikeska's assertion that industries would fail if taxed, Roach cited a number of examples of major industries existing and prospering within the taxing jurisdictions of cities. "Proximity to a viable shipping terminal and no lack of good, reliable workers is the answer to industry success, and Texas City has both. And industry should help support them," Roach said. He concluded his remarks with assurances that his critique was in no way meant to be disrespectful or to lay blame, but merely to alleviate a worsening situation.

The commissioners closed discussion from the floor and cast their votes. The outcome of two consecutive votes was a tie—two for and two against. When the third vote resulted in yet another tie, Trahan broke his neutrality and voted for annexation. The ordinance passed and Texas City immediately doubled in size.[37]

The following day, April 11, the French freighter *Grandcamp* eased into the Port of Texas City, docking in front of Warehouse O on the North Slip. Immediately, it began loading a multi-ton order of ammonium nitrate fertilizer bound for France. On Monday, April 14, four days after the annexation proposal passed, a fire erupted at the Gulf Oil Company terminal in Galena Park, near the ship channel north of Texas City. There were no injuries but the fire caused $80,000 in damage.[38]

On Tuesday, April 15, Bernice Smith picked up her daughter, Rita, from school. "Mama, let's go [to St. Mary church] and light a candle," Rita said.

"I don't have time," Smith responded. "And I don't have a coin."

"We can pay tomorrow," her daughter pleaded.

Smith agreed. She and Rita entered the church and lit their candle. As they paused to offer a prayer, they both heard the familiar sound of Father Bill's long cassock as he walked up behind them. He greeted them pleasantly and chatted in front of the statue of the Virgin Mary. At one point, Roach put his hand on the child's shoulder.

"Rita," he said, smiling. "Say a *Hail Mary* for me." Then he turned and walked briskly toward the sacristy.[39]

That evening, Father Bill visited the home of Richard and Cora Meskill. While he was there, a black Chevrolet pulled up outside. It was Bill's brother John. Normally, Father John would have come to the door and joined his brother inside with the Meskills. But this time, Bill went out to the car. John got out of the car and greeted his brother. They stood on the sidewalk talking together for a few moments. Then the brothers blessed each other, shook hands, and said goodbye. The Meskills thought the exchange was very unusual.[40]

The Roach twins, John (*left*) and Bill, as toddlers in 1909, Pennsylvania. *Courtesy of the Dominican Monastery of the Holy Infant Jesus, Lufkin, Texas.*

Father John Roach at the time of his ordination, 1939, Galveston County, Texas. *Courtesy of the Dominican Monastery of the Holy Infant Jesus, Lufkin, Texas.*

Father Bill Roach at the time of his ordination, 1939, Galveston County, Texas. *Courtesy of the Dominican Monastery of the Holy Infant Jesus, Lufkin, Texas.*

The Roach twins, Father John (*left*) and Father Bill, 1939, Galveston County, Texas. *Courtesy of the Dominican Monastery of the Holy Infant Jesus, Lufkin, Texas.*

Our Mother of Sorrows, Burnet, Texas, built almost entirely by Father Bill. *Photograph by John Neal Phillips.*

The facade of the Church of St. Christopher, Lampasas, Texas, another of the five or six churches built by Father Bill Roach in the Texas Hill Country. *Photograph by John Neal Phillips.*

St. Mary of the Miraculous Medal, Father Bill's parish church in Texas City, Texas. *Photograph by John Neal Phillips.*

A view of Father Bill's temporary rectory at Third Avenue Villa Apartments in Texas City. Maxine Montegut and Betty Laiche once waited for Father Bill on the sidewalk in the foreground. *Photograph by John Neal Phillips.*

Father Bill Roach relaxing in front of his temporary rectory at Third Avenue Villa Apartments. *Courtesy of the Dominican Monastery of the Holy Infant Jesus, Lufkin, Texas.*

The original farmhouse of the Dominican Monastery of the Holy Infant Jesus, Lufkin, Texas. *Courtesy of the Dominican Monastery of the Holy Infant Jesus, Lufkin, Texas.*

Bridge at the rear of the grounds of the Monastery of the Holy Infant Jesus. When he saw the wisteria there, as Sister Diane had foretold, Father Bill said his knees started shaking. *Photograph by John Neal Phillips.*

Pete Tarpey's house in Texas City. Father Bill spent thirty-six hours in the second-story corner room, counseling Tarpey about his chronic alcoholism. Tarpey never took another drink afterward. *Photograph by John Neal Phillips.*

Front entrance to St. Mary of the Miraculous Medal in Texas City. Sitting on the steps one evening shortly before the industrial disaster, Father Bill said, "I feel like I'm sitting on a keg of dynamite." *Photograph by John Neal Phillips.*

The sacristy entrance at the rear of St. Mary of the Miraculous Medal in Texas City. Father Bill was standing in the doorway at the far right on the morning of April 16, 1947, when he first spotted the unusual orange smoke from the docks. *Photograph by John Neal Phillips.*

The SS *Grandcamp*, on fire in the north slip, Texas City, moments before it exploded on April 16, 1947. Warehouse O stands to the right. Father Bill and Dick Benedict were standing about three hundred feet behind the photographer who took this photograph. *From the collections of the Dallas History & Archives Division, Dallas Public Library.*

An aerial view, facing southwest, of the aftermath of the explosion of the SS *Grandcamp*, April 16, 1947. In the foreground, the Monsanto plant is engulfed in fire. *From the collections of the Dallas History & Archives Division, Dallas Public Library.*

The *Longhorn II*, a barge designed to haul acid for the manufacture of tin, was berthed near the *Grandcamp*. This photograph shows where it settled after being swept inland by the blast. The bow, with the remains of a firetruck and a large piece of the *Grandcamp* draped against it, rests on a rail spur near where Father Bill Roach and Dick Benedict were standing at the time of the explosion. *From the collections of the Dallas History & Archives Division, Dallas Public Library.*

A view to the north along the dockside road. The mangled steel frame to the right is what remained of Warehouse O. The SS *Grandcamp* was berthed on the opposite side of the warehouse, in the north slip, when it exploded. Father Bill and Dick Benedict were standing at the far end of the road, at the extreme left-center of the photograph. The white, three-story building to the right of the road is the Monsanto office where Audrey Carroll worked. *From the collections of the Dallas History & Archives Division, Dallas Public Library.*

A stack of vehicles in the Monsanto parking lot after the explosion of the SS *Grandcamp*, April 16, 1947. The overturned car in the foreground on top of the pile belonged to Father Bill Roach. *From the collections of the Dallas History & Archives Division, Dallas Public Library.*

Another view of the Monsanto parking lot, with the chemical plant shrouded in smoke and fire beyond. The top floor of the white, three-story building to the right is the office where Audrey Carroll worked. *From the collections of the Dallas History & Archives Division, Dallas Public Library.*

Rescue workers examine the remains of one of two airplanes blown from the sky when the SS *Grandcamp* exploded, April 16, 1947. In the background, the Monsanto plant burns out of control. *From the collections of the Dallas History & Archives Division, Dallas Public Library.*

City hall (*right*) on Sixth Street North in Texas City, looking south toward the devastation just a few blocks away. *From the collections of the Dallas History & Archives Division, Dallas Public Library.*

At city hall, Texas City Mayor Curtis Trahan (*left*) talks with an injured survivor of the SS *Grandcamp* explosion, April 16, 1947. Note the broken glass and debris littering the floor. *From the collections of the Dallas History & Archives Division, Dallas Public Library.*

The devastation to Texas City's poorest neighborhood, located between Texas Avenue, the downtown area, and the burning industrial plants. *From the collections of the Dallas History & Archives Division, Dallas Public Library.*

Our Lady of the Snows, a Catholic missionary church serving the Latino/a community, was a total loss following the disaster in Texas City. *From the collections of the Dallas History & Archives Division, Dallas Public Library.*

=14=
"THIS IS IT"

Wednesday, April 16, 1947, dawned cool and clear. A light breeze blew from the northwest, an unseasonable direction some said.[1] The air, as always, was thick and salty. Father Bill rose early, if he'd been to bed at all, to say mass at 7:00 A.M. A young altar boy "Tookey" Mayville, arrived at the church on his bike to assist Father Bill. Cloma Frederick, a new convert of Roach's, one of his "caught fish," was in the sacristy preparing the post-Easter white vestments for mass.

Frederick, an interior decorator by trade, was remembered as a rather colorful figure by Texas City residents. A lifelong Protestant, Frederick encountered Father Bill during one of his many sojourns around the city and was swept away by his kindness, humor, and energetic charisma. Within a short time she converted to Catholicism and started doing volunteer work at St. Mary, straightening Roach's apartment/rectory, tidying the church, and whatever else was needed, much like the other "caught fish" Eddie was doing. Roach's effect on Cloma Frederick was so great that within short order, her mother also converted to Catholicism, reminiscent of what happened in Lampasas when Dana Hollister and her whole family converted to Catholicism.[2]

After mass, Father Bill and Tookey Mayville walked to the sacristy and handed their vestments to Cloma Frederick. They returned to the church to straighten up around the altar and to check the pews for lost items. Afterward, around 8:30 A.M., Roach stepped to the back door of the church for a long-overdue smoke. After lighting his cigarette, he straightened up to take the first drag—and saw smoke billowing in the air above the docks. Thick plumes of oddly colored bright orange smoke stood out against the blue sky.

"This is it!" he said, extinguishing his cigarette and heading for his car.[3]

By then, the siren mounted at city hall was sounding, calling members of the volunteer fire department. Tookey Mayville, who had also seen the smoke and heard the siren, wanted to ride with Father Bill to the docks. But Roach refused and drove off. Undaunted, Tookey jumped on his bike and headed in that direction.[4] Fires in Texas City always drew dozens, even hundreds, of curious bystanders—especially children.

Roach parked in the Monsanto parking lot, just across the shell-topped road from Frank's Café.[5] To the east, two vessels were moored in the north slip, adjacent to Warehouse O (see map 3). On the west (inland) side of the slip was a barge called the *Longhorn II*, belonging to the tin smelter. On the other side, beyond the barge, was the French oceangoing freighter, the SS *Grandcamp*, rigged to take on cargo. Coming from the aft section of the *Grandcamp* was oddly colored smoke that was changing color becoming thicker and more intense.

Longshoremen and sailors with suitcases were leaving the ship and trudging toward the café. Roach recognized some of the dockworkers. By now, as always happened, the road was crowded with townspeople coming to watch the calamity. It had happened when Monsanto burned. It had happened when the ships *Black Mountain* and *Sveaborg* exploded and sank.

Henry J. "Mike" Mikeska, president of Texas City Terminal Railway Company, arrived on the road next to Frank's Café via a footpath from the Terminal Railway office. Seeing Roach, Mikeska stopped to talk to him. A passing longshoreman who was well acquainted with both men described them "speaking in earnest tones" about towing the ship away from the dock before the fire spread.[6]

Mikeska rushed to the docks as Roach also began walking toward the burning ship. Where the apron to Warehouse O began at the end of the north slip, Roach spotted Dick Benedict and stopped to talk. Benedict was busy. All but essential workers had been ordered off the docks, and Benedict was tracking the exact minute each longshoreman working on the *Grandcamp* departed the area. Fires complicated timekeeping. If longshoremen helped fight fires, and there were many dock fires in Texas City, they were paid double time. Benedict was hurriedly noting how many longshoremen were off the jobsite and who had remained to fight the fire.

The *Grandcamp* was a war-era Liberty ship that had been sold to France as part of a program to reinvigorate European agriculture by shipping farm equipment

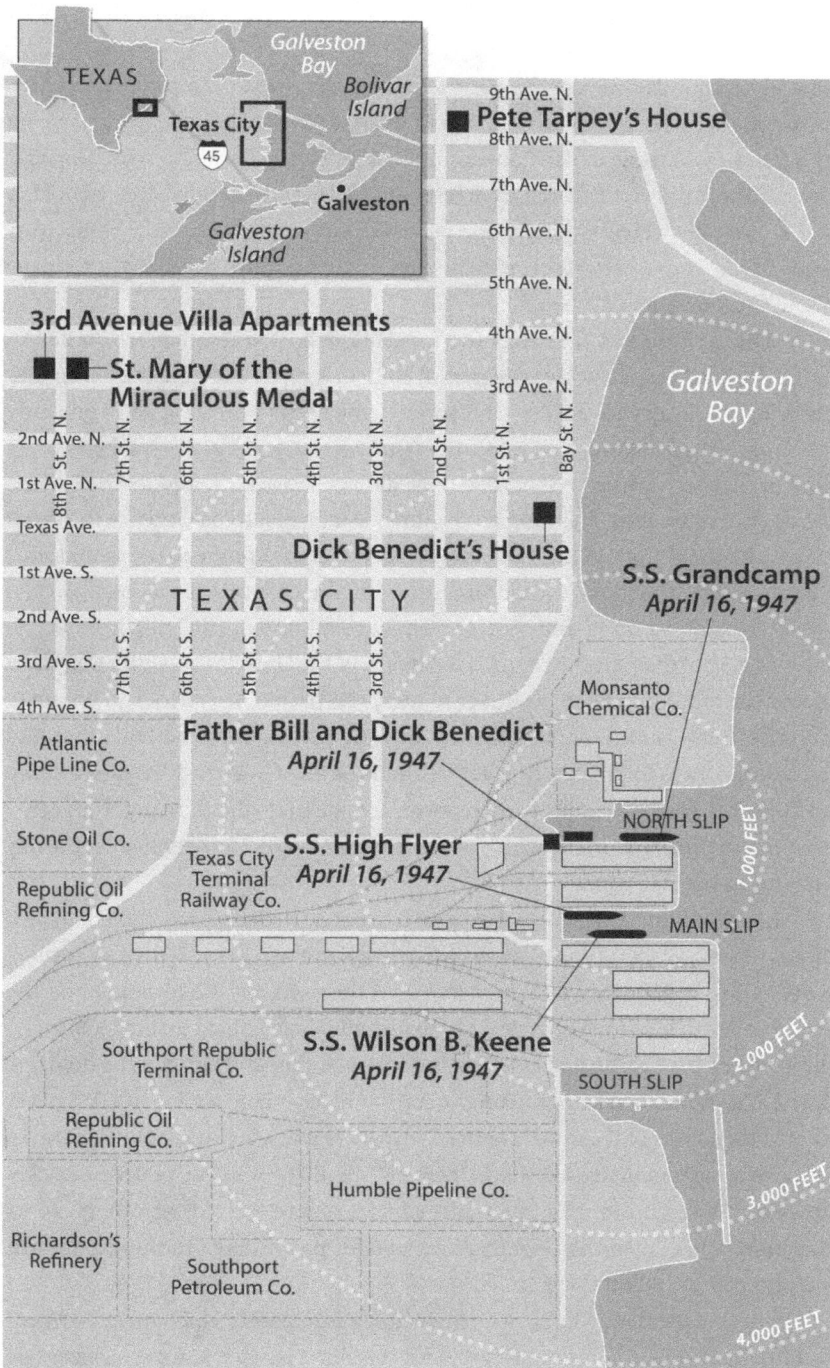

TEXAS

Galveston Bay

Texas City

45

Bolivar Island

Galveston

Galveston Island

9th Ave. N.

Pete Tarpey's House

8th Ave. N.

7th Ave. N.

6th Ave. N.

5th Ave. N.

4th Ave. N.

3rd Avenue Villa Apartments

3rd Ave. N.

Galveston Bay

St. Mary of the Miraculous Medal

2nd Ave. N.

8th St. N.

7th St. N.

6th St. N.

5th St. N.

4th St. N.

3rd St. N.

2nd St. N.

1st St. N.

Bay St. N.

1st Ave. N.

8th St.

Texas Ave.

Dick Benedict's House

S.S. Grandcamp
April 16, 1947

1st Ave. S.

TEXAS CITY

2nd Ave. S.

3rd Ave. S.

7th St. S.

6th St. S.

5th St. S.

4th St. S.

3rd St. S.

4th Ave. S.

Monsanto Chemical Co.

Atlantic Pipe Line Co.

Father Bill and Dick Benedict
April 16, 1947

NORTH SLIP

1,000 FEET

Stone Oil Co.

Texas City Terminal Railway Co.

S.S. High Flyer
April 16, 1947

Republic Oil Refining Co.

MAIN SLIP

S.S. Wilson B. Keene
April 16, 1947

2,000 FEET

Southport Republic Terminal Co.

SOUTH SLIP

Republic Oil Refining Co.

3,000 FEET

Humble Pipeline Co.

Richardson's Refinery

Southport Petroleum Co.

4,000 FEET

The industrial area and docks of Texas City, showing the locations of St. Mary of the Miraculous Medal and ship positions on April 16, 1947. *Map by Carol Zuber-Mallison.*

and related goods overseas. At 441.5 feet long, the ship could carry up to 7,176 gross tons of cargo in its five holds. A pair of large oil-fired boilers supplied steam to a three-cycle triple expansion engine that powered the screw-type propeller system. Fuel oil was stored in a large reservoir located amidships, between holds 2 and 4. Typically, a crew of forty to forty-five sailors operated the vessel. When fully loaded with cargo, crew, fuel, and supplies, the maximum deadweight tonnage of the *Grandcamp* was 10,419.[7]

Just before 8:00 A.M. that morning, longshoremen had congregated at the end of the dock to "shape out" work gangs of eight apiece. By the time the Texas City Terminal Railway whistle blew at 8:00 A.M., the gangs were assigned and ready for work. When loading a ship like the *Grandcamp*, some gangs worked on the dock and others worked onboard. Gangs did not move back and forth between the dock and the ship. The gang on the dock would attach the crates to the ship's tackle; the freight would then be lifted onboard, where another gang would stow it in the holds. That day, ammonium nitrate fertilizer was being loaded.

A night shift working from 7:00 P.M. on the evening of the fifteenth to 6:00 A.M. the morning of the sixteenth had loaded hold 2 of the *Grandcamp* with 1,600 short tons of ammonium nitrate fertilizer in hundred-pound bags. Hold 4 contained 970 short tons of ammonium nitrate fertilizer at quitting time the day before, and the day gang was to finish filling it. Within minutes of boarding the *Grandcamp* and opening hold 4, the day gang reported smoke in the hold, rising from some point on the starboard (dockside) side, between bags of fertilizer loaded the day before and the ship's hull.[8]

Carlos Suderman, outside superintendent for A. D. Suderman and Company, union contractors, was onsite supervising longshoremen loading the *Grandcamp* on behalf of his company. He was in Warehouse O with the foreman and the shipping agent, locating the cargo to be loaded into hold 4 that morning. On being informed of the fire, he immediately boarded the ship and entered the hold. He noted a "grayish" smoke rising on the starboard side, next to the hull. He never located the source of the smoke, or precisely where it was coming from. Suderman and two longshoremen, Julio Luna Jr. and William Thompson, poured a bucket of water toward the smoke, then "aimed four or five fire extinguishers" in its direction. The gray smoke only increased. Suderman ordered the longshoremen out of the hold and off the ship.

On deck, outside the hold, Suderman, gang foreman L. D. Boswell, and general foreman Jimmy Fagg conferred with the ship's master, Captain Charles de Guillebon. Onboard fires were the jurisdiction of the ship's master. Captain de

Guillebon ordered the hatches battened down and steam pumped into the holds to smother the fire. Although Suderman asked the captain not to use water in the holds because it would damage the cargo, the captain ordered the steam system turned on. Pumping steam into sealed holds was universally considered the safest and most efficient way to fight shipboard fires, despite potential cargo damage.

Within a few minutes, though, the hatch covers burst open and massive amounts of yellow-orange smoke began roiling out of hold 4. Captain de Guillebon ordered the ship abandoned. Next, Suderman contacted the shipping agent, E. S. Binnings Company, to notify them of the fire. He asked them to have a fireboat sent from Galveston. It was 8:30 A.M., just about the time Father Bill was stepping outside for a cigarette.[9]

Suderman then encountered W. H. Sandberg, vice president of Texas City Terminal Railway and informed him of the situation, adding that he had ordered a fireboat from Galveston. Sandberg had been in his office talking to Grant Wheaton, an executive of the railway company, when he noticed what he called "a peculiar smoke" floating across the main slip near two ships, a Type C2 cargo vessel called the *High Flyer* and another Liberty ship, the *Wilson B. Keane*. The company switchboard operator received a phone call from the north slip requesting a fireboat because the *Grandcamp* was on fire.

Mike Mikeska, who had left his office earlier to investigate the smoke, returned in a rush. An order was issued to set off the company siren at the powerhouse. Then calls for assistance were made to the Texas City Fire Department and the chief of the Galveston Fire Department. Tugboats from Galveston were also ordered to report to Texas City and stand by. Fortunately, despite a nationwide telephone strike at the time, emergency calls were being routed. Mikeska then left the office and returned to the docks, where he encountered Roach near Frank's Café. Just the week before, the two of them had been at city hall, arguing for and against annexation of the industries. Now they were at the epicenter of a potential disaster.

A few minutes after Mikeska left, Sandberg walked over to the apron leading to Warehouse O, astern of the *Grandcamp*, not far from Father Roach and Dick Benedict. The orange smoke made an impression on him, "just a little bit different color from any I had seen before."[10] When Sandberg returned to his office, Wheaton was still there, on the phone with J. C. Thompkins of Lykes Brothers Steamship Company, owners of SS *High Flyer*, berthed in the slip adjacent to the *Grandcamp*. It had been taking on cargo while simultaneously under repair, and was loaded with 961 tons of ammonium nitrate and 2,000 pounds of bulk sulfur, about half of its maximum cargo capacity of 6,214 tons. The steam that powered the ship was generated from a pair of boilers and delivered to two turbine engines driving a single propeller. Both turbines were down for repairs.[11] Thompkins asked whether the ship was in danger. Wheaton told Thompkins it was not in danger at the moment but that it might be wise to tow it farther away since it could not move under its own power. On seeing Sandberg returning, Wheaton held out the phone so that he might give Thompkins the latest updates. Having been intimately involved in the history of superheated bags of ammonium nitrate fertilizer arriving in Texas City, Sandberg was concerned about the cargo in both the *Grandcamp* and the *High Flyer*. After seeing that odd-colored smoke, he no longer had faith in the manufacturers' assurances that ammonium nitrate was safe. He told Thompkins that tugs had been ordered to move the *Grandcamp* and suggested the same be done for the *High Flyer*. He also said a carbon dioxide foam fire extinguisher called Foamite was en route from Republic Oil to smother the *Grandcamp* fire.[12]

Notified of the fire on the *Grandcamp*, Harley V. Bowen, general foreman of the Texas City Terminal Railway, picked up Henry Baumgarten, chief of the Texas City Volunteer Fire Department, who worked full time as the Terminal Railway purchasing agent, and drove him to Warehouse O. For twenty years, Baumgarten had held a part-time position with the volunteer fire department. It paid fifty dollars a month (the median income was $250 per month).

Bowen drove as close to the *Grandcamp* as possible, passing Dick Benedict and Father Roach standing nearby. When Baumgarten got out of the car, he told Bowen to turn in a second alarm adding, "This is a dangerous fire. We need all the help we can get." Bowen remembered a lot of yellow smoke pouring from hold 4 of the *Grandcamp*.[13]

Father Bill and Dick Benedict realized the road they were standing on, the only road to or from the dock area, was becoming overcrowded and chaotic. Vehicles were racing back and forth, people were running past, and sirens were blaring. While Roach and Benedict were considering what to do, Benedict's older brother J. W. drove up in a pickup truck and jumped out. Yardmaster for the Texas City Terminal Railway, he told Benedict and Roach that he had been instructed to have an engine pull all the freight cars away from the dock area, so the road would be momentarily blocked to pedestrian and motor traffic, and they should be careful about the rails next to them.

Roach and Benedict immediately understood that if railway officials had ordered the freight cars moved away, they clearly believed the fire onboard the *Grandcamp* was serious and getting worse. The massive column of smoke pouring from the stern of the ship, now accompanied by flames, confirmed their assessment. The scene around them was so chaotic that Dick Benedict did not notice his brother get back into his truck and drive away. Benedict was preoccupied with Father Bill, trying to persuade him to go back to St. Mary so that he would not be injured.[14] However, Father Bill would have none of it. He said he had cause to be there. As pastor of his church he was committed to serving his parish, whatever form that service might take. That was his job. He had been onsite when Monsanto caught fire, as well as when the *Black Mountain* and *Sveaborg* exploded and sank nearby. He intended to remain for this event as well.[15]

As fire equipment arrived, including all four of Texas City's pump trucks, H. D. Wray, civil engineer for the Terminal Railway, was working with Chief Baumgarten to activate the company's substantial water system. Six-inch and eight-inch water mains fed three industrial fire pumps capable of delivering 100,000 gallons of freshwater per minute from special reservoirs. Two standpipes of 100,000 gallons each pressurized warehouse risers and supplied water to fire hoses located at every warehouse door. There was also a "Y" connection for pumping additional water directly from the bay should the freshwater reserves run low. Each warehouse was equipped with its own riser and fifty feet of fire hose rack-mounted at every door. Baumgarten and twenty-six other men assembled on the dock of Warehouse O to engage the fire on the *Grandcamp*.[16] Next, Wray turned his attention to the railcars nearby and ordered J. W. Benedict to move them west, out of the area.

H. B. Williams, safety engineer for Pan American Refining Corporation, was at Frank's Café with the plant's security director, drinking coffee. He was about to pay his tab and leave to make a routine inspection of Pan American's ship-loading facilities when he spotted smoke. More ominous to Williams than the smoke was its unusual orange color. His first thought was that a chlorine drum had ruptured—clear evidence that some observers that day recognized the fire to be chemical in nature. The smoke was wafting toward Pan American, so Williams decided to warn the workers there. As Williams and the security director left Frank's Café, they encountered three men running past, heading toward town. Williams stopped one of them and asked what was wrong. The startled man blurted out that he was a sailor from the *Grandcamp*, that fertilizer was burning in hold 4, and that hold 5 was filled with small arms ammunition.

Williams assumed that the three men running away were worried about the munitions exploding, but he was much more concerned about the fertilizer. He drove to the Pan American docks and instructed all employees to leave immediately because by then the area was shrouded in orange smoke. On making inquiries, Williams discovered the fertilizer was ammonium nitrate, suggesting to him the smoke might be nitrogen oxide fumes. On smelling the smoke, he detected the odor and acrid taste of nitric acid.

Williams went to the north slip next to the *Grandcamp* to warn workers there of the dangers of breathing the orange fumes. A messenger was dispatched to ask if Chief Baumgarten and his men required acid gas masks. Within ten minutes, the answer came back: yes. Williams suggested phoning to have masks delivered but was reminded of the telephone strike. Not knowing that emergency calls could be made, he decided to drive and get the masks himself.

By then such a crush of people had gathered on the road between Frank's Café and the burning ship that Williams had a lot of trouble navigating through them. He noted the siren blasting and the fire trucks arriving, but the orange smoke against the blue, sunny sky, was a "beautiful thing to see." Unfortunately, that was causing hundreds of people to try to get as close to it as possible. Williams was finally able to squeeze through the mass of people and drive off.[17] The presence of smoke and flames in proximity to ammonium nitrate fertilizer indicated extremely volatile chemical decomposition.[18] Apart from being one of best sources of the nitrogen plants need to thrive, the key element in fertilizer, ammonium nitrate is also a component in the manufacture of explosives. In fact, it is very difficult to ignite ammonium nitrate and harder still to make it explode, but under excessive heat, it can decompose and explode.

The introduction of tremendous force (five thousand meters per second or greater) may cause ammonium nitrate instantly to decompose and explode. Contact with certain metals like aluminum, copper, cadmium, and zinc will also produce the same result. Chemical contamination may also promote decomposition of ammonium nitrate, but usually more slowly. Introduction of carbonaceous materials—particularly flammable substances like sulfur, charcoal, flour, sugar, or petroleum—will cause rapid decomposition to the point of explosion. Recall that a reservoir of fuel oil was adjacent to hold 4, separated from it by only one bulkhead.

As he drove away to find acid gas masks for the firefighters, H. B. Williams was worried about the rate of decomposition in hold 4. Decomposition produces heat. At 350–390 degrees Fahrenheit, rapid decomposition occurs, increasing heat absorption and producing orange-reddish fumes. At this point oxygen, nitrogen, and steam are being produced, which accelerate combustion. From that point, the velocity of acceleration increases substantially. At 2700 degrees Fahrenheit the decomposition is uncontrollable and producing 160,000 pounds of pressure per square inch. If the ammonium nitrate is dense enough and packed in a tight space, explosion is inevitable.[19]

Few people other than H. B. Williams had a clue about the danger of explosion. Every hundred-pound bag of ammonium nitrate was labeled "Fertilizer," which to dockworkers did not signal danger of burning or exploding. By law, the bags should have been labeled "Hazardous Chemical" and carried a warning of potential volatility. The mislabeling was a blatant cost-cutting measure: material shipped under the label "Fertilizer" cost $.85 per hundred pounds, whereas shipments labeled "Hazardous Chemical" cost $1.45 per hundred pounds. At the time, regulation of the shipping of hazardous materials was left largely up to manufacturers and shippers, with no external oversight.[20]

Mayor Curtis Trahan was at home when the city siren went off shortly after 8:00 A.M. Looking out his window he saw reddish-orange smoke rising from the docks, becoming thicker by the moment. After driving his son to Danforth School, he proceeded toward the docks. At the intersection of Fourth Street South and Fourth Avenue South, an auxiliary police officer who did not recognize the mayor stopped his car. After Trahan identified himself, the officer told him to proceed but added that the volunteer fire department was on the scene and everything seemed to be under control. Satisfied, Trahan decided not to proceed.[21]

Near the dock, Mike Mikeska told Harley Bowen to open some of the doors on the west side of Warehouse O so that fire trucks could drive through and be positioned near the *Grandcamp*. Bowen found all the doors on the south side of the warehouse blocked by bags of flour positioned for loading onboard the *Wilson B. Keane*, berthed in the main slip. Bowen started walking toward Mikeska to tell him the fire trucks could not pass through the warehouse.[22]

Opposite the north slip from the *Grandcamp*, about five hundred feet away, Audrey Carroll stood at a third-story window of the Monsanto offices with her coworkers in accounting. They watched the firefighters struggling with a tangle of hoses dockside and onboard the *Grandcamp*. Then the trickle of smoke, gray at first, grew thicker and changed to orange, then red, then dark brown, and finally black. Soon, flames were shooting high into the air from the stern of the ship.

"Shouldn't we leave?" Carroll asked a man nearby.

"No," the man said. "They can spit on it and put it out."

The office manager told everyone to get back to work. Carroll returned to her desk but was uncomfortable being there. Being close to ships on fire seemed unnatural. "What am I doing here?" she thought. Carroll's coworkers looked at her as if she were from outer space when she suggested they leave. Since she had been on the job less than a month, Carroll did not feel comfortable pressing the issue. She considered calling her father for advice but the only phone was on the office manager's desk, and a telephone strike was underway. She tried to focus on the typewriter and papers in front of her, but she could not take her mind off the firefighters.

One of the volunteer firefighters wrestling hoses on the deck of the *Grandcamp* was auto mechanic Ben L. Mitchell, who worked full time at a service station on Texas Avenue. Earlier that morning, he had removed a corroded radiator from a customer's car. He was on his way to Galveston to have it boiled out and rebuilt when he heard the siren blaring from city hall. He diverted immediately to the docks with the corroded radiator still in the back of his truck.

Onsite, Mitchell went to work, dragging a hose up to hold 4 of the *Grandcamp*. By then the deck was so hot that the soles of his boots were melting and sticking to the surface, and he could see it swelling and bowing from the growing pressure inside the hold. He returned dockside to help unroll more hoses. Then, recalling the radiator in his vehicle, the customer waiting for it, and the fact that his boss at the service station was unaware that he had diverted to fight a fire, Mitchell located Chief Baumgarten and asked to be released from the fire and continue on to Galveston. Baumgarten agreed, and Mitchell left the scene.[23]

At a few minutes past nine o'clock, Terminal Railway vice president Sandberg was pacing near the apron to the dock, watching for the tugs to arrive. He did not know it at the time, but the tugs, the *Albatross* and the *Propeller*, were already within sight of the north slip. Certainly, he must have wished local industry leaders had not backed out of their agreement to share the cost of the fireboat purchased by Texas City the year before.[24] Sandberg thought about walking out to the end of the dock to get a better look at the bay and the approaching tugs, but decided to go back to the office and call Galveston instead. When he stepped through the door, Grant Wheaton handed him the phone to speak to Thompkins. On the road near the apron to Warehouse O, about a half block from the stern of the *Grandcamp*, Dick Benedict was still trying to persuade Father Bill to leave the area. It was 9:12 A.M.

$$=15=$$

"WHERE IS FATHER BILL?"

Just nine miles from the *Grandcamp*, Father Frank Lagana was in his room at the rectory of the Shrine of the True Cross in Dickinson when the whole building shuddered, as if an earthquake had struck. The pastor, Monsignor Thomas Carney came to Lagana's door.

"What was that?" he asked.

"The windows are rattling," Lagana answered.

"I know," Carney responded. "But what caused it?"[1]

In the Monsanto office, across the slip from the *Grandcamp*, Audrey Carroll was sitting at her desk, her back to the windows where she and her fellow workers had been watching the fire. Suddenly, a massive concussion knocked her to the floor, sending her typewriter sailing across the office and slamming against a wall. Shaking off debris and dust, Carroll rose unsteadily to her feet. She could barely see a thing. A coworker looked at her and said, "Audrey, your eye is gone."[2]

To the south, in Galveston, seventeen-year-old Fred Gorzell was in chemistry class at Kirwin High School. The class was watching a 16 mm film on a large Bell and Howell projector when the whole room began shaking violently and the Bell and Howell started rocking back and forth and skittering across the projection stand. Several students jumped to their feet. Some began talking excitedly about an earthquake. One ran to the window, expecting to see the ground opening up. Then the massive blast hit.[3]

A block away from Kirwin, Mary Frances Romano was in English class at
Ursuline Academy when the whole building began vibrating, followed by a thunderous noise. The aftereffects lingered for several moments. Clearly, something
had exploded. The sound was so loud that students thought the school's boiler had
blown up. The teacher, Mother Teresa, told the class to kneel and recite a Rosary
while she went to see what had happened. Instead of praying, several students,
Romano included, ran to the windows on the north side of the classroom. The
sky was filled with what looked like dark storm clouds gathering over the bay
and moving toward Galveston. But there was no storm. It was smoke. Shortly,
Mother Teresa returned and, without offering any details, she told the class the
school was being evacuated.[4]

Catherine Medina was at her desk in the Galveston office of the US Army
Corps of Engineers, on the fourth floor of the Santa Fe Building, overlooking
Galveston Bay. At 9:12 A.M., Medina felt the building shaking, lightly at first
then growing in intensity. Her heavy, government-issue wooden desk started
skittering across the floor. Then the blast hit, momentarily knocking the breath
out of her. Someone shouted, "Texas City!" Outside, to the north, on the west
side of the bay, a massive black mushroom cloud rose high into the air. Moments
later, chunks of metal and oil rained down on the Santa Fe Building and the
whole east end of Galveston Island. Nine miles away, at Texas City, large oil
and chemical storage tanks were being struck by flaming debris and exploding. Medina immediately thought of her lifelong friend, Audrey Carroll, who
worked at Monsanto.[5]

In Houston, forty-five miles northwest of the *Grandcamp*, Rita Bouchard had
just arrived at work in a field office of Stone and Webster Company, commercial
construction contractors. The office was located on the site of oilman Glenn
McCarthy's colossal Shamrock Hotel, under construction at the time. As she
began her workday, Bouchard heard a blast so loud it seemed to have come from
somewhere on the jobsite. Stepping outside the office with coworkers, Bouchard
spotted a massive mushroom cloud of dense, black smoke rising low on the horizon
to the southeast.[6]

At the city barns in Texas City, Mayor Curtis Trahan had just pulled up
and started talking to Street and Bridge Supervisor Wylie Sloman, when the
corrugated steel building seemed to swell and bulge outward, seemingly about
to fly apart. Then the roar of a massive explosion raked past the barn and an
enormous mushroom cloud appeared over the harbor a few blocks away. Some
sheet metal panels dislodged, but the building settled down intact. Sloman ran

to his truck and Trahan sped away in his car. They did not even say goodbye to each other.[7]

Dick Benedict was unsure of where he was or what was going on. For some reason he was lying on the ground. He struggled to his feet. Most of his clothes were missing, and he was covered in some sort of black, sticky slime. He looked around. He could not recognize a thing. A handful of people were wandering nearby, all covered in the same black paste. Twisted, skeletal remains of buildings jutted from a scorched landscape. The hull of a barge loomed next to him, oddly straddling a railroad track on dry ground. And everything seemed to be on fire.[8]

Slowly, Benedict recalled what had happened. He had heard no sound but remembered two distinct concussions hitting him. The first knocked him into a pit and the second sent a wave of oily water washing over him. The *Grandcamp* had detonated and disintegrated into thousands of pieces, ranging from shards weighing a few ounces to a jagged, two-ton chunk that landed two-and-a-half miles away. Part of the ship's cargo, drill stems thirty feet long and weighing 2,700 pounds each, sailed 13,000 feet through the air like sticks and bore themselves six feet into the ground. Water from the slip spiraled 4,000 feet into the air and was redeposited hundreds of feet inland. Two light airplanes circling overhead were blown from the sky. One, passing directly above the *Grandcamp*, had its wings folded upwards by the concussion. It plummeted straight down and crashed, killing the pilot. The other, off to the side of the ship, disintegrated in midair. The pilot and one passenger were seen hurtling to their deaths. In that instant, some 430 other people were killed and another 135 were missing and later presumed dead. More than 3,500 people were injured.[9]

The *Longhorn II*, a barge in the north slip, was propelled onto dry ground, coming to rest on the railroad spur near the spot where Benedict and Father Bill had been standing. Benedict could not see Father Bill anywhere. As he looked around, he saw warehouses and most buildings within a thousand feet completely obliterated. A gnarled remnant of structural ironwork was all that remained of the largest Monsanto building. Almost everything in Benedict's line of sight was destroyed and burning. He would find out later that a thousand other structures sustained major damage or were completely destroyed and that plate glass windows were broken as far away as Galveston.

Later, Benedict surmised that the ammonium nitrate in hold 4 of the SS *Grandcamp* exploded, in turn causing the fertilizer in hold 2 to blow a millisecond later, which would account for the sensation of two concussive blasts. Several other eyewitnesses reported feeling two blasts, but just as many remembered only one.[10] The number of explosions hardly matters, though; investigators concluded that all the ammonium nitrate onboard the *Grandcamp* was consumed, and the result was devastating.

The blast ripped the SS *High Flyer* from its mooring in the main slip, five hundred feet away, and drove it against the *Wilson B. Keane* (see map 3). Whatever freight in the *Grandcamp*'s holds not immediately vaporized in the explosion was transformed into flaming projectiles sailing thousands of feet in all directions. These incendiaries landed on oil storage tanks, gasoline reservoirs, and flammable petrochemical products. Soon, dozens of new explosions rocked the area as uncontrollable flames and heavy smoke consumed the harbor and parts of Texas City. If this were not bad enough, two thousand tons of bulk sulfur loaded in an open hold on the *High Flyer* was hit by burning balls of sisal twine and started smoldering, risking decomposition of the hundreds of tons of ammonium nitrate fertilizer also aboard the vessel.[11]

Dick Benedict staggered toward his office between Warehouses O and A, only to discover the building had been sheared in half by the explosion. He started looking for his brother, J. W. Unbeknownst to him at the time, his brother, though injured, had gotten one of the company trucks; collected a load of other injured people, including Terminal Railway executive Grant Wheaton, and driven them to waiting ambulances near the offices of Republic Oil.[12]

At the Shrine of the True Cross in Dickinson, Father Lagana and Pastor Carney rushed from Lagana's room to a hallway nearby and looked southeast, toward Texas City. A huge, thick mass of black smoke filled the distant sky. Carney ran to the phone and tried to make some calls, but because of the phone strike he could not get through. Lagana suggested Carney try again and tell the operator it was an emergency. That worked. When the *Grandcamp* exploded, striking telephone operators in Texas City had dropped their picket signs and run to their posts at the switchboard inside. The tearful operator told Carney there had been a massive explosion on the docks and that many of the surrounding industries were on fire. "They need help," she cried.[13]

H. O. Wray, engineer for the Terminal Railway, was dazed, unable to hear, and encased in thick smoke. He was somewhere between Warehouses O and A, but the warehouses were gone. His clothes were soaked from a ruptured fire hydrant spraying water on him. His hat and glasses were gone. Dead bodies were all around. He had a momentary thought that it was Resurrection Day, and wondered why the bodies were not rising. Inside the Terminal Railway Company office, W. H. Sandberg had just finished his call with Lykes Brothers Steamship

Company, informing them their ship the *High Flyer* was in danger, when the office was wracked by the explosion. Sandberg was struck in the head and knocked to the floor, temporarily dazed.

Carlos Suderman had just stepped from the dock of Warehouse O to speak with a customs officer and the director of the wharf police when the *Grandcamp* exploded. Somehow Suderman survived while the other two died. Terminal Railway foreman Harley Bowen, standing just inside a door of Warehouse O, heard nothing. A powerful gust of wind struck him. The floor on which he stood rose up, buckled, and came apart, dropping him in the water. Then a second gust knocked him out of the water and dropped him upright about one hundred feet away on dry land. He fell over, one of his legs numb and mangled. His only clothing were his underpants, a piece of undershirt, and the belted portion of his upper trousers. Everything else was gone. Fire and smoke surrounded him.[14]

Dick Benedict was trudging toward the dock road, turning bodies over, looking for his brother. Then he saw Harley Bowen being dragged along the road by his wife, who had rushed to the dock after the explosion. Besides Bowen's leg injury he had a nasty gash across his throat. Benedict helped her move Bowen out of harm's way, then collapsed in place, too weak to do anything else. He had been struck in the back and legs by shrapnel and was finally starting to feel the effects. He slumped beside Bowen and his wife and waited for help. At some point, Benedict spotted Sandberg in the distance. He had a large, bloody bandage on his head but otherwise looked uninjured. Eventually, Benedict and the Bowens were transported by truck to Schmidt-Twidwell Clinic, on Sixth Street North. Using a pair of pliers from a hardware store, Dr. Schmidt removed metal slivers and bits of clothing from Benedict's head, back, and legs. Bowen was immediately transported to Galveston.[15]

Audrey Carroll was desperately trying to escape the wrecked Monsanto office building. In tremendous pain and with limited, blurred vision, she felt her way through the thick dust, chemical smoke, and debris that filled what was left of the third floor. She made it to the window where the fire escape was supposed to be, but the fire escape was gone, blown away by the blast. Everyone else in the office was stunned and wandering around aimlessly, but Carroll was determined to get out of the building and home to Galveston. She located the stairwell, but instead of steps there were only long chunks of concrete extending at a jumble of angles below. Slowly, carefully, Carroll slid down the lengths of concrete until she reached the ground and exited on the west side of the building. She started across a field just north of the parking lot. Fire was all around her. Through damaged eyes, she perceived others walking in the same direction.

Within minutes, Carroll reached a drainage ditch. By then she was covered in her own blood. Glass and wooden shards from the office venetian blinds were embedded in her back, arms, and face. Perhaps it was for the best that she did not know wood splinters had been driven through one of her cheeks and were sticking out just below her eye. The ditch was filled with chemicals, including benzol, toluene, xylene, carbon disulfide, thiophene, and pyridine, all escaping from ruptured lines at Monsanto. The smell was overwhelming. She had no idea how to get across. She was not about to wade into the chemicals, but the fires were closing in. Soon, smoke wafted over her. She waited for the flames to overtake her. Instead of fire, however, two very large men appeared, seemingly from nowhere—one white, one black. Each grabbed one of her arms, lifted her, and walked through the chemical-filled ditch holding Carroll above the sludge. They set her down on the opposite side and kept on walking, disappearing into the smoke. She never found out who they were but always thought of them as guardian angels.

Carroll was only a few steps from the road to town. A car stopped—a station wagon. The emblem on the door identified it as a Red Cross vehicle. "You're hurt real bad," said the woman at the wheel. "Yes I am," Carroll answered. "Would you please take me to the clinic?" Carroll started to get in but the woman behind the wheel waved her off, saying, "You'll get blood all over my station wagon. Somebody will pick you up." As she drove off, Carroll was left standing alone on the smoky road, injured and bleeding. Alas, this was only one of several times local Red Cross officials were criticized for their disaster response and arrogant attitude.[16]

In Dickinson, Father Carney and another priest, Father Cary Fowler, rushed to one of the parish cars for the short drive to Texas City. Father Lagana grabbed oils for last rites, then followed in another car. Within minutes the three priests arrived in the midst of what looked like a war zone. Not really expecting to survive, they quickly heard each other's confessions, blessed each other, and charged into the conflagration. The three priests searched for injured people in need of help, but all they found was death—severed arms, legs, heads, and mangled torsos. The whole area was blackened. Large drops of oil fell for several minutes like some unnatural rain. And an odd silence (apart from fires burning) had descended over the whole area. After anointing the dead, the priests made their way one by one into Texas City to help out at the clinics.[17]

At the Danforth Clinic on Sixth, Dr. Clarence Quinn had his hands full. Having been an army medic in World War II, he had dealt with mass casualties often, including during the Battle of the Bulge. His son, C. F. Quinn, a seminarian at St. Mary's in La Porte, was already there, assisting his father. He set out from La Porte with several fellow seminarians shortly after receiving word of the explosion of the *Grandcamp*. They and the priests from Dickinson went to work. The younger Quinn helped his father attend to an eight-year-old boy who had been placed on the doctor's desk. The boy died—but nothing stopped, or even slowed. "In the X-ray room, Father, please," one nurse called out. "On the operating table, Father, please talk to this boy," cried another. Dr. Quinn pointed outside to a truckload of injured people. Father Carney followed the direction of Quinn's finger and jumped onto the rear of the truck. "Help the priest [get on that truck]," Quinn instructed.[18]

In the midst of all the activity, someone arrived with a baby to be baptized. Father Lagana and Father Fowler pushed everything off the surface of a desk in the outer office and baptized the infant. It was like that—life and death, death and life. Outside the clinic, on Sixth Street, someone grabbed Father Lagana and spun him around to face a woman. "Here's your sister!" Lagana just stared at her, overjoyed to see her. He knew she had been at work in the offices of Republic Oil and was worried about her. She told him the roof collapsed in her office but no one there was hurt.

At some point, Carney, Lagana, and Fowler went back to the disaster site, leaving C. F. Quinn and the other seminarians to assist at Danforth Clinic. As the Dickinson priests neared the flames and smoke, they parked one of their two cars and continued in the other. But even so, they could not get much closer and finally had to continue on foot. The African American and Latino/a working-class neighborhood south of Texas Avenue was destroyed—every last home. Most of the inhabitants had been killed, and those that survived were severely injured. The area was part of Father Bill's regular nocturnal sojourns among the city's poor and homeless inhabitants. Lagana found it strange he had not yet seen Father Bill. It was completely out of character for him to not be there helping.

The Catholic mission church, Our Lady of the Snows, had collapsed. The only thing unharmed was the statue of the Virgin Mary. The priests worked the neighborhood, helping the injured get to clinics or loading them into vehicles for transport to Galveston or some other place farther away. In at least one case, a dislodged door was used as a stretcher. The dead were anointed, covered, and the spot where they lay marked as best as possible for body recovery later.

Those able to move on their own were assisted in evacuating the area. Monsignor Carney arranged for the two large halls and other spaces at the Shrine of the True Cross in Dickinson to be opened for refugees. By the end of the day, about one hundred displaced people were housed there, mostly children. Three women transported there were pregnant and close to giving birth. There was also a mumps outbreak among the children. Area doctors and nurses were diverted to Dickinson to assist the sick and injured people pouring into the Shrine of the True Cross. There was really no concerted organization to the rescue and recovery. The many priests and seminarians, a handful of Protestant clergy, and local citizens just banded together and did what they could. Vehicles appeared, seemingly from nowhere, mostly private citizens from as far away as Houston, San Antonio, and Dallas wanting to help.[19]

Father Carney encountered a young man who approached excitedly. He pointed to a group of men charging into the flames at Monsanto, only a few yards away, to find injured victims. The young man was not Catholic, but he wanted some kind of religious blessing before proceeding. "I want to go in there and help, Father," he said. "Do something for me." Carney led the young man in an act of faith and contrition, blessed him, and sent him on his way.

Not long thereafter, Carney, Lagana, and Fowler met four other priests from the seminary who had been on the site since about 10:00 A.M. Father Kermiet and Father Nelson had been working at the wrecked dock where the *Grandcamp* had been moored, while Father Deslatte and Father Griffin joined the Dickinson priests at Monsanto. The five men ranged through the property, as close to the flames as they could get, helping the injured and anointing the dead.

They heard a loud scream from the third story of the office building Audrey Carroll had escaped from earlier. Several men nearby climbed up the corner of the building. Father Griffin, who was nimble and athletic, climbed along with them and entered the upper floor of the building, Audrey Carroll's floor. Everyone inside was dead. A rescuer removing a victim from another part of the building fell, but other rescuers caught both him and the victim.[20]

Explosions continued erupting all around. Rumors of more and greater blasts circulated everywhere the priests went. The thick smoke had somehow settled a few feet above the heads of the rescuers, creating a surreal undulating ceiling. Steel projectiles from explosions dropped nearby. Eventually the fire at Monsanto became so intense that all the rescuers had to abandon the area. Everyone converged on what was left of the north slip, where the *Grandcamp* had been. Father Carney noted a remnant of the ship's hull embedded in the massive, nearly dry hole the explosion had created.[21]

Father James Nelson gravitated to the *High Flyer*, where victims remained onboard, some calling for help. Scaling a rope ladder to the deck, Nelson collected an injured man, hauled him over his shoulder, and started back down the ladder.

But a rung failed and Nelson fell about twenty-five feet to the wrecked dock below. The victim landed on top of him, breaking Nelson's collarbone.[22] Nelson was helped to a vehicle for transport to a clinic, but the victim died at the scene. The rest of the injured on the *High Flyer* were successfully evacuated, and the priests moved on.

By noon, Carney, Lagana, and the other priests began to question why they had seen nothing of Father Bill. "Where's Father Bill?" they asked. They all knew it was not at all like him to avoid being directly involved in an event such as this. Eventually, they began hearing rumors that he had been injured in the blast.[23] In town, others were also wondering about Father Bill. He was not at the church, and no one had seen him on the streets or around the docks. Katherine Hunter walked to Richard and Cora Meskill's house to ask about Roach. They said they were sure they had seen him drive past the house earlier, but it turned out to be Father John, cruising the streets, searching for his brother. The twins looked so much alike that people in Texas City often mistook John for Bill, sometimes thinking they had seen Bill in two different parts of town at almost the same time.[24]

At Danforth Clinic, Father Harris drove up with the other seminarians he brought from La Porte and collected young C. F. Quinn. "Let's all go to Galveston to see if we can find Father Roach," he said.[25] Harris and the others had heard multiple reports that Father Bill had been injured in the explosion of the *Grandcamp*, but he was not at any of the clinics in Texas City. Harris thought a Galveston hospital, most likely Marine Hospital, would be where Father Bill would have been taken if he had been seriously injured. Marine Hospital, built in 1931, was established as part of a nationwide program to provide free medical treatment to merchant marines, longshoremen, and other employees of maritime services.[26] Also eligible for services was anyone injured in an incident on a dock, which would include victims of the *Grandcamp* explosion.[27]

Harris, Quinn, and the other seminarians crossed the old causeway into Galveston and proceeded down Broadway to Marine Hospital. Traffic was heavy because of all the incoming casualties. However, cars were able reach speeds of seventy to eighty miles per hour along Broadway because a network of volunteers, mostly students from Kirwin High School, spontaneously posted themselves at strategic corners, redirecting cross-traffic to prevent collisions with the hundreds of speeding vehicles entering the city. The whole time, large drops of oil, like black rain, were falling on them.[28]

The group of searchers from the seminary rushed into Marine Hospital. Injured people were everywhere—sitting in chairs, stretched out in hallways, leaning against doors—and doctors and nurses were rushing in all directions. They spotted

Father George Rhein, busily helping the living and anointing the dead. They asked about Father Bill, and Rhein told them the priest had been there. He had come across Roach, naked, sitting on the floor, slumped against the wall in a room. He was covered in ash and some sort of black, sticky goo. There was a tag around his neck, identifying him as Father Bill Roach. Rhein was a close friend of Father Bill's, having been a fellow seminarian with Bill and John. He liked both brothers a lot, especially Bill—everyone liked Bill. Rhein remembered him as sunny and very optimistic, always looking at the bright side of things and always ready for the next adventure.[29] Rhein was shocked at the sight of Father Bill on the floor, rail thin, almost emaciated, from his practice of penitent fasting. Father Bill was barely breathing and unable to speak, but he recognized Rhein and smiled faintly. Rhein greeted him, administered last rites, and prayed. At 2:30 P.M. on April 16, 1947, Father Bill exhaled audibly and died.[30] He was thirty-eight years old.

$$=16=$$

"HOW CAN WE HELP?"

After learning of Father Bill's death, Father Harris and the seminarians left Marine Hospital and drove to Malloy and Sons Funeral Home, a few blocks away, on Broadway. Father Rhein said he thought Father Bill's body had been taken there.

"Do you have Father Roach here?" they asked at the funeral home. "Yes," the representative replied, leading them to a room in the back of the building. Roach was on a preparation table. He had already been embalmed. All around were so many dead bodies yet to be prepared that there was not enough space even to lay them out on the floor. Bodies were sitting up against walls, all around the room, and outside in the hall. All of them had sustained massive injuries. But not Roach. There were no marks on him at all. Not the slightest sign of trauma.[1]

After the explosion of the SS *Grandcamp*, Father Bill reportedly emerged from the smoke and fire on the dock road near the wreckage of Frank's Café, staggering but walking on his own. His clothes, cassock and all, had been ripped from his body by the blast. He was covered with either molasses from a nearby storage tank or oil, or perhaps a combination of both, depending on the witness.[2] He was next seen on Sixth Street North. Dr. Quinn's Danforth Clinic was on Sixth, and so was city hall where Fred Linton was helping coordinate transportation for the injured. His family owned Emken Funeral Home in Texas City. After the explosion, Linton went to city hall to offer the use of his company's vehicles, including an ambulance, for rescue and recovery, but wound up staying to organize and

manage the effort. At 9:50 A.M., he and a young woman helped Father Bill onto
a bus filled with other injured victims bound for Galveston. Roach never spoke.
"He was beyond speaking," Linton later wrote.[3]

At the offices of Pan American Refining Company, two miles from the burning
Grandcamp, safety officer H. B. Williams had located several gas masks for the
firefighters on the docks. He was walking to his car when the ship detonated.
He saw a massive column of smoke rising to about fifteen hundred feet, with a
classic mushroom-shaped cloud at the top. As Williams watched, a second, more
powerful explosion occurred. Debris sailed through the air in all directions, some
of it toward him and the refinery. He ducked behind the brick office building
momentarily, then peeked out toward the blast area. An immense shaft of fire
was moving from the north slip across the entire Monsanto property, followed
by an even larger mass of thick, black smoke that obscured every building and all
the industrial stacks and risers. At the same time a tank at Stone Oil Company
Refinery exploded in flames. Then others did as well. Williams again retreated
behind the brick building until the concussions passed.[4]

Those concussions were so powerful that they were felt as far away as Palestine,
Texas, 160 miles from Texas City. Port Arthur, 100 miles away, felt earthquake-like
tremors. Glass was shattered as far away as Houston and Freeport.[5]

After feeling the blast concussion that nearly brought down the city barns,
Mayor Curtis Trahan drove home to make sure his family was safe. Then he
went to his office at city hall. All the glass on the south side of the building was
shattered and the walls were cracked, but no one had been injured. Trahan began
formulating and directing rescue and recovery efforts, working with Chief of
Police W. L. Ladish to manage relief services already arriving by land, sea, and air.

Trahan soon contacted Governor Beauford H. Jester in Austin. Jester alerted
Colonel Homer Garrison, director of the Texas Department of Public Safety, who
coordinated with Mayor Trahan and Chief Ladish, first by phone, and later in
person. Garrison was quick to assert that his role was not to boss everyone around.
Instead, he told Trahan and Ladish that his department had many resources to
offer and simply asked, "How can we help?"[6]

The amount of help needed was unfathomable. Between 2,000 and 2,500
people were made homeless by the blasts. In and around Texas City, 3,300
structures were severely damaged, including 90 percent of homes. Crews from
Galveston County were assembled to enter residences and remove all food
and other perishables to control the spread of disease. Health inspections of
restaurants and grocery stores commenced, with officials issuing special permits

before these establishments could reopen to the public. More than two hundred broken mains, spraying water throughout the city, had to be isolated and shut off. Water service to the rest of the city was restored by noon the following day, April 17, when electric power was restored to city pumps. The concrete ground reservoir at Tenth Street North and Ninth Avenue North was cracked in the explosion but was deemed safe for use. Nevertheless, Galveston County health officials ordered water tests five times daily and closely monitored sewer and garbage to prevent outbreaks of cholera, typhus, and other diseases. Some electricity service was restored by April 17, and miraculously, only one natural gas pipeline was ruptured in the city. It was repaired and service restored a few hours after the *Grandcamp* exploded.[7]

Damage to the business district was particularly heavy. The largest buildings suffered the most, including two movie theaters whose roofs collapsed. Fifteen businesses were so structurally unsound they had to be condemned and demolished, while 186 other retail businesses sustained moderate to heavy damage but were repairable. In all, 539 structures would be razed.

Six hundred cars and trucks, all parked in the Monsanto parking lot, were consumed by fire, crushed by the blast concussion, or hit by shrapnel. One of those cars, of course, had belonged to Father Bill. Five hundred more vehicles were damaged in town and elsewhere in the area, mostly involving broken windshields from concussions and flying debris. Twenty-six of the city firefighters were dead and the department's four engines destroyed. Forty percent of the population fled Texas City, some never to return.[8]

The port area was almost totally obliterated. A half-mile of wharves were flattened. Three ships were lost, their hulks still blocking the north slip and main slip. The oil docks at the south slip, clear of tankers at the time of the explosions, was almost totally destroyed. Only an isolated section of the dock located southeast of the slip remained intact.[9]

Many of the large industries had been reduced to rubble. Monsanto, the one closest to the SS *Grandcamp* when it exploded, suffered a $20 million loss, equivalent to $243,673,562 in 2021.[10] A wave of bay water was blown out of the slip and washed over the Monsanto property, coating everything with fuel oil and other chemicals. The force of the wave ripped open pipelines filled with benzene, styrene, and other petroleum derivatives, which showered the landscape and ignited. Flaming projectiles pierced chemical storage tanks, causing them to explode and burn. Two 11,600-barrel benzol tanks burned for more than a week. The warehouse, office, laboratory, and various petrochemical processing units were completely wrecked by the blast. Among the Monsanto workforce, 154 employees were killed and 200 others hospitalized, including Audrey Carroll.

Also nearby was Republic Oil Refining Company, which had 80,000-barrel petroleum storage tanks located a mere seven thousand feet from the blast. All caught fire and were completely incinerated. Humble Pipeline Company, Southport-Republic Terminal Company, Sid Richardson Refining Company, and Stone Oil Company all sustained similar damage.

The Tin Processing Corporation, the only producer of tin in the nation, was substantially damaged and six of its key equipment operators were killed. At the Texas City Terminal Railway Company, the offices and all eleven warehouses were gone. Three of its locomotives were destroyed and two others severely damaged, while 362 freight cars were wrecked. Petroleum storage tanks, 250 of them ranging from 25,000 to 80,000 barrels in capacity, were partially damaged by combinations of explosion, fire, and debris. Twenty-two others were completely destroyed. Thick columns of black smoke rose three thousand feet in the air, visible for thirty miles in all directions. Fires burned for more than a week.[11]

Mayor Trahan named Dr. Clarence Quinn of the Danforth Clinic as medical coordinator, charged with managing the medical response. Firefighters from Galveston, Houston, and dozens of other cities as far away as Dallas began arriving on the scene. The Texas City Police Department quickly received assistance from other departments throughout Texas, in addition to the support coming from the Texas Department of Public Safety. The US military deployed troops and equipment to the scene from nearby Camp Wallace, the Fourth Army Disaster Team, Fort Sam Houston in San Antonio, Naval Air Stations at Dallas and Corpus Christi, and the Naval Bureau of Medicine and Surgery. Meanwhile, military and civilian hospitals in Houston, San Antonio, Corpus Christi, and Galveston took in casualties.

The first wave of injured people was placed in the city hall auditorium. When that space soon filled, they were surged into the park behind city hall. Merchants along Texas Avenue and Sixth Street donated medical supplies, clothing, blankets, food, and other necessities from their wrecked stores. A temporary morgue was established at McGar Motor Company, but the dead soon overflowed into the high school auditorium. When that filled, facilities at nearby Camp Wallace were pressed into service.

A lighthouse tender, the *Iris*, arrived near the dock area and was quickly refitted to serve as a floating hospital. The Coast Guard, alerted by a small column of orange smoke, dispatched several vessels that used their high-capacity onboard pumps to extinguish a burning mass of ammonium nitrate fertilizer in the area where Warehouse O had stood. They then turned their attention to the raging fires engulfing Monsanto.[12]

The Shrine of the True Cross in Dickinson may have been the first to open its facilities to refugees, but Camp Wallace and the Federal Works Agency Bureau of Community Facilities in Hitchcock, Texas, soon followed. The Salvation Army arrived promptly in Texas City, handing out tens of thousands of dinners, sandwiches, mugs of coffee, bottles of milk, clothing, and beds to rescue workers and refugees. The Mexican consulate in San Antonio was also deeply involved in relief activities, particularly for survivors emerging from the wreckage of the Latino/a community south of Texas Avenue. In addition, thousands of private citizens poured into the area to help out in any way they could.

In contrast, Mayor Trahan was not at all impressed with the work of one relief organization: the Red Cross. Trahan charged Red Cross officials with arriving late to the disaster, then working harder on press releases and publicity than on actual relief. At the time of the disaster and even years later, Trahan articulated his disappointment, claiming that by the time the Red Cross finally arrived, a disaster relief system had been established without their help. The blatant arrogance of the Red Cross officials who treated Trahan and other city officials like lowly subjects expected to bow and scrape before royalty was also hard to stomach. To the *Chicago Tribune*, Trahan revealed the Red Cross independently established a refugee center at Camp Wallace, a military base several miles from Texas City but failed to set up any form of transportation to or from the center. In a 1981 interview, Trahan said, "We didn't wait for the Red Cross . . . when the Red Cross finally got [to Texas City], . . . I told them what they could do. And I guess that they were used to people just being prostrate."[13]

In Galveston, Catherine Medina witnessed the giant mushroom cloud. She left the Santa Fe Building as soon as she could and went to Marine Hospital to look for her friend Audrey Carroll. She reckoned if Carroll survived the blast at all, she must have been injured, and the injured would have been taken to Marine Hospital.

When Medina walked into Marine Hospital, she encountered a shocking sight of bloody, injured people standing, sitting, and lying everywhere. The first uninjured person she saw was Father Ruddy, a priest she knew quite well, who was helping arriving victims. Medina asked Ruddy if he had seen Audrey Carroll. He had not. Medina next saw a man being brought in on a stretcher. Someone was carrying the man's boot, with the victim's severed foot still inside. Charging deeper into the hospital, Catherine somehow found her friend. Medical personnel were removing fragments of wood, glass, and fabric from her face. All around, rescuers were bringing more and more people into the hallways and rooms, placing them wherever there was enough space—"just dumping them," Medina recalled. After the medical technicians left, Catherine tried to talk to Audrey, but her friend only winced and complained that her back hurt. Catherine turned Audrey over, and as she did jagged pieces of glass fell all over the sheet. Other shards remained embedded in her skin, protruding like little crystal blades.[14]

At about five o'clock on the afternoon of April 16, Monsignor Carney returned briefly to the Shrine of the True Cross in Dickinson. The church halls were packed with refugees, mostly children. He opened the schoolrooms and meeting spaces as well, and before long those spaces were also crammed with victims. A group of volunteers was working closely with the Red Cross to set up beds and food service facilities. The meals came from army field kitchens erected by units from Camp Hood then handed over to the Red Cross for operation.[15] Medical personnel, mostly from nearby Camp Wallace, were treating injuries and illnesses. Among other issues, an outbreak of mumps was spreading through the crowd of refugees. After ensuring the personnel on scene had all the resources he could give, Carney grabbed a quick bite to eat and returned to Texas City at seven o'clock in the evening.

Because of fears that another ship, the *High Flyer*, was in danger of exploding, very few relief workers were being allowed into the blast zone. As the apparent danger subsided, volunteers were allowed to return to the area and help with rescue and recovery. Among them were about twenty-five priests, including Father Jack Davis who had knowledge of heavy machinery. He had mounted a bulldozer and was using it to carve roadways through the debris so that emergency vehicles could approach the scene.[16] After several hours of night work illuminated by uncontrolled fires and a pair of military searchlights from Fort Crockett, Carney was exhausted. Unable to continue, he returned to Dickinson at midnight and climbed into bed. Not long afterward, at 1:10 A.M. on April 17, the windows of Carney's room began to rattle and vibrate, as they had the previous morning. Then, for the second time in sixteen hours, a blast concussion struck the building. Carney was almost thrown from his bed by the blast. He hurriedly dressed and rushed back to Texas City.[17]

Once again, the docks at Texas City were rocked by an exploding ship. The *High Flyer*, loaded with both ammonium nitrate fertilizer and sulfur, had detonated in a massive fireball rising several thousand feet in the air. Sulfur, an ingredient in gunpowder, is one of the most dangerous materials to mix with ammonium nitrate, even without flames. Sulfur contamination makes ammonium nitrate very unstable and prone to heat-accelerated explosion.[18] There had been fears very early on that the *High Flyer* might either be in danger or become a danger. Grant Wheaton and Swede Sandberg of Texas City Terminal Railway had phoned the owners of the *High Flyer* as soon as the fire started, recommending they have their vessel towed to a safer place. However, after the *Grandcamp* exploded sending the *High Flyer* crashing into the *Wilson B. Keane*, the subsequent fires and secondary explosions made it difficult to move either of the latter ships. Nevertheless, throughout the day E. S. Binnings officials were repeatedly advised that the *High Flyer* should be moved. By the afternoon, it was on fire. Crews along the waterfront were being kept up-to-date with news about the *High Flyer* and other developments by means of a loudspeaker system mounted on a truck that drove back and forth near the docks.[19] Throughout the afternoon of April 16, the loudspeaker blared warnings that the *High Flyer*, too, could blow. Yet, by evening, when Monsignor Carney was on his way to Dickinson for a quick break, those fears had subsided.

Suddenly, later that night, word of an imminent explosion spread quickly. By midnight, Sandberg, still on the job despite his head injuries from the first explosion, had ordered the flaming *High Flyer* towed out to the middle of the bay. Shortly before one in the morning on April 17, the *High Flyer* was lashed to a tugboat and began being towed. It was too late. The tug had only moved the ship fifty feet when the hatches and tarps covering the holds blew open. Massive flames rose from the openings and large balls of burning sulfur shot high into the air. The skeleton crew onboard the *High Flyer* was ordered to evacuate, and the tug cast off its lines. Ten minutes later, the *High Flyer* detonated.

US Army Air Corps photographer Sergeant Don Lynn had been within one hundred feet of the *High Flyer* when he ran out of film. He rushed to city hall to get more film. While he was there, the *High Flyer* blew. Lynn described two concussions. The first felt like "a fairly light blast . . . a terrific shaft of flame and smoke shot up, and then the big blast hit . . . it sounded like a string of empty boxcars running over a dance floor . . . it came, building up in force and sound until, when it hit, it was deafening . . . flames shot up very high." Lynn was knocked to the floor.[20]

A reddish-orange column of roiling fire shot four thousand feet into the air. As the fireball reached its peak, smaller tendrils of fire peeled off in every direction like a massive fireworks display. Hot metal fragments and burning chunks of sulfur descended all around, starting new fires everywhere. Fortunately, because the danger of explosion had been recognized early, injury and loss of life was less than it might have been. Still, one person was killed and fifty to one hundred others were injured. Father Davis, still operating the bulldozer, was knocked to the ground. Though completely covered in black soot and shaken, he was otherwise unharmed.[21]

One of the *High Flyer*'s turbines, weighing two thousand pounds, had been removed from the ship and placed on the dock in front of Warehouse A for repair. The explosion hurled the turbine into the cooling towers of Republic Oil Refining Company, four thousand feet away. The blast split the SS *Wilson B. Keane* in half from starboard to port and tossed the stern of the ship end-over-end onto a line of already damaged railway cars several hundred feet away. A length of heavy steel pipe, ten inches in diameter, was driven right through the brick walls of the Republic Oil fire station, then through the wall of an adjacent boiler room. Shrapnel penetrated a nearby grain elevator, causing 400,000 bushels of wheat to pour out and collect at the base of the structure. Burning sulfur immediately ignited the grain. At 7:30 A.M., a cloud of wheat dust lingering inside the perforated grain elevator detonated, destroying the structure.[22]

When the *High Flyer* exploded, a high school student volunteering at St. Mary's Infirmary in Galveston was trying to help an injured man get comfortable in one of the hospital's crowded hallways. The victim, who had just received a shot of morphine from a nurse, lifted his head and shouted, "I'll bet those SOBs on the *High Flyer* are really flying high now!" He then slumped back on the floor and passed out.[23]

A few hours after the explosion of the *High Flyer*, a Pontifical Requiem Mass was offered for Father William Roach at the Cathedral of St. Mary in Galveston. The cathedral was overflowing, with crowds spilling outside into the streets. A somber Bishop Christopher Byrne was the celebrant. Responses were sung by the choir from the seminary in La Porte. Like Byrne, most of the choristers had been close to Roach. Among them were Dick Meskill and C. F. Quinn, whom Father Bill had encouraged to join the seminary and who were part of the group that located his body in Galveston the day before. Also in attendance were fifty area priests and dozens of parishioners from Texas City. Many of the attendees from Texas City wore torn and tattered clothes, stained with blood, oil, and mud. Texas City had been sealed by a military cordon to prevent looting and to assess safety, so even those citizens who still had homes were unable to return to clean up and change clothes.[24]

Of course, no one in the cathedral that day had a bond with Father Bill approaching that between him and his identical twin brother, Father John. They had been inseparable all their lives. Stoic but visibly shaken, John participated from the front pew.[25] Shaken as well was the bishop. Indeed, Byrne withdrew completely from public life for a time following the death of Father Bill, his "cowboy priest." During the sermon, Byrne tearfully said, "Greater love no man hath than he lay down his life for his friend."[26]

After the mass, Father John left by train with his brother's body for the journey home to Media, Pennsylvania. He was accompanied by another priest, Father John Lane. At five o'clock on the morning of Saturday, April 19, the train arrived in Philadelphia. A funeral home collected the casket and transported it to Media, accompanied by the two Texas priests.

At eleven o'clock that very morning, John Roach celebrated a solemn requiem mass for his brother at the Church of the Nativity of the Blessed Virgin Mary in Media, the same church where John and Bill had said their first masses after ordination nearly eight years earlier. Among those in attendance were Bill and John's father, William F. Roach, stepmother, Mabel, and three half siblings, Leo, James, and Mary. Among the pallbearers was Bill and John's childhood friend Dan Barrow. Burial followed at the Nativity of the Blessed Virgin Mary Calvary Cemetery, four miles from the Roach family service station where the twins had worked in high school and when they came home from the seminary in the summer.[27]

On Saturday, April 19, the same day Father Bill was buried in Pennsylvania, a thousand Texas City residents gathered at the local high school football stadium to participate in a memorial for the missing victims of the explosions. Buildings all over town were too damaged and unsafe for people to congregate inside. Fires still raged, black smoke wafted skyward, and secondary explosions continued to shake the ground.

The following Tuesday, April 22, the Texas state senate passed a resolution recognizing the heroism and self-sacrifice of Father Bill Roach, killed in the explosion of the *Grandcamp*, and of Reverend Roland P. Hood of the First Baptist Church and Reverend Ervin Jackson of the First Methodist Church, both of whom suffered severe injuries. The three clerics carried out their duties, "without prejudice as to creed or race . . . [and] administered courage, patience, and the hope of Heaven at an hour when all earthly things seemed Hell," the resolution read.[28]

By this time, the last major fires were finally extinguished in Texas City, including those at Monsanto where fireboats summoned from Galveston had battled the flames all weekend. Explosions had ceased and, although small fires would continue to erupt for days to come, the people of Texas City began to realize the danger was passing.[29]

Father Bill's parish church, St. Mary of the Miraculous Medal, had sustained heavy damage. Every one of the church's roof beams had been sheared in two by the blast. Long shards of glass from the stained-glass windows had been driven into the pews and walls like nails. Although still standing and with its roof intact, the building was too dangerous for occupancy and initially condemned and slated for demolition. Fortunately, St. Mary was saved from the wrecking ball when engineers realized the beams overhead could be repaired after all.[30]

A solemn requiem mass for all the victims of the Texas City disaster, including Father Bill, was scheduled for 8:00 A.M. on Thursday, April 24. Due to the instability of the structure, the service was conducted on the lawn beside the church, where an improvised altar was set up before rows of lawn chairs. Monsignor Joseph Valenta of St. Mary's Seminary in La Porte led the mass. In attendance were Mayor Curtis Trahan, city official John Hill, Police Chief W. L. Ladish, and a large crowd of residents.

During the sermon, Father Carney described Father Bill's crushed car being found in the wreckage of the Monsanto parking lot. He continued, "Before Father Roach came here, I told you a saint was coming into your midst. A saint came and a saint has been taken away. Father Roach was very close to you. I think he died just as he would have wished to die." Then, turning to Mayor Trahan, Carney added, "Father Bill would want me to tell you not to be discouraged, but to rebuild your city into a greater, safer place."[31] As a matter of fact, all around the attendees, the sounds of repairs and general construction filled the air. The city was already rebuilding.

Even as fires still burned in and around the Monsanto property, Monsanto Chairman Edgar M. Queeny announced in Texas City on Saturday, April 19, that the company intended to rebuild and expand its operation. He promised that during the period of reconstruction all surviving hourly employees would remain on the payroll.[32] By mid-May, the wreckage on the Monsanto property had been completely cleared. On July 1, contracts were awarded to rebuild the styrene plant. By the end of the year, seventy-one acres adjacent to the original property were purchased, including sailors retreat and fifteen acres of the devastated Latino/a and African American neighborhood between Texas Avenue and Monsanto. The mission church, Our Lady of the Snows, was bulldozed and never rebuilt. Where it once stood is now part of the Monsanto plant.[33]

Carbide and Carbon, Pan American, and Republic Oil also rebuilt and expanded their operations, the last increasing its capacity by 50 percent. Initially, neither insurance companies nor the federal government would accept financial responsibility for the massive damage sustained by the Texas City Terminal

Railway Company. Nevertheless, the company cleared the salvageable part of the south slip on its own and started handling petroleum products just two weeks after the explosions.

In May, just weeks after the explosions, the SS *Pan Pennsylvania* was the first ship to dock at the refurbished south slip wharf. It was severely damaged on May 18, when a fire broke out onboard, igniting 150,000 barrels of gasoline loaded in the ship's hold. Flames shot hundreds of feet in the air and smoke roiled four thousand feet above the docks, once again terrorizing local residents. The *Pan Pennsylvania* was followed two weeks later by the SS *Henry S. Dawes*, which docked uneventfully. The pace of ship traffic increased substantially thereafter. Later, Seatrain Lines rebuilt its massive loading crane, which had been located on the north slip, adjacent to Monsanto.[34]

For the next three weeks, bodies drifting in Galveston Bay continued to be recovered, some as far as ten miles away from Texas City. On May 11, the last body found was recovered from the dock area. In all, estimates are that 576 people were killed, 398 of whom could be identified; 63 sets of remains were unidentifiable; and 115 people reported missing were never located. The number of injured was estimated at four thousand, including many schoolchildren cut by flying glass as they sat at their desks in school.[35]

Two weeks before the last body was found, twenty-six victims previously reported dead were discovered alive and recovering in various area hospitals. It is likely that many other such cases were never discovered because the injured people did not return to Texas City afterward. Equally likely, some victims may never have been reported missing and included in the death toll. Six months after the conflagration, Chief of Police Ladish was still receiving inquiries about missing individuals.[36]

On June 22, Texas City officials and citizens gathered at Memorial Cemetery on the northwest corner of Twenty-Ninth Street North and Highway 197 to witness the interment in a common grave of the unidentified victims of the explosions. In 1950, the last piece of wreckage, the bow of the SS *Wilson B. Keane*, was removed from the main slip. The event marked Texas City's final physical departure from the devastation of the explosions.[37] The legal battles were just getting underway however.

— 17 —

REVELATIONS AND REPARATIONS

On April 16, 1948, exactly one year after the explosion of the SS *Grandcamp*, private citizens filed twenty-four lawsuits against the federal government. All alleged that negligence with respect to improper labeling of ammonium nitrate fertilizer resulted in the disaster that claimed hundreds of lives and destroyed million of dollars of property. The week before, Monsanto had filed its own lawsuit. Combined, the suits sought two hundred million dollars. Eventually, the numerous private suits were combined in a single class-action suit, *Dalehite v. United States*, named for plaintiff Elizabeth Dalehite, whose husband died in the disaster.[1]

For much of its history, the federal government had been immune from lawsuits. In 1946, however, Congress passed the Federal Tort Claims Act, allowing lawsuits to proceed with congressional approval. *Dalehite v. United States* was approved, and the case went to trial in 1949 before Federal Judge T. M. Kennerly of the US District Court, Southern Division of Texas.

The claim of negligence resulted from a series of investigations by federal and industry agencies. Only days after the explosions of the SS *Grandcamp* and SS *High Flyer*, the US Coast Guard had convened a board of investigation in Washington, DC. On May 28, 1947, the board released a press statement summarizing its findings. The investigation concluded that during loading operations of the *Grandcamp*, longshoremen received no specific instructions with respect to safe handling or stowage of ammonium nitrate, particularly regarding the danger of smoking. Although the US Coast Guard had declared ammonium nitrate a dangerous substance in 1941, no shippers had followed the regulation requiring them to give advance written notification to the vessel regarding the dangerous properties of ammonium nitrate. "Hardly without exception, all persons who testified before the board and were concerned with the handling, stowage, and transportation of the ammonium nitrate material displayed a lack of knowledge of the provisions of regulations governing the safety of the operations either by land or water," the report stated.[2]

The Coast Guard report blamed a lit cigarette from a longshoreman for causing the fire that was discovered in hold 4 of the *Grandcamp* on the morning of April 16, 1947. The board also recommended that the US Department of Justice file criminal charges against the ocean shipper, the captain of the *Grandcamp*, and several other individuals and institutions. What the report failed to mention was that the reason everyone involved had "displayed a lack of knowledge" of how to handle ammonium nitrate was because the US Coast Guard had never informed anyone of its own regulations. The nature of the actual labels affixed to each bag provided evidence of this. Apart from the words "ammonium nitrate," there was no indication by declaration or color code that the product was in any way hazardous. Thus, although a lit cigarette may have been the immediate cause of the explosion, improper federal oversight and a lack of proper labeling of the fertilizer bags had led to habitual mishandling of the material. The labels read:

FERTILIZER
(Ammonium Nitrate)
32.5% Nitrogen
100 lbs. Net
101.5 lbs. Gross
1.6 cu. ft.
Made in U. S. A.[3]

The National Board of Fire Underwriters conducted an independent investigation that was critical of the Coast Guard's assessment. Although not dismissing the Coast Guard's conclusion that a cigarette ignited the ammonium nitrate, the report pointed out that the docks at Texas City handled a wide variety of products, any one of which might cause ammonium nitrate to become unstable. Substances like sulfur, flour, cotton, various grains, and metals such as tin, zinc, and copper were ever present in Texas City and often in close proximity to or in actual contact with ammonium nitrate. Moreover, the multi-ply bags holding the fertilizer contained at least one layer of asphalt for moisture prevention. Contact with any petroleum product, including asphalt, could cause ammonium nitrate to decompose and become unstable.

The bags of ammonium nitrate frequently broke open during shipment to Texas City. When this happened, workers simply scooped up the material and placed it in a fresh bag. They never received guidelines or reasons to do otherwise. Because no one handling the ammonium nitrate understood the chemical reactions it might be susceptible to, the fertilizer would often be swept up along with other substances that might have spilled on warehouse floors or outside on the docks. Frequently, dripping oils from forklifts and other machinery would be collected along with the spilled fertilizer and end up contaminating bags of ammonium nitrate, initiating chemical decomposition reactions. In addition, the National Board of Fire Underwriters found that broken bags of fertilizer were treated the same way at the manufacturing point of origin. This fact explained why longshoremen in Texas City were having to handle superheated bags of fertilizer arriving by rail, which prompted Swede Sandberg of the Texas City Terminal Railway to write letters of concern to the manufacturer. The board also discovered that the manufacturer often packed and shipped ammonium nitrate at 240 degrees Fahrenheit from its point of origin.[4] Another factor identified in the report was that the hull of the *Grandcamp*, like many other vessels, contained zinc, which would promote decomposition of ammonium nitrate.

Overall, the National Board of Fire Underwriters concluded that in all likelihood contamination by reactive substances like asphalt, sulfur, oil, and certain metals contributed more to the events in Texas City than smoking did. In other words, the way ammonium nitrate was handled at both the manufacturer and the docks in Texas City created an accident waiting to happen. It was also emphasized that such contamination was possible because the agency responsible for oversight, the US Coast Guard, never informed the parties involved of its own regulations regarding safe handling of ammonium nitrate. Regulation of such hazardous materials was left to parties with the greatest motivation to cut costs by taking safety risks—shippers, carriers, and manufacturers—as a 1971 special report of the National Transportation Safety Board documented.[5]

In fact, the practice of improperly handling ammonium nitrate fertilizer continued after the Texas City explosions. Representatives of the National Board of Fire Underwriters observed longshoremen in Galveston loading broken bags of ammonium nitrate fertilizer onto a ship just days after the explosions at Texas

City. And they witnessed the same thing again in Baltimore. Then, three months after the Texas City catastrophe, on July 28, 1947, the SS *Ocean Liberty*, filled with ammonium nitrate fertilizer from the United States, exploded in the harbor at Brest, France. The master of the ship and twenty-one townspeople were killed, while hundreds were injured. Chemical plants and warehouses up to nine hundred yards away were destroyed. The accident could have been much worse had an alert dockworker not noticed the smoke arising from a hold, remembered the *Grandcamp*, and issued a prompt warning. One week later, the Coast Guard amended labeling requirements on ammonium nitrate products.[6]

Other reports found serious discrepancies in how various federal agencies classified ammonium nitrate. The *US Army Ordinance Safety Manual* classified the substance as a "high explosive." In contrast, regulations for the transportation of dangerous articles published by the US Interstate Commerce Commission (ICC) classified ammonium nitrate as an oxidizer, not an explosive. Meanwhile, scientists with knowledge of ammonium nitrate described the material as a chemical substance capable of exploding under a special set of circumstances. No scientist referred to it definitively as an explosive. ICC regulations required a yellow label for bulk shipments of oxidizing materials but not for the same material shipped in bags. Thus, federal regulations did not require bags of ammonium nitrate to have safe handling instructions printed on them or to be labeled in red letters as containing a "hazardous chemical."

All this information and much more was revealed during trial testimony. During the trial, Audrey Carroll was visited by agents of the Federal Bureau of Investigation, who initially refused to show identification, bullied their way into her home, and questioned her aggressively about her part in the lawsuits. She refused to cooperate with them.[8] In the end, the government lost its case and the 8,485 plaintiffs were awarded monetary restitution. Subsequently, however, the decision was overturned by the Fifth Circuit Court of Appeals. In 1953, the US Supreme Court upheld the circuit court decision, thus ending the class-action suit without compensation to the victims.

In 1955, US Congressman Clark Thompson, who represented Texas City, introduced a bill to compensate the victims of the explosions. The bill passed the following year as the Disaster Relief Act for Texas City. Subsequently, 1,755 cases were processed, $10, 064,771.37 was paid on death claims, and $5,428,780.78 paid on injuries, for total restitution of $15,493,552.15. The last of these payments was distributed in March 1957.[9] Then, in 1959, the Disaster Relief Act for

Texas City was amended to allow for claims to be submitted through September 1961. By November 1960, an additional $528,034.60 in death benefits and $102,248.26 in personal injury claims had been paid, bringing the total to at least $16,123,835.01.[10]

One of those receiving a death benefit payment was Jesús Jiménez, who had lived with his wife and children in the African American and Latino/a neighborhood south of Texas Avenue. Jiménez and his family, who lived just two blocks from Monsanto, attended the mission church Our Lady of the Snows. When the *Grandcamp* exploded, Jimenez's home was heavily damaged and his wife injured by flying glass. His oldest daughter, Ernestine, who worked on the docks, was killed. Jiménez found her body himself, digging through the rubble of the industrial office where she worked. When the compensation arrived, Jesús Jiménez gathered his wife and surviving children together and showed them the check. It was for $25,000. He explained to his family that because the payment came as a result of Ernestine's death, it was "blood money and very sacred" and had to be treated as such. Jiménez put the money in a college fund for his children. All three used it and graduated from college.[11]

Just a few hours after the explosions in Texas City, as fires still raged, Mayor Trahan experienced one pleasant, though unexpected, outcome—an influx of cash donations to the city. Trahan became aware of this when he was informed that the Busch family of St. Louis (owners of Anheuser-Busch) wished to donate $50,000 to a Texas City relief fund. After that, he discovered that donations were pouring in from all over the world. Some money had been sent to local newspapers, which then publicized the fact, resulting in even more donations. Churches, too, were receiving money for general relief. Catholic Charities, under the direction of Father John Roach, had created a fund as well. Trahan appointed a prominent local banker and former mayor of Texas City, Carl Nessler, to manage the donations and steer them toward a general Texas City relief fund.[12]

Then entertainers joined the donors. Their involvement began with an attempt by promoters to cancel scheduled performances in Houston and Galveston by Lauritz Melchior, principal tenor of the Metropolitan Opera of New York, in deference to the developing events in Texas City. The Galveston performance was set for Friday, April 18, while fires were still raging after the explosion of the *Grandcamp*. Melchior, however, insisted on performing both concerts, as well as a concert in New Orleans, and donating his compensation toward relief for the residents of Texas City. While Melchior was negotiating with promoters,

Galveston entrepreneur Sam Maceo contacted his friend, band leader and jazz trumpeter Phil Harris, and proposed organizing a gala benefit that would include some of the best-known entertainers of the day. Working with Maceo; Ed Leavell, vice-president of the *Galveston News-Tribune*; as well as Ed Leach, president, and G. Martini, general manager, of the Greater Galveston Beach Association, Harris lined up entertainers and scheduled the performance for Monday, April 28, in the Galveston City Auditorium. Harris also arranged for two additional benefit performances, in Houston and New Orleans. In addition to Phil Harris and his band, Frank Sinatra, Jack Benny, and Gene Autry, among numerous other stars of screen and radio, performed. All proceeds went to the relief fund for Texas City. In the end, the fund received more than one million dollars from private and public donations.[13]

Over the next decade, Texas City rebuilt itself anew. By 1957, its physical boundaries were three times those of 1947 and its population had increased by 30 percent. The total employment of Texas City residents had tripled, with 80 percent of the workforce living in Texas City, compared to 52 percent before the explosions. Gross tonnage handled at the port increased nearly 23 percent and all the industries rebuilt and expanded. Only two small businesses in town failed to reopen after 1947.[14]

As the port was restored and reopened, it moved toward the exclusive handling of petrochemical products. Agricultural products, once a major part of the port's activities, rapidly disappeared from Texas City docks. The cotton press and grain elevator were never rebuilt, and plans to resume handling breakbulk, or general, cargo (individually packaged products, in contrast to bulk shipments of commodities like oil), never materialized. Where cotton had once been king, oil was the new monarch. Meanwhile, in town, the Texas City infrastructure was completely overhauled. In 1948, all storm drains and streets were repaired and upgraded through a bond initiative. The city also created more full-time positions within the fire department and started moving away from an all-volunteer force.[15]

The events of April 1947 revealed multiple problems on the local, state, and national levels with respect to emergency response preparedness. Recall that just five weeks before the explosions at Texas City, Marie Luppold, director of nursing at Houston's Methodist Hospital, had warned that local medical professionals would be caught unprepared if some catastrophe struck. Subsequent events proved her right.

The closest thing to an officially coordinated response in Texas was the emergency proclamation from Governor Beauford Jester putting Colonel Homer Garrison of the Texas Department of Public Safety in charge of relief to Texas City. However, Garrison was aware of jurisdictional issues involved with this proclamation. At the time, Texas state government tended to defer to local governments on issues directly affecting counties and municipalities. Learning a lesson from the nature of the Texas City explosions, where the municipality had been severely damaged, Texas and many other states developed and implemented statewide disaster plans.[16]

On the federal level, although Congress occasionally appropriated money for disaster relief, there was no government agency overseeing disaster relief in 1947. Volunteer agencies, private enterprises, and individuals would funnel money and assistance independently, which could be counterproductive and inefficient. Although charitable institutions like the Salvation Army, Red Cross, and Catholic Charities maintained a national presence, their structure was often decentralized. Not until President Jimmy Carter established the Federal Emergency Management Agency (FEMA) in 1979, thirty-two years after the Texas City explosions, was there a way to efficiently coordinate relief on a national scale.[17]

Safety, particularly with respect to the transportation of hazardous materials, became a national priority after Texas City. On August 7, 1947, the US government issued an order requiring permits for loading and unloading ammonium nitrate in quantities of five hundred pounds or more. The order also required that hazardous material be handled in isolated terminals and at remote anchorages, away from heavily populated areas and major industrial zones. The order further specified that shipments over water must be made as full cargoes, preventing the need for secondary calls at other ports. Finally, only selected, specially equipped terminal points in Louisiana, Alabama, and Florida would be allowed to handle ammonium nitrate in bulk.

In another development, the Federal Interagency Committee on Ammonium Nitrate was established in 1947 to examine dangers of fire and explosion involving the chemical. The committee, composed of eighteen representatives from ten government agencies, heard testimony from dozens of scientists, manufacturers, and shipping agents. Two reports were issued. Part 1, published August 20, 1947, dealt with the hazards of handling ammonium nitrate on ships. Part 2, published November 10, 1947, addressed transportation of the material on land and how best to store it safely.[18] These findings led to requirements for handling other hazardous materials as well. Federal mandates for systemic generation of material safety data sheets for all chemicals and their derivatives were imposed in the 1960s. Then, in 1970, the US Congress passed the Occupational Safety and Health Act and President Nixon signed it into law. This act created the Occupational Safety and Health Administration, which assumed much more oversight with regard to hazardous materials—but not necessarily enough.

Despite multiple inspections and citations, a cache of ammonium nitrate fertilizer caught fire and exploded in the town of West, in Texas, on April 17, 2013. Fifteen people were killed and another 150 were injured. Then, on August 4, 2020, 2,750 tons of ammonium nitrate destroyed the entire harbor area of Beirut, Lebanon. The blast killed 220 people and injured 6,500. The same material that nearly destroyed Texas City in 1947 is still causing fatalities, injury, and destruction to this day.

In Texas today, there are few to no safety and environmental regulations, particularly when it comes to the petrochemical industry. A trio of at-large elected officials, collectively called the Texas Railroad Commission, are charged with regulating the petrochemical industry in the state. Because election campaigns are heavily funded by that industry, however, the commissioners who are elected are little more than pawns of the very companies they are supposed to regulate. An example of this involves flaring, the burning of so-called unusable natural gas created during the refining process. These flares, burning day and night in Texas City, caused Father Bill to remark that he felt like he was "sitting on a keg of dynamite." Although legal at the time, flaring has since been outlawed on the federal level, but it is habitually tolerated in Texas and ignored by the Texas Railroad Commission.

Then, in February 2021, Texas experienced one of the coldest months on record. The extended period of freezing temperatures (subzero in many parts of the state) caused the power grid to fail almost catastrophically. A University of Texas study of the power failure reported the situation was so dire that the state came within five minutes of the entire power grid shutting down completely, a shutdown that would have taken months to restart. The same study concluded that the February freeze and related power failure caused more damage than any other natural disaster in the state.

The state's power grid is regulated by the Electric Reliability Council of Texas, or ERCOT, which is completely unregulated. The council consists of a board of appointed officials, and after February 2021, the public discovered most of those officials lived outside of Texas. Because Texas refuses federal funding to support its power grid and is unwilling to become linked to any other grid in the country, it avoids regulation. The state political machine that keeps the state unregulated at all cost is the same one Father Bill and others fought against in Texas City in the 1940s. After the disastrous month of February 2021, many Texans demanded action. But because of the political power structure in place, the changes made to ERCOT and the Texas power grid were largely superficial. It would appear the state has learned little from the lessons of the Texas City explosions of 1947.[19]

18

CLOSURE

News of the devastation in Texas City and the death of Father Bill was very slow to reach the Monastery of the Holy Infant Jesus in Lufkin. Roach had last visited the Monday before, bringing the usual array of doughnuts, fresh fruit, and vegetables for the nuns. As always, he said mass, heard confessions, stayed for lunch, and ate little if anything on his plate.

The news arrived when the prioress of the convent summoned Sister Mary William Montegut and Sister Mary Catherine Laiche to her office. That alone was unusual. Then, when they reported to her office, they saw a number of newspapers spread out on the desk before the prioress. That was unusual as well. News of the outside world was typically of little consequence to a community of cloistered nuns. Yet the distressed look on the prioress's face told them this was different.

Without being able to offer any details whatsoever, the prioress abruptly said there had been a terrible explosion in Texas City and that Father Bill had been killed. She added that she had absolutely no news about Montegut's and Laiche's families. News trickled in over the next hours, days, and weeks. Sister William's brother sustained an eye injury but was safe, as was the rest of her family. Sister Catherine's family was safe as well. However, the entire community was stunned and completely devastated by the death of Father Bill. Their deep faith and spirituality helped them to recognize it as part of God's unknowable plan, despite the pain and grief they felt.

Sister William and Sister Catherine, both novices at the time Texas City was destroyed, professed their solemn final vows on August 15, 1948. They remained the closest of friends and cloistered nuns for the rest of their lives. Including her time in the novitiate, Sister Mary William Montegut spent fifty-eight years at the Monastery of the Holy Infant Jesus in Lufkin. She died on December 22, 2004, at the age of seventy-seven. Sister Mary Catherine Laiche followed her friend eight years later, on February 13, 2012, after sixty-five-and-a-half years at the monastery. Throughout their lives, their memories of both Father Bill and Father John seemed forever fresh in their minds. When they spoke of either priest, broad smiles would break across their faces, followed by laughter. Those memories were joyous.[1] Sister Diane, also a novice at the time of the explosions in Texas City, chose to leave the convent before taking final vows. She returned to the Great Lakes area and eventually married. Occasionally, she visited the monastery she helped found. She died of cancer in the late 1980s.[2]

Father John Roach never had much chance to grieve the loss of his brother. He returned to Pennsylvania to arrange for and officiate at Father Bill's funeral and burial, but Bishop Byrne called him back early and ordered his return to Texas on diocesan business. According to some people who knew him, he never really got to say goodbye to Bill, and that was something he battled with for the rest of his life. It is hard enough for anyone to lose a close family member, but for the surviving half of identical twins who completed each other's sentences when speaking, the pain must have been immense. Every year on the anniversary of his brother's death, Father John would disappear for the day. He always returned the next day, ready to tackle whatever business was at hand. But April 16 was forever his day to be alone.

Father John continued to be a major force in the sustained development of the Galveston Diocese, supporting its transformation into the Archdiocese of Galveston-Houston. From 1943 on, he was the chaplain of the Novitiate of the Sisters of Charity of the Incarnate Word in Houston. In 1952, he became the sixth pastor of Sacred Heart Church (later Co-Cathedral of the Sacred Heart), in downtown Houston. In 1956, Father John was made a domestic prelate and elevated to the title of monsignor. The *Houston Press* named him one of the thirty most distinguished citizens of Houston in 1962. In 1965, he became a Houston coordinator of the federal War on Poverty. In 1969, he was raised to prothonotary apostolic, or honorary prelate, by Pope Paul VI. Then, in 1971 he was appointed the Bishop's Liaison of Religion and Human Decency and the Bishop's Representative on Pastoral Formation.

In addition, for thirty-five years Father John remained the director of the Texas chapter of Catholic Charities, the organization he created almost single-handedly on his return to the diocese after receiving his master's degree in social work from Fordham University in 1943. He was a longtime member of both the Academy of Certified Social Workers and the National Association of Social Workers. A recipient of the Brotherhood Award from the National Conference of Christians and Jews, he was also instrumental in founding St. Elizabeth Hospital in Houston. Father John also maintained close ties to the Monastery of the Holy Infant Jesus, visiting there as often as possible on his days off. Because he and Bill had located that property in Lufkin and helped the nuns from Detroit establish a successful foothold in Texas, the place had always been very special to both brothers. So much so that on his death in 1987 at the age of seventy-nine, Father John Roach was buried at the Monastery of the Holy Infant Jesus.[3]

Despite being treated at Schmidt-Twidwell Clinic following the explosion of the *Grandcamp*, Dick Benedict had trouble standing and his legs grew progressively weaker. He returned to the clinic and Dr. Schmidt gave him a pair of crutches to use. Sometime afterward, Father Karl Kermiet spotted Benedict on Sixth Street, hobbling along on his crutches. Kermiet took one look at Benedict's legs, loaded the sufferer into his car, and drove him to a hospital in Pasadena, forty miles north of Texas City. There, Benedict was placed under the care of a specialist. He remained hospitalized in Pasadena for two months, finally emerging under his own power without crutches. Benedict went back to work for the International Longshoremen of America, first in Houston, then in Galveston, for the rest of his career. He retired in 1967 after more than thirty years with the union.[4]

As for the other characters who played roles in Father Bill's story, the onetime alcoholic Pete Tarpey never took another drink after Father Bill's intervention. He became a civic leader and labor advocate, then found a permanent position with the Texas Employment Commission, where he worked until his death in 1970.[5] Along with the remains of more than one hundred other victims, the body of H. J. "Mike" Mikeska, president of Texas City Terminal Railway, was never found. Mikeska was last seen standing just outside a dock door of Warehouse O, next to the *Grandcamp*. Only the week before the ship exploded, he and Father Bill had appeared before the mayor and city commissioners, arguing respectively against and for Texas City annexation of the portside industries. Both perished that day. Two members of the Texas City Heights Fire Department and twenty-four members of the Texas City Volunteer Fire Department were killed, including Chief Baumgarten. Like Mikeska's, most of their bodies were never found.[6]

Eddie, the blond-haired, blue-eyed, strikingly handsome young worker who caught the eye of teenaged Maxine Montegut (later Sister Mary William) was killed by the blast of the *Grandcamp*. He died on the docks while driving his truck, exactly as Father Bill had predicted months before.[7] Clarence "Tookey" Mayville, the young altar boy who followed Father Bill to the docks, also died that day. His body was never recovered. The handlebars of his bicycle were the only trace of him ever found.[8]

Because of the seriousness of her eye injury, Audrey Carroll was transferred from Marine Hospital to John Sealy Hospital, also in Galveston. She was placed in an ambulance belonging to Malloy Funeral Home, where Father Bill was taken after his death. En route to the hospital, the rear doors of the ambulance swung wide open and Carroll's gurney began inching toward the traffic-filled roadway outside. "You're going to lose me!" she yelled. "You're going to lose me!" Looking over his shoulder, the driver saw his patient rolling slowly toward the open back doors. He screeched to a stop right in the middle of Broadway Avenue, slid Carroll's gurney back into position, and secured the doors. Carroll started laughing. "I live through an explosion and now you're going to lose me on Broadway, to get run over?" At John Sealy Hospital, Carroll underwent the first of multiple surgeries to save her eye. For years afterward, bits of glass and wood still embedded in her body slowly worked their way to the surface of her skin and fell out. In 1949, after Monsanto rebuilt, expanded, and reopened, Audrey Carroll returned to work there. Despite the new facility, to her the area always "reeked of chemicals and death." She said the odors lingered for years.[9]

Curtis Trahan, described as tall and charismatic in news reports, garnered much public adulation in the wake of the explosions at Texas City. When he was introduced onstage in Houston during one of the benefit performances organized by bandleader Phil Harris, the auditorium erupted into a thunderous standing ovation. Trahan, still emotionally and physically tied up in the dynamic, ever-changing situation in his city, was taken completely by surprise.

While fires still burned in Texas City, Trahan received a call from a manufacturer of fire engines in Lansing, Michigan. The company wanted to donate a brand-new fire engine to Texas City, but only if Trahan agreed to visit Lansing. It was a ploy to generate publicity for the company and Trahan knew it, but he agreed to go anyway. A new fire engine was a new fire engine, he reckoned. Trahan journeyed to Lansing to accept the gift, only to discover he was also expected to deliver a speech to the Michigan state legislature. He stood facing the assembly, totally unprepared and wondering what to say.

Then Trahan thought about how, before he left for Michigan, some of his follow Texans had derisively chided him for accepting a gift from a bunch of "damned yanks." Most of the chiding was good-natured, but some of it was not. Knowing some Texans were still fighting the Civil War well into the twentieth century, Trahan began his impromptu speech by alluding to the recent end of World War II against Germany and Japan. Then he described the remarks from his fellow Texans and concluded, "I'm sure you have seen the publicity [about Texas City] . . . and know that I'm here [because] one of your good companies has given us a fire engine. I've had fantastic treatment since I've been here. And when they [his fellow Texans] said 'damn yanks,' they should have said 'damn swell yanks!'" The reaction was spontaneous, thunderous applause throughout the state house. "I thought the roof would cave in," he said later.

Afterward, a group of people approached Trahan, suggesting he run in a special election for US Congress to replace an incumbent who died suddenly. Trahan resigned as mayor and started campaigning. It was already very late in the race, and for months eight other candidates had been pounding the pavement for votes. Trahan did not have time to put together an efficient campaign organization and consequently was unable to raise much money. He came in third, losing to Clark Thompson, who went on to a long career in the House of Representatives. Thompson is the one who initiated the congressional act giving relief to victims of the Texas City explosions, after the class-action lawsuit failed.

After his defeat, Trahan left politics completely. He became successful in the hotel industry, and on his retirement moved to McAllen, Texas. He always thought of himself as lucky to have been stopped by that officer as he drove toward the docks on April 16, 1947, to monitor the fire onboard the *Grandcamp*. The officer's assurance that everything was under control caused Trahan to change his plans and visit the city barns instead. That decision placed him just far enough away to survive the blast.[10]

Like many details of the explosions of April 16 and 17, 1947, there are multiple, conflicting stories about the death of Father Bill. Most of the stories have Father Bill arriving on the scene after the explosion of the *Grandcamp*. Some sources maintain Roach heard the first explosion and rushed to the scene, pushing past perimeter guards and saying that he was needed by his people. Most sources have Roach administering last rites. One source has Roach comforting mourners at a morgue.

How Father Bill was fatally injured has been a matter of much debate in published works on the Texas City disaster as well. Ron Stone merely states that "an explosion killed him." Hugh Stephens and many other sources have Roach being killed in the explosion of the *High Flyer*. Wheaton comes closest to the accounts of eyewitnesses, writing, Roach "was mortally wounded in the explosion . . . [and he] died in the Marine Hospital, after having received the Last Sacraments at the hands of Rev. George Rhein, with Bishop Byrne at his bedside."[11] Indeed, Father George Rhein did administer last rites to Father Bill moments before his death. As Rhein described, however, Roach was slumped on the floor, not in a hospital bed, and Rhein was alone with Roach when he died. Bishop Byrne was not present, as has been widely reported.[12] Perhaps the best evidence of what happened to Father Bill, and when, is found in four entries on his death certificate:

> *Date of Occurrence*: April 16, 1947
> *Manner or Means*: ship explosion
> *Primary Cause*: blast injury
> *City or Precinct*: U.S. Marine Hospital, Galveston[13]

The date listed, April 16, eliminates the possibility of Roach being injured by the explosion of the *High Flyer* on the morning of April 17. "Ship explosion" and "blast injury" indicate Roach was injured by the explosion of the SS *Grandcamp*, rather than in a secondary blast from one of the chemical plants or refineries, as has also been reported. Dick Benedict recalls that Roach was not ministering to the dead and dying, also widely reported. Rather, he was talking to Father Bill near the burning *Grandcamp* before it exploded; that is, before any injuries or deaths occurred. The entry "U.S. Marine Hospital" is the only fact nearly every source agrees on.[14]

Regardless of the exact circumstances, Father Bill's death garnered headlines across the nation, many lauding Roach as a "hero priest," something he certainly would not have liked.[15] Something he would have found amusing is a handwritten entry in the Sharon House Journal, a daily diary maintained by the nuns who once taught young Bill and John Roach at Holy Spirit School in Sharon Hill. The entry, dated April 17, 1947, mentions the death of Father Bill and that he had once attended Holy Spirit School. There is no mention of what terrors Bill and John were during their time at that school. Instead, like so many other contemporary accounts, the entry stated, "Father Roach risked his life, and gave it, in an heroic attempt to bring final absolution to dying persons in the inferno of burning oil and gas." Father Bill would have winced at the word "heroic," but he would have appreciated the irony of the entry. It was the principal of Holy Spirit School, from the same convent of nuns, who had written the letter for Bill and John before they departed for the seminary in Arkansas, saying that they were in no way suited for the priesthood.[16]

In Texas, Bishop Byrne established the Reverend William Roach Burse, a perpetual endowment for St. Mary's Seminary in La Porte. A Dallas priest was the first to contribute to the fund. After being deemed repairable, the church of St. Mary of the Miraculous Medal in Texas City was saved from demolition. At the rebuilt church on Christmas Day 1947, the recently installed carillon bells were dedicated in memory of Father Bill. Bishop Byrne joined parishioners, fifty area priests, and an honor guard of Fourth Degree Knights of Columbus for the ceremony. A memorial plaque reads:

> To the glory of God and in honor of the Queen of Heaven, the carillon in this church is dedicated in loving memory of Father William F. Roach and the victims of the disaster of April 16, 1947. Installed Christmas 1947.[17]

The multiplicity of errors leading to the explosions in Texas City, along with the collision of inconsistent responses to more recent dire global issues, including pandemics and climate change, may suggest that humankind, despite our intellect and capacity for abstract thought, is too arrogant and selfish to survive as a species. Our supposedly great achievements may in the end wipe us from the face of the earth. It is probably for this reason that humans, ensconced in their little worlds of self-absorbed satisfaction, find people like Father Bill Roach and Father John Roach intriguing. They were absolutely selfless human beings, the antithesis of most of the rest of us.

The legacy of Father Bill's short life is built on earlier legacies of Catholic social awareness. That Catholicism should be thought of as an institution of social awareness may appear to some to be out of step with reality. The devastating revelations of systemic sexual abuse at the hands of Catholic priests and nuns going back decades, probably even centuries, would be quite enough reason to reject the idea. In addition, the fact that some Catholic institutions, like Georgetown University, were once sustained solely by the slave trade, as Catholic priests bought and sold humans into bondage with the complete approval of the Vatican, would certainly, justifiably add to that rejection. Yet, as is the case with any human institution, Catholicism is a great deal more complex than priests and nuns harming the very people their faith demands they protect. There are just as many Roman Catholics who follow the commands of their faith as a solemn duty.

Father Bill and Father John were certainly among the latter. The Roach brothers were part of a new generation of Catholics emerging in the early twentieth century, focused on issues of race relations, labor equity, and economic justice for all. Like many Catholics, Father John, and especially Father Bill, would ignore their own well-being to achieve those goals. The root of this movement dates to a series of papal encyclicals collectively referred to as *Rerum Novarum* (Of New Things), named for the first such encyclical, issued by Pope Leo XIII (1879–1903) in 1891. *Rerum Novarum* addresses social issues involving labor and fair wages within the borders of sovereign nations. This document became the basis for a push toward a global Catholic Christian labor movement, touching all parts of the world where factors of religion and politics exist. A major theme of the *Rerum Novarum* is that freedom of association, or the right to create associations of fellow workers (unions), should be viewed as an essential element in establishing relations between industry and labor. Father Bill cited this idea many times in Texas City. The document also declares trade unions to be the key to resolving labor issues and economic injustice.[18]

This new social awareness was a seismic break from the church's history of close alliances with the aristocracy. Indeed, past popes had been members of some of the most elite, wealthiest families in Christendom. By the late nineteenth century, however, the church was aligning itself more with its poor and working-class faithful. In addition to economic justice, issues of racial inequality became part of Catholic social teaching.[19] By the time the Roach brothers entered the seminary, Catholic social justice was a major movement in the United States and elsewhere. It was definitely not universally accepted by all Catholics, as evidenced by the popularity of the reactionary priest Father Charles Coughlin (1891–1979), who had a radio audience of thirty million listeners in the 1930s. Although the heart of his speeches dealt with the plight of the poor and working classes, his rhetoric was laced with foul and bigoted racism.

The Roach brothers and other Catholics remained closer to the core of the *Rerum Novarum*. Under the guidance of Bishop John Baptist Morris in Little Rock, Bishop Christopher Byrne in Galveston, and the organizers of Friendship House in Harlem, among others, Father Bill and Father John honed their social philosophies. In keeping with this orientation, John Roach earned a master's degree in social work from Fordham University.

Other friends and contemporaries of the Roach brothers were prominent in the social justice movement. Thomas Merton, whom the Roaches met at Friendship House, went on to become deeply involved in the civil rights movement of the 1950s and 1960s. By then, he was one of the most prolific and respected Christian philosophers of his time, with dozens of books and articles to his name. Much of Merton's work continued in the vein of *Rerum Novarum*.[20] Another contemporary of the Roach brothers was Father John M. Corridan (1911–84). Corridan championed union rights in his parish on the New York City waterfront. His experiences became the basis for one of the main characters in the Academy Award–winning film *On the Waterfront*, starring Marlon Brando. Corridan's character, portrayed by Karl Malden, was named Father Barry.[21]

Regarding civil rights, the Roach brothers were part of a Catholic surge in the first half of the twentieth century that openly proclaimed injustices against their fellow humans as precisely that—injustices. Up to that point, the formal Catholic position had been to treat the poor underclasses, particularly African Americans, in a paternalistic manner. There were notable exceptions, including Saint Katherine Drexel of Philadelphia and the priests of the Society of the Divine Word, the Josephites. These were rarities however.

Beginning in the late 1920s, the Roach brothers came under the influence of the writings and deeds of Father John LaFarge (1880–1963). LaFarge, then a staff writer for *America* magazine, began publishing a series of articles analyzing contemporary issues of race and methods by which to reverse racial injustices. LaFarge had already established an industrial institute providing job training for African American men in Maryland. In 1934, he founded the Catholic Interracial Council of New York, which collaborated with Friendship House in Harlem and like-minded organizations.

In 1937, LaFarge published *Interracial Justice: A Study of the Catholic Doctrine of Race Relations*. In this book he argued that human rights were natural to all people regardless of race, class, or creed. These ideas led Pope Pius XI to ask LaFarge to assist with drafting an official encyclical on the subject in 1938 (*Humani Generis Unitas*/The Unity of the Human Race). LaFarge became executive editor of *America* in 1942 and editor-in-chief in 1944, while Father John was at Fordham, volunteering at Friendship House alongside Thomas Merton and occasionally Father Bill, who was by then already known as the "builder of churches" in the Texas Hill Country.[22]

In the decades following Father Bill's death, the Catholic presence in civil rights issues increased. Native Southerners like Bishop Vincent S. Waters, Bishop Joseph A. Durick, and Bishop Joseph Brunini, among others, created a frontline force calling for racial equality. Dozens of priests and nuns marched for civil rights in the 1950s and 1960s, often at great peril. The Second Vatican Council (1962–65) produced many landmark church decisions, including ones regarding race relations. To that end, Pope Paul VI began, among other things, appointing African American priests to high church positions, including the Vatican episcopacy.[23]

Likewise, labor continued to receive much church support. In the 1950s, Father Donald McDonnell introduced the *Rerum Novarum* encyclical by Pope Leo XIII, along with other works, to a young César Chávez. These ideas deeply influenced Chávez, first as an organizer for the Community Service Organization, then in 1962, as cofounder of the United Farm Workers union.[24] In this way, Father Bill lives on.

In the wake of Father Bill's death, parish volunteers entered his temporary rectory at the Third Street Villa Apartments, across from the church. They came to pack Father Bill's few possessions and clean up before the new pastor, Father John Lane, arrived. Lane, a close friend of the Roach brothers, had accompanied Father John to Pennsylvania to assist in the funeral of Father Bill.

Despite the near absence of physical possessions, or perhaps because of it, reminders of Father Bill's personality were everywhere in the little apartment. The simple frame bed was neatly made, as if it had never been used. A crucifix hung above it. The refrigerator, as usual, was nearly empty—containing nothing other than a pitcher of water and a half-consumed carton of ice cream. The place was littered with books, however. They were on shelves; on the bed, table, and chairs; stacked on the windowsills; and on the floor. Most were biographies of saints, including Francis of Assisi, Catherine of Siena, and Teresa of Ávila. There was also a copy of Saint Augustine of Hippo's *Confessions* and a tattered copy of his *City of God*, formative works not only for Western culture but for Father Bill's life as well. *City of God* was the book Bill and John Roach irreverently referred to as bathroom reading when they were together in the seminary in La Porte. Despite their jokes, both brothers were deeply affected by that book, particularly its emphasis on renouncing possessions and helping those in need. One look around the apartment told visitors how serious Father Bill was about renouncing possessions.

As already noted, nearly every book in the apartment had cash and checks stuffed in it, donations from people Roach encountered on his daily sojourns around town. "Money didn't mean anything to him," said Katherine Hunter, one of the volunteers there to pack up the apartment. "He gave it away." Befitting the life of Jesus and the writings of Saint Augustine, Roach would hand out the money he received, cash in particular, to homeless and destitute people south of Texas Avenue and in sailors retreat, or distribute it to families living in the poorest neighborhoods nearby. "He loved anybody who needed help. He just didn't live long enough to give it [the money] all away."[25]

NOTES

Preface

1. "William F. Roach Diocesan File," n.d., Archives and Records, Archdiocese of Galveston-Houston, Houston, TX; also available, "Roach, William," Catholic Directories, Catholic Archives of Texas, Austin, Texas.
2. Rev. Thomas A. Carney, quoted by Sr. Mary William (Maxine) Montegut, interview by author, Lufkin, TX, 1 July 2000. Father Bill Roach's work, not surprisingly, was deeply influenced by scripture and major works of Western philosophy, such as *The City of God* by St. Augustine of Hippo. Matthew 23:12 contains a passage that meant a lot to Roach: "Whoever exalts himself will be humbled; but whoever humbles himself will be exalted" (Hiesberger, *Catholic Bible*).

Prologue: April 16, 1947

1. Father William F. Roach, quoted by Cloma Frederick to Sr. Mary William Montegut, interview by author, 1 July 2000.

Chapter 1

1. Certificate of Death, File #82004, Registered #19444, Helen Elizabeth Roach, August 7 1908, Commonwealth of Pennsylvania Bureau of Vital Statistics.
2. Sr. Mary William Montegut to the author, 19 February 2004.
3. Eclampsia is a postpartum high blood pressure disorder that can cause seizures and coma.
4. Sr. Mary Jeremiah, "Biography of Bill and John Roach," 1989, Archives of the Monastery of the Holy Infant Jesus, Lufkin, TX, p. 1; Helen Roach death certificate.

5. Barbara Williams, curator, Drexel University College of Medicine Archives and Special Collections, interview by author, Philadelphia, PA, 1 October 2003.

6. Jeremiah, "Biography of Bill and John Roach," 1; Helen Roach death certificate.

7. Helen Roach death notice, *Public Ledger* (Philadelphia), 8 August 1908.

8. Jeremiah, "Biography of Bill and John Roach," 1; Montegut interview by author, 1 July 2000.

9. US Census, 1920; Media, PA, deed records, 1919, pp. 340–41, Delaware County Historical Society, Chester, PA.

10. "Chester County" and "Delaware County," Philadelphia Historical and Museum Commission website, available at http://www.phmc.state.pa.us/bah/dam/rg/di /IncorporationDatesForMunicipalities/pdfs/chester.pdf?catid=15#:~:text=Chester %20County-,One%20of%20the%20three%20original%20counties%20formed%20by %20William%20Penn,borough%20on%20March%2028%2C%201799'; and http://www .phmc.state.pa.us/bah/dam/rg/di/IncorporationDatesForMunicipalities/pdfs/delaware .pdf?catid=23; Weigley, *Philadelphia*, 5, 24. The county was named after the Delaware River, itself named for Lord De La Warr (Sir Thomas West, 1577–1618), the first British governor of Virginia.

11. Weigley, *Philadelphia*. Apart from nearby Philadelphia where the Continental Congress drafted, among other documents, the American Declaration of Independence, the pivotal 1777 Battle of Brandywine took place in Delaware County, and Washington's winter encampment, Valley Forge, is just a few miles to the north, bordering neighboring Chester and Montgomery Counties.

12. Weigley, *Philadelphia*, 337, 339, 356–57, 530–32, 548, 590–92. An organization called the Protestant Crusade fomented anti-Catholic sentiment, leading to a bloody riot in 1844 that was a pretext for disrupting a rapidly expanding Irish labor movement. But even Catholics could not maintain a unified front. Vicious quarrels between Irish and Italian parishioners resulted in even more flight to the suburbs.

13. Delaware County deed records, 10 July 1919, Delaware County Historical Society, Chester, PA. Apart from the social unrest in Philadelphia, there might have been another, more practical reason for the Roaches' move from the city: Mabel Roach is listed as a resident of the Borough of Norbeth, Lower Merion, in neighboring Montgomery County, and she had relatives in Delaware County. Moreover, the sale price of the house the Roaches purchased in Sharon Hill was one dollar, a low sum that was, and still is, often used for the legal transfer of real property meant as a gift from one party to another. Of course, the transfer might just as easily have come from a relative of William Roach's, but I was unable to associate Roach with any other family of the same name living in the Philadelphia area. This fact lends credence to the idea that the gift, if indeed it was a gift, came from someone close to Mabel.

14. In addition to the Gibbstown explosion, accidents occurred at Oakdale, NJ, on 15 September 1916; Aetna Chemical Plant, Pittsburgh, PA, in May 1918, killing one hundred people; Morgan, NJ, on 4 October 1918, where 4,500 tons of fertilizer detonated, forming a crater 150 by 140 by 20 feet and killing ninety-four; and Nixon, NJ, 1 March 1924. Davis, *Explosibility and Fire Hazard of Ammonium Nitrate Fertilizer*; Georges

Guiochon, "On the Catastrophic Explosion of the AZF Plant in Toulouse," presented at the Eighth Global Congress on Process Safety, Houston, TX, April 1-4, 2012, http://azf.danieldissy.net/Guiochon/AZF-Toulouse-Houston.htm; Sean Gillis and Sreenivasan Ranganathan, "Variables Associated with the Classification of Ammonium Nitrate—A Literature Review," final report to the Fire Protection Research Foundation, March 2017, https://www.nfpa.org/-/media/Files/News-and-Research/Fire-statistics-and-reports/Hazardous-materials/RFANHazardClassification.pdf.

15. Jeremiah, "Biography of Bill and John Roach," 1; Sr. Helena Mayer to the author, 22 March 2004.

16. Sr. Mary William Montegut and Sr. Mary Catherine Laiche, interviews by author, Lufkin, TX, 1 July 2000; Jeremiah. "Biography of Bill and John Roach," 1; Eleanor Barrow Schoch, interview by author, Glen Ridge, NJ, and Ed Barrow, interview by author, Villa Nova, PA, both 10 December 2000.

17. Schoch, interview by author.

18. Helen Elizabeth Roach was described as very beautiful. The brothers had at least one photograph of her. It has been lost, but many who saw it agree with the brothers' descriptions. Montegut and Laiche, interviews by author, 1 July 2000; Jeremiah, "Biography of Bill and John Roach," 1.

19. Sr. Helena Mayer, archivist of the American Provinces Archive of the Society of the Holy Child Jesus wrote, "I must say, I am surprised at the numbers of children [at Holy Spirit School] 'remaining' in various grades each year, sometimes as many as a third of the class! I am wondering what that was based on. This was not the case later on." Mayer to the author, 8 October 2003.

20. Based on economic statistics placing the average household income at $1,236 in 1920 and at $1,368 in 1930. Gordon and Gordon, *American Chronicle*, 190, 284.

21. Rev. Larry Lee, interview by author, Houston, TX, 1 August 2000.

22. Lee, interview by author; Montegut and Laiche, interviews by author, 1 July 2000; Jeremiah, "Biography of Bill and John Roach," 1; Schoch and Barrow, interviews by author.

23. Emily Wilson, interview by author, 8 October 2003.

24. LeRoy F. McHugh, "Death of a Media Priest—'They Figured He Had Courage—They Call It Guts,'" *Chester* (PA) *Times*, 17 April 1947; *Journey of Faith: The History of St. Philomena Church, Centennial Journal, 1898–1998*, Archives of St. Philomena Church, Lansdowne, PA; *Suburban Telephone Directory of Delaware County, Pennsylvania, 1933*. Media, PA: Bell Telephone Company, 1933. Specifically, the sale date of the Sharon Hill house was June 23, 1926. The Stratford Arms on Lansdowne was northwest of old Route 1 (West Township Line Road).

25. Ed Barrow recalls a relative saying that the twins had their own apartment, but Barrow and Schoch both recall the boys living at the Stratford Court Apartments (interviews by author, 10 December 2000). Even after they had begun their seminary studies, the twins would return to Pennsylvania during the summer break and work for their father. During those visits they likely stayed with the rest of the family at the Stratford Court Apartments, which would account for the memories of them living there.

26. *Southern Messenger*, April 24, 1947; McHugh, "Death of a Media Priest; Schoch and Barrow, interviews by author.
27. Age estimated based on the twins finishing seventh grade in spring 1923.
28. "History," Penn AC Rowing Association website, accessed 6 November 2021, https:// www.pennac.org/about/history/. Indeed, rowing has been called the oldest organized sport.
29. Penn AC Rowing Association, "History."
30. Arguably one of the greatest rowers ever, John Brendan "Jack" Kelly won 126 consecutive races between 1909 and 1920, along with numerous national and international championships. At the 1920 Olympics in Antwerp, Belgium, he won two gold medals within an hour of each other, then went on to win a third gold medal in the 1924 Olympics. Kelly was also a brilliant businessman, building a small construction company, John B. Kelly, Inc., into a world-class corporation during the 1920s and making himself a very rich and powerful man. But Kelly's passion remained sports, and particularly rowing.
31. Barrow and Schoch, interviews by author; *History of St. Philomena Church, Centennial Journal*.
32. Schoch, interview by author.
33. Schoch, interview by author; Jeremiah, "Biography of Bill and John Roach," 1.
34. Penn AC Rowing Association, "History."
35. Barrow, interview by author; Heiland, *Schuylkill Navy*.

Chapter 2

1. Jeremiah, "Biography of Bill and John Roach," 1.
2. Rev. Frank Lagana, seminary classmate of the Roaches and eyewitness to the Texas City disaster, interview by author, Houston, TX, 24 January 1999; Richard Meskill, interview by author, San Antonio, TX, 10 July 2000; Monsignor George Rhein, seminary classmate of the Roach brothers and eyewitness to the Texas City disaster, interview by author, Houston, TX, 15 August 2000; Sr. Mary William Montegut to the author, 19 February 2004.
3. Jeremiah, "Biography of Bill and John Roach," 1.
4. Jeremiah, "Biography of Bill and John Roach," 1; Montegut and Laiche, interviews by author, 1 July 2000.
5. It seems likely the Roach brothers entered into St. John's seminary in the fall of 1931.
6. Watkins, *Hungry Years*, 31–33; Gordon and Gordon, *American Chronicle*, 276; Kennedy, *Freedom from Fear*, 11–12, 57–58.
7. Watkins, *Hungry Years*, 37, 43.
8. Gordon and Gordon, *American Chronicle*, 297. In Detroit, 30 percent of the workforce was out of a job. In Chicago, the unemployment rate was 40 percent.
9. Watkins, *Hungry Years*, 44–45, 87, 118, 57, 59, 69.
10. John Roach, quoted by Montegut, interview by author, 3 July 2000.
11. Jeremiah, "Biography of Bill and John Roach," 2–3; Montegut and Laiche, interviews by author, 1 July 2000.

12. Moorhouse, *Sun Dancing*, 122–25, 157–66. The concept of peregrinatio, with its emphasis on exile and blind acceptance of chance outcomes, likely predates Christianity but it is most associated with Irish monks of the early Christian era. References to *peregrinatio pro Dei amore* date back as far as the sixth century, when Irish monks began traversing the European continent. One of these monks, Columbanus (b. 540), left Ireland at the age of forty-five with a handful of followers and established at least two monasteries along the way before crossing the Alps and founding the great monastery at Bobbio in northern Italy. In 891, three Irishmen cast themselves adrift in a boat with no oars. They wished to live in exile for the love of God and they cared not where. They packed only enough food for seven days, trusting their fates to chance and to God. On the night of the seventh day they landed in Cornwall, England, whence they were presented to King Alfred. Such peregrinatios spread Irish-Celtic monastic life and culture from the Atlantic seaboard of France and Spain to the Ukraine on the Black Sea. Many of the religious communities so founded became great seats of learning, precursors to our modern universities. Yet the intention of these wanderings, almost always involving trips to regions already populated with Christians, appears to have had little if anything to do with spreading the faith, or even with education. Peregrination pro Dei amore appears to have been purely a means of personal salvation, in the tradition of the desert hermits of the early Christian church.

13. Gordon and Gordon, *American Chronicle*, 17–18, 305; Watkins, *Hungry Years*, 44–46, 476; Jack Hammett, interview by author, Denton, TX, 20 February 1982; McCullough, *Truman*, 145–51.

14. Watkins, *Hungry Years*, 127–30, 6–7. Nearly a year later, on March 7, 1932, three thousand marchers seeking jobs at Ford's River Rouge plant were met with tear gas and machine gun fire. Four were killed and sixty wounded in what has since been called "the River Rouge Massacre."

15. Watkins, *Hungry Years*, 382–83.

16. Watkins, *Hungry Years*, 384; Smith, *Redeeming the Time*, 815; Waskow, *From Race Riot to Sit-In*, 121–74.

17. Watkins, *Hungry Years*, 109.

18. Watkins, *Hungry Years*, 125.

19. Gordon and Gordon, *American Chronicle*, 298.

20. Jeremiah, "Biography of Bill and John Roach," 3.

21. Montegut and Laiche, interviews by author, 1 July 2000.

22. John Baptist Morris (1866–1946) had been appointed bishop of the Diocese of Little Rock by Pope (later Saint) Pius X, in 1907 and served in that office until his death in 1946.

23. Sloane, "Arkansas." In 1931 the Diocese of Little Rock had been in existence eighty-eight years, having been carved out in 1843 from the much larger Diocese of Saint Louis. The new diocese had originally included what was then called "Indian Territory," the future state of Oklahoma, but in 1876 that area became a separate diocese. Thereafter, the Diocese of Little Rock largely aligned with the state of Arkansas and was part of the Archdiocese of New Orleans. Whereas Catholics had long been plentiful south

of Natchitoches, Louisiana, such was not the case in northern Louisiana and Arkansas.

24. Jeremiah, "Biography of Bill and John Roach," 3; Rev. James Mancini (former seminarian at St. John the Baptist Seminary) to the author, 22 August 2000.

Chapter 3

1. In 2000 only 3.4 percent of the state population was Catholic.

2. Lucey, "Diocese of Little Rock," accessed 5 January 2022, http://www.newadvent.org /cathen/09295a.htm.

3. The cofounder of the *Liberator*, Rev. Joseph A. Scarboro, proposed that Catholics be banned from voting in any election. That never happened, but his partner, Ben Bogard, wrote and secured passage of state legislation requiring the Protestant Bible to be read daily in all Arkansas public schools. The US Supreme Court did not strike down that law until 1963, almost thirty years later. The Scarboro-Bogard newspaper should not be confused with others of the same name. In the nineteenth century the abolitionist William Lloyd Garrison published a periodical also called the *Liberator*. From 1918 to 1924, a magazine emphasizing American sociopolitical art was published under the same name. A member of its staff was Dorothy Day, a longtime advocate of social change who would become founding editor of the *Catholic Worker*. Barnes, *Anti-Catholicism in Arkansas*, 174; Jim Forest, "The Catholic Worker Movement," Catholic Worker Movement website, accessed 14 August 2021, https://www .catholicworker.org/forest-history.html; Tom Cornell, "A Brief Introduction to the Catholic Worker," Catholic Worker Movement website, accessed 14 August 2021, https:// www.catholicworker.org/cornell-history.html.

4. Alexander, *Ku Klux Klan*, 18–19, 22, 25, 89–90, 112–18.

5. Barnes, *Anti-Catholicism in Arkansas*, 102.

6. Barnes, *Anti-Catholicism in Arkansas*, 109.

7. Sloane, "Arkansas"; Alexander, *Ku Klux Klan*, 18–19, 22, 25, 89–90, 112–18.

8. Sloane, "Arkansas"; Barnes, *Anti-Catholicism in Arkansas*, 130.

9. Based on Federal Bureau of Investigation statistics for 1935, quoted in Smith, *Redeeming the Time*, 814–15.

10. Unger, *Union Station Massacre*, 36–37; Phillips, *Running with Bonnie and Clyde*, 138–39; Barrow and Phillips, *My Life with Bonnie and Clyde*, 101–3, 108–9, 215–16, 262–63 n.12. Gangsters from Johnny Lazia's Kansas City, Al Capone's Chicago, and even as far away as New York and other East Coast cities frequented the state, especially the beautiful resort town of Hot Springs. Bank robbers and outlaws, including John Dillinger, Pretty Boy Floyd, and the Barker brothers, also visited Hot Springs, roaming freely and openly under the apparent protection of local law enforcement officials. Local crime boss Richard Galatas and Hot Springs Chief of Detectives Herbert A. "Dutch" Akers promised members of the underworld "a quiet stay in their town," for a substantial fee.

11. Joseph Murray, quoted by Montegut, interview with author, 4 July 2000; Forest, "Catholic Worker Movement"; Cornell, "Brief Introduction to the Catholic Worker."

Bill Roach made a similar remark several years later in Texas City, Texas. Vincent Schmidt, interview by author, 7 November 1999.

12. John Roach, quoted by Montegut, interview by author, 14 July 2000.

13. Rev. James Mancini to the author, 22 August 2000; Jeremiah, "Biography of Bill and John Roach," 4. Murray later attained the rank of monsignor and was appointed vicar-general to Bishop Albert L. Fletcher, who succeeded Bishop Morris in 1946.

14. Murray, quoted by Montegut, interview by author, 14 July 2000. These traits would also have been noticed almost immediately by the bishop of the Galveston Diocese once the brothers arrived in Texas.

15. Sloane, "Arkansas."

16. John Roach, quoted by Montegut, interview by author, 14 July 2000; Alexander, *Ku Klux Klan*, 89–90. Although the Ku Klux Klan in 1932 was nothing like the presence it had been even seven years earlier, it was still quite active and influential, particularly in the rural South and Southwest. Indeed, one of Arkansas' leading Klan members of the day was the minister of a Pine Bluff Baptist church. The priest's last statement is intriguing in that it indicates his previous experience of, or at least awareness of, other acts of Ku Klux Klan intimidation.

17. Father John LaFarge was one of the seminal figures in American civil rights and labor movements from the 1920s until his death in 1963. Keane and McDermott, "Manner Is Extraordinary." In 1933 Dorothy Day would found the *Catholic Worker* at the urging of fellow social democrat Peter Maurin. Forest, "Catholic Worker Movement"; Cornell, "Brief Introduction to the Catholic Worker Movement." The *Catholic Worker* and other similar publications would influence the thinking of both Bill and John Roach after their move to Texas. Lagana and Meskill, interviews by author.

18. Not long after the Roach brothers left Arkansas, the SCU was destroyed by a series of violent incidents. Watkins, *Hungry Years*, 378–90.

19. Jeremiah, "Biography of Bill and John Roach," 3. The word ROACH was finally removed when the buildings were renovated in the 1990s. Rev. James Mancini to the author, 22 August 2000.

Chapter 4

1. McHugh, "Death of a Media Priest"; Lee, Schoch, and Barrow, interviews by author.

2. Schoch, interview by author.

3. Rhein, interview by author.

4. Montegut, interview by author, 7 November 1999.

5. Jeremiah, "Biography of Bill and John Roach," 3–4; González, "St. Mary's Seminary."

6. Marthaler, *New Catholic Encyclopedia*, 1:845–47; Lisa May, email to the author, 27 July 2000. Indeed, today Spanish is the dominant language in large parts of Texas. But there was a time in the nineteenth and early twentieth centuries when German, French, Italian, and multiple Slavic and Asian tongues were the only languages spoken in portions of the state. The immigrant population was as diverse as the Native American cultures it replaced. The first non-indigenous settlement in what was then

called New Spain was near the present-day city of El Paso, founded at a time when Spain was one of the most powerful European nations. A major presence in the New World, the Spanish Empire at one time controlled much of the southern and western regions of what later became the United States, including Texas. Following a lengthy revolt against Spanish rule, the Federal Republic of Mexico was founded in 1821. Texas was part of the new republic, a large part, encompassing hundreds of thousands of square miles from the Gulf Coast to as far north as present-day Wyoming. To populate this enormous territory, the new Mexican government opened Texas to foreign immigration. Thus began the influx of US pioneers and land speculators. Initially, only Catholics were allowed to immigrate, but after 1825 entrepreneurs like Stephen F. Austin and other colonists were allowed to accept "nominal" Catholicism. In reality, there were so few priests to serve the region that these new residents were left largely to their own religious practices. After Texas fought for and won its independence from Mexico in 1836, much of the population remained Catholic, and those Catholics were still governed from Mexico, by the bishop of the Diocese of Linares o Nuevo León. This situation was further complicated just nine years later when Texas joined the United States as the twentieth-eighth state in 1845.

7. May, emails to the author, 27 July 2000, 5 January 2005, and 14 August 2008. The Galveston Diocese was formed in a manner designed to avoid political problems arising from the US War with Mexico. It was hoped that once territorial issues were finalized, the diocese would encompass all of Texas. The exception was El Paso in far west Texas, claimed by the bishop of Durango and never part of the Diocese of Galveston.

8. Marthaler, *New Catholic Encyclopedia*, vol. 13; Under Odin, Catholicism spread rapidly. By the time he was reassigned to another diocese in 1861 many new churches had been established, funding and priests were flowing into the area, and the Ursuline sisters had established a convent and major school for girls in Galveston.

9. Rhein, interview by author.

10. Katherine Hunter recalls the car being a Model A (interview by author, 11 July 2000); Sr. Mary William Montegut believes it was a Model T (interview by author, 7 November 1999).

11. Rhein, interview by author.

12. McComb, *Galveston*.

13. Jeremiah, "Biography of Bill and John Roach," 7.

14. Bishop Joseph Lynch and Bishop Lawrence J. Fitzsimmons, quoted in Jean Baker, "Tributes to Late Bishop Byrne Pours [sic] in from All Quarters," *Galveston Daily News*, 5 April 1950; González, "St. Mary's Seminary"; Ryan, "Galveston-Houston."

15. Hunter, interview by author; Jeremiah, "Biography of Bill and John Roach," 7; Montegut, interview by author, 7 November 1999.

16. González, "St. Mary's Seminary"; Kolodzy, "LaPorte, TX."

17. Lagana, interview by author.

18. "St. Mary's University Boarding College for Young Men, Catalogue, 1935–1936," 7, 23, 24, 27, Archives and Records, Archdiocese of Galveston-Houston, Houston, TX.

19. Jeremiah ("Biography of Bill and John Roach," 5) states that the old hotel was put into use in 1902, but González ("St. Mary's Seminary") gives the date as October 1901.

20. Jeremiah, "Biography of Bill and John Roach," 7; Montegut and Laiche, interviews by author, 1 July 2000.

21. Montegut, interview by author, 14 July 2000.

22. Jeremiah, "Biography of Bill and John Roach," 5, 7; Lagana, interview by author; Montegut and Laiche, interviews by author, 1 July 2000.

23. Rhein, interview by author; introduction to "St. Mary's University Catalogue, 1935–1936."

24. "St. Mary's University Boarding College for Young Men, Catalogue, 1934–1935," 12, 15; introduction to "St. Mary's University Catalogue, 1935–1936"; May, email to the author, 5 January 2005, and letter to the author, 23 August 2004.

25. Lagana and Rhein, interviews by author; "St. Mary's University Catalogue, 1935–1936," 8.

26. Rhein, interview by author; Brown, *Augustine of Hippo*, 16, 74–77, 184–88, 282–85, 378–80.

27. "Take care to guard against all greed, for though one may be rich, one's life does not consist of possessions," Luke 12: 13–15; "The Parable of the Good Samaritan," Luke 10: 29–37; "You cannot serve God and wealth," Luke 16: 13. Hiesberger, *Catholic Bible*.

28. Rhein, interview by author; St. Augustine, *City of God*, books 1 and 12; St. Augustine, *Confessions*, 177–78; O'Meara, introduction to *City of God*, by St. Augustine, vi, ix, xvi, xvii.

29. Rhein, interview by author.

30. Lee, interview by author; descriptions of Bill Roach from Lagana, interview by author; Rhein, interview by author; Jeremiah, "Biography of Bill and John Roach," 14; Montegut and Laiche, interviews by author, 1 July 2000.

31. Rhein, interview by author.

32. Lee, interview by author; Jeremiah, "Biography of Bill and John Roach," 7; Montegut and Laiche, interviews by author, 1 July 2000.

33. Lagana, interview by author.

34. Barrow, interview by author; Penn AC Rowing Association, "History"; Heiland, *Schuylkill Navy*.

35. Barrow, interview by author; Rev. James Vanderholt, "Biography of Father William Roach," 27 May 1999, Catholic Archives of Texas, Austin; Lagana, interview by author; Schoch, interview by author; "Flock of Priest Who Died In Blast Gather for Mass," *Galveston Daily News*, 20 April 1947; "Bishop's Tribute."

Chapter 5

1. Lee, interview by author; *More Than Brick and Mortar*.

2. Jeremiah, "Biography of Bill and John Roach," 1.

3. Vivian B. Maldonado, June 18, 1972, *Dedication of St. Mary's Catholic Church, Lampasas, Texas*, Catholic Archives of Texas, Austin; Lampasas History Book Committee,

Lampasas County, Texas, 76; Nancy Jones, email to the author, 4 October 2006; Joe Wittenberg, interview by author, Lometa, TX, 10 July 2000.

4. Podbielski, *Celebrating the Golden Jubilee*, 8; Dr. Patrick Foley and Joe B. Frantz, quoted in Marty Perry, "History of Immigration, Texas Question Raised in March," *Texas Catholic*, April 21, 2006.

5. Wittenberg, interview by author.

6. Rev. Charles V. Grahmann, "Extension Society Meets Needs of Rural Parishes," *Texas Catholic*, 21 October 2005, 2.

7. Nancy Jones, "A Brief History of the Good Shepherd Parish, Lometa, Texas," St. Mary's Parish website, accessed 27 April 2000, http://www.stmaryslampasas.org/; Beth King, interview by author, Lampasas, TX, 11 July 2000; Wittenberg, interview by author.

8. Jones, "A Brief History of St. Mary's Parish, Lampasas, Texas," St. Mary's Parish website, accessed 27 April 2000, http://www.stmaryslampasas.org; Alfredo Cárdenas, "Lampasas Parish Thrives with 'Can Do' Spirit," *Austin Diocese Newsletter*, May 2006; Lampasas History Book Committee, *Lampasas County, Texas*, 76. See also Marthaler, *New Catholic Encyclopedia*, vol. 13. Father Thomas A. Ryan was the first resident pastor of St. Mary's Catholic Church in Lampasas. Lampasas History Book Committee, *Lampasas County, Texas*, 76.

9. Wright, "St. Dominic's Villa," 63.

10. The Klan, most associated with the South, actually had tremendous support in many western and northern states, particularly Colorado, Indiana, Ohio, New Jersey, and the Roaches' own home state of Pennsylvania, where Jews and Catholics were principal targets. This new incarnation of the Klan was also deeply involved in politics, helping to elect many officials across the nation, including governors in Georgia, Oregon, Colorado, and Maine and a US senator from Texas. Alexander, *Ku Klux Klan*, 25, 111–12, 159.

11. Most sources agree that the Ku Klux Klan was responsible for the demise of St. Dominic's Villa. See Castañeda, *Church in Texas*, 337; Hackett, *Dominican Women in Texas*, 115–22; Wright, "St. Dominic's Villa," 63; Wittenberg, interview by author; Dana Hollister, interview by author, Lampasas, TX, 29 May 2000. In contrast, Nancy Jones, secretary at St. Mary's Catholic Church, stated that the villa closed solely because of financial problems. Jones, interview by the author, Lampasas, TX, 27 April 2000. When I interviewed her, Beth King recalled a persistent rumor, still widely believed to this day among non-Catholics in the region, that St. Dominic's Villa closed because all the sisters contracted tuberculosis.

12. Margarite and Mike Medina, interview by the author, 25 July 2000; Wittenberg, interview by author. For purposes of continuity, I use "Latino/a" throughout the text, knowing that such labeling is ever-changing and often annoying. For much more on the definitions of categorical terms such as "Spanish-speaking," "Mexican," "Mexican American," "Texas Mexican," "Chicano/a," "Tejano/a," and "Latino/a," see Treviño, *Church in the Barrio*, 223–24 n.4. See also "Ethnic Compartmentalization" in Márquez, *Black-Brown Solidarity*, 20–23.

13. King, interview by author. The anti-masking law was passed by the Thirty-Ninth Texas Legislature and signed into law by Governor Miriam Ferguson in 1925. Alexander, *Ku Klux Klan*, 222–23.

14. King, interview by author; Hollister, interview by author. Statements by Luther and White quoted in Wade, *Fiery Cross*, 181–82.

15. King, interview by author; Hollister, interview by author. Wittenberg told me in an interview that he did not recall anti-Catholicism in Hill Country. He added, "And I was a *German* Catholic," referring to the very real hatred of German Americans in the era of World Wars I and II.

16. Wade, *Fiery Cross*, 194; "Shooting in K. K. K. Parade," *Waco Times-Herald*, 2 October 1922.

17. Bernstein, *Ten Dollars to Hate*, 55–66, 76–81, 140–44, 223–24.

18. In Pennsylvania, Catholics were leading Klan targets in the 1920s. Alexander, *Ku Klux Klan*, 159; John Roach, quoted by Montegut, interview by author, 14 July 2000.

19. Rhein, interview by author; Bill Roach, quoted by Montegut, interview by author, 14 July 2000.

20. St. Augustine, *City of God*, book 12.

21. In 1997, a Lampasas lumberyard burned down, revealing what is believed to have been the foundation of a Franciscan mission. Cárdenas, "Lampasas Parish Thrives"; "Lampasas Courthouse," Texas State Historical Marker 12795, Courthouse Square, Lampasas, TX, erected 1965. The Higgins-Horrell feud, as it came to be known, began at the Gem Saloon in Lampasas on January 22, 1877, when Pink Higgins accused the Horrells—Tom, Mart, Sam, and Merritt—of cattle rustling. Shots were exchanged and Merritt Horrell was killed. On March 26, Tom and Mart Horrell were ambushed by unseen attackers, thought to be the Higgins family, at the Battle Branch fork of Sulphur Creek where it crosses present-day US Highway 190. Tom was wounded. On June 7, a gunfight on the town square of Lampasas resulted in the deaths of one Higgins and one Horrell. The Texas Rangers then intervened and forced a truce. "Horrell-Higgins Feud," Texas State Historical Marker 12017, US Highway 190, Lampasas, TX, erected 1999.

22. Kallus, *St. Mary's Open House* (brochure). The priest who fell ill was Rev. Louis A. LeBlanc. Some believe LeBlanc died in 1939 (see Jeremiah, "Biography of Bill and John Roach," 8–12). Diocesan records indicate however that LeBlanc was reassigned to parish duty upon his release from the hospital, first to Christ the King parish in Houston, in 1944, then to St. Francis parish in Giddings, in 1945. LeBlanc fell ill again in 1946 and died on July 19, 1947, three months after Bill Roach was killed in Texas City. "St. Mary's Church, Lampasas, Texas, List of Pastors 1932–72," 1973, Archives and Records, Archdiocese of Galveston-Houston, Houston. A few years later, Bill would tell his brother John that he was resigned to "dying young." John Roach, quoted by Montegut, interview by author, 14 July 2000. Some have interpreted this statement as a premonition of the catastrophic events in Texas City in 1947, but it might be that Bill Roach suspected he actually had diabetes.

23. Kallus, *St. Mary's Open House*; "History of Lampasas," n.d., p. 7, Catholic Archives of Austin, Texas. In "Lampasas Parish Thrives," Cárdenas states only four priests served in twelve years.
24. Hollister, Wittenberg, King, and Margarite Medina, interviews by author.
25. Wittenberg, interview by author; "History of Lampasas," 76; Kallus, *St. Mary's Open House.*
26. The rectory had been built by the parish's first resident pastor, Rev. Thomas A. Ryan, shortly after his arrival in Lampasas in 1927. Maldonado, *Dedication of St. Mary's*; "History of Lampasas," 76.
27. Rhein, interview by author.
28. In an email to the author on 6 October 2006, Nancy Jones stated that Roach did not build the rectory first; it was built at the same time as the church, later than Rhein's visit. When I interviewed him, however, Rhein was adamant that he remembered the rectory being in place, with no church yet attached, in late 1939.
29. Bill Roach was described in the local newspaper as accomplishing seemingly daunting tasks "with bewildering rapidity." Untitled clipping from *Lampasas Record*, 1 July 1945.
30. Bishop Byrne added Marble Falls and Bertram to St. Mary's Parish in 1945. Maldonado, *Dedication of St. Mary's*; Jones, "Brief History of St. Mary's Parish." In interviews, both Nancy Jones and Bill Wittenberg recalled Father Bill having overseen Leander as well.
31. Rhein, interview by author. The Holy Cross fathers of Austin assisted Roach during holidays such as Christmas and Holy Week, and on the rare occasions Roach needed time off. The Holy Cross fathers had assisted prior pastors of St. Mary's parish and would continue to do so after Roach's reassignment to Texas City in 1945. The mission church at Bertram was eventually placed officially under the control of St. Mary's Parish in 1945, a few months before Roach was reassigned to Texas City. Maldonado, *Dedication of St. Mary's.*
32. King and Wittenberg, interviews by author; "Bishop's Tribute."
33. Hollister, interview by author.
34. Hollister, interview by author. "He went to convert the West. Well, Bill made more converts than anybody ever thought of" (Rhein, interview by author).
35. Wittenberg, interview by author. "Roach loved children. He would visit children in the hospital to hold in his arms a child who had to undergo a painful treatment, the child having asked for him." Untitled clipping from *Lampasas Record*, 1 July 1945.
36. Initially, Good Shepherd Church was a four-room house purchased along with the property in Lometa. After 1927, a red brick building replaced the house. King, interview by author. In "Brief History of the Good Shepherd Parish," Nancy Jones writes that the money for the purchase of the original house was actually bequeathed by Augusta, who died in 1921.
37. King, interview by author.
38. For more on the Texas Farmers' Alliance, see Palmer and Macune, "Macune, Charles William (1851–1940)." Though outsiders might disagree, local residents definitely

consider Lampasas and environs part of the Texas Hill Country. Mike Medina, interview by author.

39. Among Roach's few possessions was a chalice given to him in Pennsylvania upon his ordination and a photograph of his mother. Montegut, interview by author, 11 November 1999.

40. Wittenberg, interview by author. Similar sentiments about Father Bill were published in the local newspaper: "He was unmindful of his own discomfort, and always dispensed pleasure." Untitled clipping from *Lampasas Record*, 1 July 1945. "Roach endeared himself to everyone, regardless of race, color, creed." "Bishop's Tribute."

41. St. Augustine, *City of God*, vi–xxxv, 55–70, 146. Colleagues confirm Roach was a serious student of the philosophy of St. Augustine of Hippo. Rhein, Lagana, and Montegut (1 July 2000), interviews by author.

42. Montegut, interview by author, 11 November 1999. Antony of Egypt, A.D. 251–356, is a good example of Coptic asceticism. He ate once daily, and then only salted bread. He slept on a thin mat spread on the ground. He also worked at difficult physical jobs in mines, prisons, and elsewhere. His aim was to perform penance for his own sins and the sins of others, especially for those unwilling or unable to do so for themselves. See Farmer, *Oxford Dictionary of Saints*, 25–26; Moorhouse, *Sun Dancing*, 159–72. The term "green martyrdom" comes from an early Christian directive written in Irish at the end of the seventh century. It describes three official types of martyrdom: "white martyrdom," or abandoning everything one loves for the sake of God's love; "green martyrdom," or fasting and suffering in toil for penance and repentance; and "red martyrdom," or endurance of the cross or death for Christ's sake. Moorhouse, *Sun Dancing*, 177–78.

43. Untitled clipping, *Lampasas Record*, 1 July 1945.

44. Jones and Wittenberg, interviews by author. Roach "set out to change the face of Catholic worship in the Hill Country," according to Cárdenas, "Lampasas Parish Thrives." In a 1998 brochure, Thad Podbielski characterized Roach's work as "Herculean." *Celebrating the Golden Jubilee*, 4. Sources universally agree that Father Bill built St. Mary's and St. Christopher's in Lampasas, Our Mother of Sorrows in Burnet, Our Lady of Lourdes in Gatesville, and Sacred Heart in Killeen. See "History of Lampasas," 76; "Bishop's Tribute"; Kallus, St. *Mary's Open House*; "Priest, Hero of Texas City Blast, Burial," *Media Times* (PA), 21 April 1947; Jeremiah, "Biography of Bill and John Roach," 8–12; Jones, interview by author; Montegut to the author, 11 July 1999; Wittenberg, interview by author. To these five structures, some add one or more of the civilian chapel at Camp Hood (later Fort Hood), St. Margaret Mary in Leander (now St. Andrew Kim), and even Good Shepherd in Lometa. Jones, Montegut, and Wittenberg, interviews by author; Podbielski, *Celebrating the Golden Jubilee*, 4, 18. The inclusion of Good Shepherd is certainly incorrect, and there is some debate about the others, particularly St. Margaret Mary. In *History of Leander*, Elizabeth Bailey states that St. Margaret Mary, begun in 1941 and finished in 1943, was "initiated by Father Frederick A. Schmidt, Father Thomas Culhane, and Father Joseph Houser" (63). Possibly Roach may have taken over the project at some point.

The construction of Our Mother of Sorrows in Burnet is a case in point. Others had proposed the idea of building a Catholic church in Burnet before Roach was assigned to the Hill Country, but nearly all of the principal construction and finish work was overseen by, and at times actually performed by, Roach. See Debo, *Burnet County History*, 216–17; Montegut and Laiche, interviews by author, 1 July 2000. Roach may have been the first priest attached to Camp Hood where he served eighty thousand troops.

45. Montegut to the author, 11 July 1999.

Chapter 6

1. Kallus, *St. Mary's Open House*; Maldonado, *Dedication of St. Mary's*; "History of Lampasas," 76. The original St. Mary's dated from 1885 and was conceived as a mission of the first Church of the Good Shepherd on the Wittenbergs' property, seven miles west of Lometa. When the area was elevated to the status of a parish in 1901, St. Mary's, located in Lampasas rather than on private property, became the parish headquarters. Nancy Jones, quoted in Cárdenas, "Lampasas Parish Thrives."

2. Jeremiah, "Biography of Bill and John Roach," 10.

3. Local residents adamantly pronounce Burnet as "burn-it." "Burn-it, durn-it" they say humorously to drive home the point. Jones, interview by author.

4. Burnet was originally called Hamilton, after a settler and landowner named John Hamilton. A creek in town still bears the Hamilton name. Fort Croghan was named for George Croghan, an officer serving under General (later President) William Henry Harrison. It was part of an initial network of eight Texas outposts erected by the US government in 1848–49, ostensibly for protection against Native American raids. Debo, *Burnet County History*, 8. The forts were just as likely to have been created as a line of defense against Mexico, with which the United States had just concluded a war. See Perry, "History of Immigration"; Anderson, *Conquest of Texas*, 4–7.

5. Debo, *Burnet County History*, 216–17; "Bishop's Tribute."

6. The Lion's Club was "closed to worshippers without notice." Debo, *Burnet County History*, 216–17. This closure may have been motivated by more than anti-Catholic fervor. The fact that the majority of Burnet's Catholics were Hispanic, many of whom were incredibly poor migrant workers living in tents and shacks west of town, may have contributed to the Lion's Club's decision. Perhaps for the same reason, only two of Burnet's twelve Anglo-Catholic families used the Lion's Club or any other local venue for worship, preferring instead to venture to Lampasas, Llano, or other distant churches for mass. "When Father Roach arrived, there was a terrible race problem between Anglos and Hispanics," Joe Wittenberg recalled in an interview with the author.

7. Father Frederick A. Schmidt, CSC, was actually stationed in Georgetown, Texas, thirty-five miles east of Burnet. He and another priest had been caring for twelve missions when Bishop Byrne decided to reduce their burden by reassigning some of the missions to existing parishes. Marble Falls, Bertram, and Burnet were transferred

to St. Mary's Parish under Father Bill. At Roach's request however, Schmidt was retained as his assistant. Schmidt continued to serve Burnet while still being stationed in Georgetown. It was Schmidt who experienced the unpleasantness over use of the Lion's Club hall. And it was Schmidt who usually celebrated mass in Burnet and heard confessions, at times seated on his suitcase. "Fiftieth Anniversary Celebration of 'Our Mother of Sorrows Catholic Church,' Burnet, Texas," 9 June 1991, Catholic Archives of Texas, Austin; Debo, *Burnet County History*, 216–17.

8. Debo, *Burnet County History*, 216; "Fiftieth Anniversary Celebration," 1. Burnet County was historically staunchly Democratic. In the 1928 election, however, county residents did not vote for the Democratic presidential nominee, Al Smith, who was a Catholic. Vanderholt, "Biography of Father William F. Roach."

9. Dobyville was founded in the 1850s. Its name derived from the bright white limestone hill (adobe) where it once stood. The earliest grave in its cemetery is dated 1857. "Dobyville," Texas State Historical Marker, US Highway 281, Burnett, TX, erected 1996.

10. Migrant workers were not the only poor people in Burnet County. During the Great Depression, half of all farms in the county lay idle. Vanderholt, "Biography of Father William F. Roach."

11. *More Than Brick and Mortar*, 1.

12. Montegut, interview by author, 1 July 2000. "Father Bill could wriggle things out of people, Catholic, Protestant, it didn't matter. He didn't have a bulldozer personality. He made you feel good about everything. He got a lot donated to his causes." Laiche, interview by author.

13. Debo, *Burnet County History*, 216.

14. Established 1898. "School of Architecture," University of Notre Dame, 2021, https://architecture.nd.edu/.

15. Debo, *Burnet County History*, 216–17.

16. The Catholic Extension Society was founded in 1905 by Father Francis Kelly, a Michigan parish priest. Worried about the dire conditions of some small-town and rural Catholic communities, Kelly began a campaign to establish a permanent fund to help finance the building of churches, community centers, and schools; seminary education; and even sacraments. Within a few years Pope Pius X elevated the group to the status of a Papal Society. The Diocese of Galveston was at the time very large, very rural, and very poor, so the Catholic Extension Society funding helped greatly. Rev. Charles V. Grahmann, "Extension Society," *Texas Catholic*, 21 October 2005, 2.

17. Barrow and Schoch, interviews by author.

18. Lee, interview by author.

19. Belle Mullin, Friendship House volunteer, interview by author, Jersey City, NJ, 8 August 2000.

20. Mullin, interview by author. See also Duquin, *They Call Her the Baroness*. Baroness de Hueck was born Catherine Fyodorovna Kolyschkine in Czarist Russia. Friendship

House was not the only such undertaking at the time. Dorothy Day and Peter Maurin, Catholic socialist activists and publishers of the *Catholic Worker*, founded a similar organization called Hospitality House in 1933. Day, who was well aware of de Hueck's work, stated, "We have lived with the poor, with . . . the unemployed, the sick . . . and we have learned that the only solution is love and love comes with community." Smith, *Redeeming the Time*, 877–78.

21. Smith, *Redeeming the Time*, 878.

22. Derived from Greek, "apostolate" refers to a sending, commission, or expedition. The word came to signify the active mission of the church in the world. "Apostolate," in Marthaler, *New Catholic Encyclopedia*, 1:578. For people like de Hueck, Dorothy Day, Peter Maurin, and later Bill Roach, it meant positive social activism. Mullin and Lee, interviews by author; Smith, *Redeeming the Time*, 878.

23. In *Redeeming the Time*, Page Smith claims many seminaries and schools of theology became hotbeds of radical socialist thought in the 1930s. Many churches, embracing a nonviolent, non-Marxist socialism, rendered aid, food, and shelter to the homeless, viewing capitalism as dead (871–73). Such views were not universally accepted, however. Claude Williams, pastor of a church in Paris, Arkansas, and a graduate of Vanderbilt Theological Seminary, was badly beaten for his association with the Southern Tenant Association. A plethora of popular radio evangelists of the time, including Cyclone Mack, Billy Sunday, and Aimee Semple McPherson, denounced liberal Christianity.

24. Mullin and Lee, interviews by author.

25. Bill Roach met Lee and Mullin sometime in 1942.

26. Bill Roach probably encountered Merton in 1941. In a letter to Catherine de Hueck, Merton writes, "First, thanks very much for letting me stand around Friendship House for a couple of weeks." The letter is dated two months before Merton entered the Abbey of Gethsemani and became a Trappist monk. Merton to de Hueck, 6 October 1941, "Merton's Correspondence with Doherty, Catherine de Hueck, 1896–1985. 'The Baroness,'" Thomas Merton Center at Bellarmine University, http://merton.org /Research/Correspondence/y1.aspx?id=528.

27. Jim Knight, "The Thomas Merton We Knew," blog, n.d., http://www.therealmerton .com/tommie.html.

28. Knight, "Thomas Merton We Knew."

29. The company was reportedly the Tippies of Burnet. Debo, *Burnet County History*, 216–17.

30. "Fiftieth Anniversary Celebration"; Debo, *Burnet County History*, 216–17. The completion of such a building was considered "impossible, or at least remote" ("Bishop's Tribute").

31. A group referred to only as "the Simon brothers" and men from Clark's Produce Company were among those who helped Roach finish the job. "Fiftieth Anniversary Celebration."

32. "Fiftieth Anniversary Celebration." One wing of a transept and a tall, enclosed bell tower were later added to this original floor plan.

33. "Heavy Rains Ended Wednesday. Trinity Five and One-Half Feet Above Flood Stage. Twelve Swept to Their Deaths in Albany, Texas. Harvest of Small Grains Halted Because of Rains," *Dallas Times Herald*, 11 June 1941.

34. At first there seemed to be no Catholics to speak of to support the new church, few permanent families and "Hispanics away many months of the year." Debo, *Burnet County History*, 216–17. Roach loved the new church and its poignant name so much that some thought he had chosen the name. But Our Mother of Sorrows was the idea of Roach's assistant, Father Schmidt. "Fiftieth Anniversary Celebration."

35. "Green-Byrne Deed of Transfer," 27 May 1941, Lampasas County Recorder of Deeds, Lampasas Courthouse, Lampasas County, TX. That portion of old Texas State Highway 66 was renamed Texas State Highway 281 and includes sections of today's Texas State Highways 183 and 190. Smyrl, "Burnet County."

36. Materials and labor were very difficult to find at the time. Maldonado, *Dedication of St. Mary's*.

37. Many sources report the church was built in 1940. See Kallus, *St. Mary's Open House*; Maldonado, *Dedication of St. Mary's*; "History of Lampasas," 76; "Bishop's Tribute." However, the property was not purchased until late spring 1941, clearly contradicting the 1940 date. War news from "Secretary of the Navy Frank Knox Said Japanese Caught U.S. Off Guard in Hawaii," *Dallas Morning News*, 16 December 1941; "Javanese Dance Troupe Performing at SMU Held by Inspector of Detectives Will Fritz" and "Russians Defeat Three German Divisions at Klin," *Dallas Times Herald*, 16 December 1941.

38. Anderson, *Conquest of Texas*, 4–8.

39. Captain Frank Hamer, quoted in A. B. McDonald, "Ace Man Hunter of Texas Says No. 1 Criminal in America Can Be Seized," North American News Agency, 6 June 1934.

40. Wittenberg, interview by author.

41. Margarite Medina, interview by author.

42. The Society of the Sacred Heart is an organization of Catholic women who raise money for and provide goods and services to migrants, indigenous people, and refugees (among others) in schools, colleges, universities, parishes, retreat centers, and prisons. Sociedades Guadalupanas are groups of Mexican American Catholic women who offer community leadership and perform charitable works. The name refers to Nuestra Señora de Guadalupe, patron saint of Mexico. Margarite Medina, interview by author. See also Treviño, *Church in the Barrio*, 66–67, 69–70, 131.

43. Margarite Medina, interview by author.

44. Margarite Medina, interview by author. "Jamaica" is pronounced *ha-MY-aw-kaw*. Rev. Hilario Guajardo, email to the author, 23 August 2000.

45. I was unable to locate information regarding the dedication of the Church of St. Christopher.

46. One of several sources referring to Roach as "the builder of churches" is McHugh, "Death of a Media Priest," *Chester Times*, 17 April 1947.

47. Rogers, "History of Our Lady of Lourdes"; Podbielski, *Celebrating the Golden Jubilee*, 4; "Bishop's Tribute"; "Eisenhower Promoted to Four-Star General," "Rommel Pushed

Hard in North Africa," and "Japanese Driven Back in New Guinea," *Dallas Times Herald*, 11 February 1943; "New Guinea" and "Attack on Rommel," *Dallas Morning News*, 11 February 1943.

48. Lee, interview by author.

49. Some suggest that this would have been Roach's seventh church (see chap. 5 n.44).

50. Prior to the establishment of Camp Hood, only twelve Catholic families resided in Killeen. *More Than Brick and Mortar*, 2.

51. *More Than Brick and Mortar*, 2. Lee, interview by author. Father Roach's weekly Sunday circuit included Lometa, Gatesville, Camp Hood, Killeen, and Burnet.

52. Named for the proprietor, Marsden Ogletree, it was part of the Lampasas-Belton stage line. In 1891, after railroads had overtaken stage lines in the mass transportation market, Jesse Clements bought the site and used the buildings as the headquarters of his enormous ranching empire. Lee, interview by author. Copperas (also spelled Coperas) Cove was founded in 1882 by the Gulf, Colorado, and Santa Fe Railroad. It is said to have been named for the coppery-tasting spring nearby. "Ogletree Stage Stop and Post Office," Texas State Historical Marker 3681, US Highway 190, Copperas Cove, TX, erected 1979.

53. Jones, interview by author; "Silver Jubilee"; *More Than Brick and Mortar*, 1.

54. Lee and Rhein, interviews by author; Montegut and Laiche, interviews by author, 1 July 2000.

55. Farmer, *Oxford Dictionary of Saints*, 268–69, 455–56; "St. Teresa," in Marthaler, *New Catholic Encyclopedia*, 7: 1037–41.

56. "Silver Jubilee."

57. Jeremiah, "Biography of Bill and John Roach," 8; "Bishop's Tribute"; "Big Three Plan Conference Report," "US & Britain South of Rome," and "Russians Retaking Ukraine." *Dallas Morning News*, 12 May 1943; "85,000 Reported Killed in Berlin Raids," *Dallas Times Herald*, 12 May 1943.

58. Montegut, interview by author, 1 July 2000; "History of Lampasas," 76; Jeremiah, "Biography of Bill and John Roach," 8–10.

59. Untitled clipping, *Lampasas Record*, 1 July 1945. Established by the American Catholic hierarchy in 1940, the NCCS continued until 1980. It was founded to serve the spiritual, social, educational, and recreational needs of military and defense workers and their families. The NCCS rendered service with both professional personnel and volunteers in the United States and overseas. It was a member agency of the United Service Organization (USO) and the Voluntary Service National Advisory Committee of the Veterans Administration and operated a VA hospital program with the assistance of a Veterans Administration diocesan hospital committee. The organization produced numerous publications, including *NCCS-VA Hospital News, NCCS Chairman's Newsletter, USO Notebook*, and various prayer books and pamphlets. "National Catholic Community Service (NCCS): 1940-1980," Virginia Commonwealth University Social Welfare History Project, accessed 5 January 2022, https://socialwelfare.library.vcu.edu/religious/national-catholic-community-service/

60. "William F. Roach Diocesan File," n.d., Archives & Records, Archdiocese of Galveston-Houston.

Chapter 7

1. Mabry, *Texas City Diamond Jubilee*, appendix B, 20.
2. The name Karankawa, or Carancahua (as in Carancahua Point and Carancahua Reef not far from Texas City), actually refers to several different bands of Native Americans with similar languages and cultures who once lived along the Texas Gulf Coast between Galveston Bay and Corpus Christi. The Karankawa, derived from a name roughly meaning "dog lovers," were nomadic, never camping in one location more than a few weeks. They traveled in dugout canoes along the coast or walked overland. The men, tall and muscular, were fast runners. The bands sustained themselves by hunting the plentiful coastal game and gathering native plants, but their staple foods were fish, turtles, and shellfish. European diseases and systematic extermination brought about the eventual annihilation of the Karankawa, beginning in 1528. Anderson, *Conquest of Texas*; Lipscomb, "Karankawa Indians."
3. Benham, "Texas City, TX"; Mabry, *Texas City Diamond Jubilee*, 2–6.
4. Benham ("Texas City, TX") gives the date as 1891; Mabry gives 1892 (*Texas City Diamond Jubilee*, 3).
5. Benham, "Texas City, TX"; Mabry, *Texas City Diamond Jubilee*, 2–6; "Fluid Catalytic Cracking Is an Important Step in Producing Gasoline," Today in Energy, US Energy Information Administration, 11 December 2012, https://www.eia.gov/todayinenergy/detail.php?id=9150.
7. Montegut and Laiche both referred to Mexican Oil and Pan American (or "Pan Am"), rather than Mexican Petroleum and Pan American Refining. Montegut, interviews by author, 7 November 1999 and 1 July 2000; Laiche, interview by author; Mabry, *Texas City Diamond Jubilee*, 8–9; Benham, "Texas City, TX."
8. Mabry, *Texas City Diamond Jubilee*, 9. Maxine Montegut and Betty Laiche both remembered going to the beach with their families as children and seeing row after row of new houses almost everywhere they looked. Montegut, interviews by author, 7 November 1999 and 1 July 2000; Laiche, interview by author, 1 July 2000.
9. Montegut, interviews by author, 7 November 1999 and 1 July 2000; Laiche, interview by author. The average per-capita annual income was $495.00 annually in 1933, compared to Montegut's and Laiche's annual salaries of $480. But thirty-four million people, 28 percent of the population, had no income whatsoever that year. Watkins, *Hungry Years*, 44.
10. The port was fourth behind New Orleans, Houston, and Galveston. Mabry, *Texas City Diamond Jubilee*, 12.
11. Mabry, *Texas City Diamond Jubilee*, 12, 18; Benham, "Texas City, TX"; Ferling, "Texas City Disaster," 49.
12. Lagana, Meskill, Sauer, and Quinn, interviews by author; "St. Mary's Dates to 1900," clipping from the *Texas City Sun*, n.d., St. Mary of the Miraculous Medal archives, Texas City.

13. There is also mention of a church being built in 1912. "St. Mary's Dates to 1900."
14. Alice Ramsower, "How It Grew, St. Mary's Church Was Only Dream at Turn of Century," clipping from the *Texas City Sun*, n.d., St. Mary of the Miraculous Medal archives, Texas City.
15. "St. Mary's Dates to 1900"; Montegut, interviews by author, 7 November 1999 and 1 July 2000; Laiche, interview by author.
16. "St. Mary's Dates to 1900"; Ramsower, "How It Grew"; Montegut, interviews by author, 7 November 1999 and 1 July 2000; Laiche, interview by author. In addition to his other accomplishments, Carney was a former pastor of St. Mary's in Galveston, building a rectory there, and serving as president of the University of Dallas. He was forced to resign from the latter position in 1928 due to ill health. "Reverend Thomas A. Carney," n.d., Catholic Directories, Catholic Archives of Texas, Austin. Carney is quoted in "Bishop's Tribute" as announcing that a saint was coming to Texas City. Montegut remembers Bishop Byrne having said something similar to the congregation at a different time: "I'm sending you a saint. I'm sending you my saintly priest." Montegut, interview by author, 7 November 1999.
17. Mabry, *Texas City Diamond Jubilee*, 12; Lagana, interview by author; "St. Mary's Dates to 1900"; Ramsower, "How It Grew."
18. Lagana, interview by author.
19. Lagana, interview by author; Montegut, interview by author, 1 July 2000. Father Frank Lagana, assistant to Pastor Thomas A. Carney, played a major role in construction of the new church. He sang the solemn high mass at its dedication, while Carney assisted the bishop. A friend of Maxine Montegut's and Betty Laiche's, C. F. Quinn, who was a seminarian at La Porte where the Roach brothers were ordained, was assistant master of ceremonies. Initially, the construction budget was set at $34,000, but the final cost was $47,000, an increase of 28 percent. "Saint Mary's Church at Texas City to Be Dedicated March 18 by Bishop," *Texas City Sun*, March 15, 1945; "St. Mary's Dates to 1900"; Ramsower, "How It Grew."
20. A news report at the time of the March 1945 dedication of the new church still referred to it as a mission attached to the Shrine of the True Cross in Dickenson, and to Father Thomas Carney as the parish pastor. "Saint Mary's Church at Texas City to Be Dedicated March 18 by Bishop." In June a small item appeared in the local Texas City newspaper announcing that the bishop had elevated St. Mary of the Miraculous Medal to the status of parish. "Saint Mary's Church at Texas City To Be Dedicated March 18 by Bishop."

Chapter 8

1. Montegut, interview by author, 5 November 1999.
2. Quinn, interview by author, 25 July 2000; Meskill, interview by author.
3. Montegut and Laiche, interviews by author, 1 July 2000; Laiche, handwritten account of first impressions of Father William Roach, n.d., Monastery of the Holy Infant Jesus, Lufkin, TX.

4. Many have commented about the apparent need of both brothers, and especially William, to mask the depth of their faith and devotion with large doses of humor. Montegut and Laiche, interviews by author, 1 July 2000; Laiche handwritten account; Lagana, Meskill, and Mikulik, interviews by author; Quinn, interview by author, 7 February 1999.

5. "Bishop's Tribute"; Montegut to the author, 23 October 2003; Montegut, interviews by author, 7 November 1999 and July 1, 2000; Laiche, interview by author. The Meskills, one of the oldest Catholic families in Texas City, had established a long tradition of caring for and aiding the local priests. It may have been at John Roach's suggestion that he and Bill made the Meskill home one of their first stops. Meskill, interview by author.

6. Laiche, interview by author.

7. *Going My Way* had been a major hit movie the year before. It won Oscars for Best Picture (1944), Best Director (Leo McCarey), Best Actor (Bing Crosby), Best Supporting Actor (Barry Fitzgerald), Best Screenplay (McCarey, Frank Butler, and Frank Cavett), and Best Song ("Swinging on a Star"). The movie was clearly very much in the memories of both Betty Laiche and Maxine Montegut, who were still making the correlation more than a half century later. Montegut and Laiche, interviews by author, 1 July 2000.

8. Montegut, interviews by author, 7 November 1999 and 1 July 2000; Laiche, interview by author; Laiche, handwritten account. Federal immigration authorities and other agents frequently stopped buses and trains in Galveston County and spoke to passengers, listening for hints of German or Japanese accents, in an attempt to thwart spies and saboteurs during World War II. Although Germany had already surrendered when Roach arrived in Texas City, the war with Japan still raged. Quinn, interview by author, 7 February 1999.

9. Laiche, handwritten account. Richard Meskill, who was present that night, described William Roach as "an uncomplicated man, but very, very spiritual . . . less conspicuous than John, quieter . . . he had a wonderful sense of humor and a real fine laugh, an open laugh." Meskill, interview by author. Others mentioned a complexity to William Roach, a mix of spirituality and humanness. "One always sensed a deep faith hidden beneath an endless onslaught of jokes and boisterous, self-effacing humor. Father Bill was ever so human, a man of prudence, nobility, and one who was delicately considerate of others." Montegut to the author, 15 March 2003.

10. When I interviewed Sr. Mary Catherine Laiche, she variously mentioned a crowd gathered around Roach and that few people attended the Wednesday devotions. Perhaps the historical lack of attendance prompted her and Montegut to try and initiate a conversation with Roach, thinking it would be easier then, but that night they encountered a crowd.

11. Montegut, interviews by author, 7 November 1999 and 1 July 2000.

12. Several people recalled Roach's activity around the shrine, a ritual performed almost every time he entered the church. It came to be recognized as part of his deep

devotion to the Virgin Mary. Bernice Smith, interview by author, Texas City, TX, 4 July 2000; Laiche, handwritten account; Montegut and Laiche, interviews by author, 1 July 2000. It was Katherine Hunter who recalled that on occasion, when Roach was in a hurry, he would simply rush past the shrine, wave a hand in the direction of the statue, and call out, "I'll talk to you later." Hunter, interview by author, Lampasas, TX, 11 July 2000.

13. Laiche, handwritten account.

14. The Second Vatican Council (1962–65) changed the way the Roman Catholic mass is conducted. In 1945, however, during the Transubstantiation, a medieval term signifying the moment when, for Catholics, the bread and wine become the body and blood of Jesus Christ, the priest's back was usually turned to the congregation. See the *Catholic Encyclopedia*, 14:158–60 and 14:407–18 for more on Transubstantiation and the Second Vatican Council.

15. Montegut, interview by author, 1 July 2000.

Chapter 9

1. "The Community was growing in number. What was God saying? Mother Mary Imelda considered the possibility of a new foundation." "Our History—Part VI." *Echoes* 54, no. 2 (2009) 3, Dominican Cloistered Nuns, Monastery of the Blessed Sacrament.

2. "Our History—Part VI," 3; Montegut to the author, 3 October 2000; Quinn, interview by author, 25 July 2000; Hunter, Meskill, and Bernice Smith, interviews by author.

3. Quinn, interview by author, 25 July 2000.

4. Quoted from "Welcome to the Monastery of the Blessed Sacrament," Monastery of the Blessed Sacrament, accessed 30 May 2020, http://www.opnuns-fh.org/. Exceptions to the cloister rule include emergencies and outsiders who need to enter out of necessity, such as builders, repair workers, and first responders. Additionally, within the community there is a position called the "extern." Like the role of "Mother," the prioress of the monastery, the extern is an elected position with term limits. The extern acts as the direct contact between those living in the outside, material world and the cloistered community. Externs buy groceries and other supplies. They also greet visitors and show them to the meeting room, a space divided by a substantial screened barrier, where relatives and others may talk with the nuns—visitors on one side of the screen, nuns on the other. Because of this, the extern lives apart from the rest of the community for the duration of her term, typically a year. It is a rather lonely position, but one that is typically viewed as an act of faith and penance, a major aspect of the contemplative life. Quinn, interview by author, 25 July 2000.

5. Latourette, *Beginnings to 1500*, 437–39; Murray and Murray, *Oxford Companion to Christian Art*, 139–40; Previte-Orton, *Shorter Cambridge Medieval History*, 673–79; Quinn, interview by author, 25 July 2000.

6. The prior was Blessed Jordan of Saxony (d. 1237) and Dominic's mother was Blessed Jane of Aza. "Jordan of Saxony: Handbook on the Origins of the Order of Preachers,"

Medieval Sourcebook, Fordham University, 28 April 1996, https://sourcebooks
.fordham.edu/basis/jordansax1.asp.

7. From the moment he arrived in Texas City, Father Bill visited individuals in need,
whether or not they were his parishioners, at all hours of the day or night. Meskill
and Bernice Smith, interviews by author.

8. Although today the property is within the city of Lufkin, surrounded by housing and
industrial plants, including Coca-Cola and Lockheed Martin, in 1945 it was well
outside the city limits in farm and ranch country. Montegut, interviews by author,
7 November 1999 and 1 July 2000; Laiche, interview by author.

9. Quinn, interview by author, 25 July 2000.

10. "Our History–Part VI" identifies the nuns only as "Mother Imelda and a companion"
(p. 3). In interviews by the author, Meskill and Montegut (7 November 1999) named
the companion as Sr. Diane.

11. "Our History—Part VI," 3.

12. "Our History—Part VI," 4. The Monastery of the Blessed Sacrament had been established in 1906 by a group of nuns who came from the Monastery of St. Dominic in
Newark, NJ. That monastery, in turn, had been founded in the nineteenth century
by a group from a monastery in France.

13. John Nolan, Ed Peterson, and Marni Zarin, "Texas Purchase and Sale Issues for
Buyers," pp. 19–20, the Practical Real Estate Lawyer, March 2017, https://www.winstead
.com/portalresource/lookup/wosid/cp-base-4-92102/overrideFile.name=/Texas
%20Purchase%20and%20Sale%20Issues%20for%20Buyers.pdf; Montegut, interview
by author, 1 July 2000.

14. Sr. Mary Veronica, interview by author, 1 July 2000. Sr. Veronica, who joined the
Lufkin monastery in 1946, was from Nacogdoches and was personally acquainted
with both the seller and his wife.

15. Montegut (1 July 2000), Laiche, and Sr. Veronica, interviews by author.

16. Montegut to the author, 3 October 2000.

17. In addition to Sr. Diane, there was a second mystic in the monastery, Sr. Mary Rose,
another transplant from the Detroit house. However, the name of Sr. Diane is mentioned most often in relation to Father Bill Roach. Meskill and Bernice Smith,
interviews by author. In an interview with the author, Katherine Hunter claimed Sr.
Diane displayed the stigmata, the wounds Jesus Christ sustained when he was
crucified.

Chapter 10

1. US Dept. of Justice, Records of US Attorneys, Southern Judicial District of Texas,
Texas City Torts Claims as Consolidated for Joint Trial, Record Group 118, vol. 44,
pp. 11, 966–69, National Archives and Records Administration.

2. Deposition of W. H. "Swede" Sandberg, 3 June 1949, US Department of Justice, Texas
City Torts Claims as Consolidated for Joint Trial, RG 118, vol. 24, pp. 6839–7029.
Sandberg's testimony was supported by much evidence, including reports, memo-
randa, and letters in Texas City Torts Claims, vol. 10, pp. 1882, 1888, 1890, 2075;

"Roosmann 44-C, Report of Improper Shipment to Cornhusker Ordnance Plant," 24 February 1947, 12 February 1944; "Roosmann OCO 65-C," 12 February 1944, and "Starr 54-C, "Improper Packing and Car Loading," memorandum to commanding officer, 25 June 1947, 54-A, Nebraska Ordnance Plant.

3. Deposition of J. Curtis Trahan, 31 May 1949, Texas City Torts Claims, vol. 21, p. 6246.

4. Benedict, transcription of interview by Moncla, pp. 23–24, Texas City Oral History Project, Moore Memorial Public Library, Texas City.

5. Meskill and Lee, interviews by author.

6. Lee, interview by author.

7. Jeremiah, "Biography of Bill and John Roach," 8–10; Meskill and Lee, interviews by author.

8. Meskill, interview by author.

9. Margie Sauer, daughter of Pete Tarpey, interview by the author, 10 July 2000; Meskill, interview by author.

10. Benedict, interview by Moncla, pp. 23–24.

11. Deposition of Curtis Trahan, May 31, 1949, US Department of Justice, Texas City Claims as Consolidated for Joint Trial, RG 118, vol. 21, p. 6246; Montegut and Laiche, interviews by author, 1 July 2000.

12. Matthew 4:19 (Hiesberger, *Catholic Bible*). Also see Mark 1:17, among other places. Montegut said ministering to homeless and poor people, prostitutes, and other outcasts living south of Texas Avenue was "very much to his [Roach's] liking," adding, "I mean, he'd be, you know, in the back alley!" It was also in tune with the words and actions of Jesus, as described in the Gospels and elsewhere in the New Testament. Roach's work also reflected the main thesis of rejecting possessions and helping those in need in St. Augustine's *City of God*. Montegut, interviews by author, 7 November 1999 and 1 July 2000.

13. Montegut, Laiche, and Sr. Veronica, interviews by author, 1 July 2000; deposition of Curtis Trahan, p. 6246.

14. Hunter, interview by author; Montegut, interview by author, 7 November 1999. See also Mark 2:1–22, "Healing the Paralytic," where Mark emphasizes the value of associating with sinners and outcasts. "The Samaritan Woman" (John 4:7–9) also focuses on associating with outcasts. Jesus asks a Samaritan woman for a drink of water, despite the practice of Jews never using anything in common with Samaritans, including water from the same well. The disassociation dated to the Babylonian Exile, when Jews were enslaved and held captive in Babylon. Jews claimed the Samaritans had mingled with and intermarried with the Babylonians and were thus traitors. Jesus, as always, was trying to erase the human penchant for being tribal and alienating other humans considered to be somehow different from the tribe. Hiesberger, *Catholic Bible*.

15. Bernice Smith and Hunter, interviews by author.

16. Hunter, interview by author.

17. Sauer and Meskill, interviews by author.

Chapter 11

1. "Tanker Explodes at Texas City," *Texas City Sun*, 21 September 1945.
2. The Interstate Commerce Commission had regulated and enforced both the safety and economic concerns of transporting goods domestically since its inception in 1887.
3. C. F. Quinn, a barrel inspector in Warehouse O at Texas City in 1943, described the US Coast Guard searching him for cigarettes and matches before he was allowed to start work each day. The guardsmen even inspected the soles of workers' shoes for nails that might create sparks and ignite the flammable materials moving through the warehouse. After the war ended, such safety oversight disappeared. Quinn, interview by author, 7 February 1999.
4. Curtis Trahan, mayor of Texas City, 1946–48, transcribed interview by Susie Moncla, Texas City Oral History Project, Moore Memorial Public Library, Texas City, TX, 12 June 1981.
5. Janie Meskill, Maxine Montegut, and Betty Laiche, quoted in Montegut to the author, 15 March 2003.
6. In an interview, Benedict insisted the union's name was the International Longshore-men of America. But the union's webpage states the name has always been Interna-tional Longshoremen's Association. Richard Benedict, International Longshoremen's Association local union agent and timekeeper, transcribed interview by Susie Moncla, 1981–82, Texas City Oral History Project, Moore Public Library, Texas City, TX; "Overview of ILA History," International Longshoremen's Association, 13 August 2021, https://ilaunion.org/ila-history/.
7. Kennedy, *Freedom from Fear*, 640. In April 1942, the Office of Price Administration (OPA) announced its General Maximum Price Regulation, nicknamed "General Max," which capped prices at the level they were in March of that year.
8. The War Production Board (WPB) was designed to lean in favor of labor and small business, but it failed there as well. The old guard of military procurement ignored the WPB and created its own policies—policies that enriched businesses, particularly the thirty-three largest US corporations, with military "cost-plus" contracts. OPA, estab-lished by executive order on August 28, 1941, before the US entry into World War II, became part of the WPB in 1942. Created to control inflation at the end of the Great Depression, OPA continued these efforts throughout the war years, with mixed success, until it was abolished in May 1947. By the war's end, OPA controlled a great deal of pricing. With the exception of farm products, the agency was generally successful in controlling most other expenses, including rents. OPA also rationed scarce materials, such as tires, automobiles, sugar, gasoline, coffee, meat, and a host of other items. Beginning in the fall of 1945, OPA began relaxing price and commodity restrictions, but did so slowly because of fears of initiating rampant inflation and other economic problems. Meanwhile, Congress increased individual tax rates. Before the war, Ameri-cans making less than $1,500.00 annually were exempt from federal income tax. In 1939, 70 percent of US households qualified for the exemption. In 1942, the exemption was lowered to $624.00. Taxation was a proven hedge against inflation, a very real

worry at the time. Yet ordinary citizens increasingly felt that the odds were stacked against them. The First and Second War Powers Acts (Act 55, Stat. 838, 1941, and Act 56, Stat. 176, 1942), initiated because of the Japanese attack on Pearl Harbor and the US entry into the war, gave the executive branch enormous powers, including over all economic measures that applied directly to the war effort. Kennedy, *Freedom from Fear*, 620–24, 638, 640–41; Goulden, *Best Years*, 93–94; McCullough, *Truman*, 469.

9. McCullough, *Truman*, 468.

10. To be fair to the United Mine Workers, there were more than three thousand strikes in 1943. Most lasted only a few days and all but a handful happened in the first six months of the year. See "Strikes in 1943." The War Labor Disputes Act, enacted on June 25, 1943, was a reaction to those strikes. Designed to be temporary, it was repealed in 1948. The Labor Relations Management Act, known as the Taft-Hartley Act, imposed new restrictions on unions, including a ban on closed shops that hired only union members. After it became federal law on June 23, 1947, several states passed similar legislation. Kennedy, *Freedom from Fear*, 641.

11. The War Labor Disputes Act, enacted 25 June 1943, not only broadened presidential war powers, it established criminal penalties for strike leaders and outlawed union contributions to political campaigns.

12. "Pan American Refining Corporation's Position on the Recent Strike," *Texas City Sun*, 5 October 1945.

13. "Refineries Back in Operation under Navy Control," *Texas City Sun*, 12 October 1945.

14. "Housing Shortage in Texas City," *Texas City Sun*, 2 November 1945; "Altar Society of St. Mary's to Meet," *Texas City Sun*, 9 November 1945.

15. O'Rourke quoted in "Rev. O'Rourke to Speak at Catholic Men's Club," *Texas City Sun*, 2 November 1945.

16. Mabry, "Work Incidental," 9.

17. Mabry, "Work Incidental," 6–7.

18. Mabry, "Work Incidental," 11–28.

19. Quoted in Montegut to the author, 15 March 2003.

20. "Tin Smelter, Monsanto Go on 40-Hour Week," *Texas City Sun*, 23 November 1945.

21. "Pan Am: Those Not at Union Meeting to Begin 40-Hour Week," *Texas City Sun*, 27 November 1945.

22. "Sinclair Workers Given Wage Increase," *Houston Chronicle*, 17 December 1945.

23. See the *Texas City Sun*: "Monsanto Damaged by Fire," 4 December 1945; "Partial Operation Begins at Monsanto," 26 March 1946; "Monsanto at Capacity," 14 June 1946. Also "$500,000 Fire at Monsanto," *Houston Chronicle*, 4 December 1945.

24. Accounts of the explosion throughout the chapter are from the *Texas City Sun*: "Swedish Tanker Explodes," 28 December 1945; "Tanker Explosion Still Unexplained," 1 January 1946; "Tanker Blast Still Called a Mystery," 4 January 1946; "Fifth Body Recovered in Tanker Blast," 8 January 1946; "Nine Still Missing from Sveaborg," 11 January 1946; "Eighth Victim Recovered," 18 January 1946; and "Crews Still Searching Wrecked Tanker," 22 January 1946; "Swedish Tanker Sveaborg Explodes," *Houston Chronicle*, 27 December 1945.

25. "Crews Still Searching Wrecked Tanker," *Texas City Sun*, 22 January 1946.

26. It was not until February 1946 that oil workers at Republic voted to accept an 18 percent pay increase with a forty-hour workweek and the US Navy relinquished control of the refinery. See the *Texas City Sun*: "Oil Workers Reject 18% Offer," 22 January 1946; "Pan Am: Workers May Have Misinterpreted Offer," 25 January 1946; "Oil Workers Take 18% Offer," 29 January, 1946; "Navy Releases Republic Refining Co.," 19 February 1946.

27. See the *Houston Chronicle*: "Oil Barge Explodes," 7 February 1946; "Two Men Still Missing in Explosion," 9 February 1946; "One Injured in Pipe Line Explosion" and "Tank Explosion at Galena Park, 29 April 1946; "Explosion Rocks Houston Refining Co.," 8 May 1946.

28. See the *Houston Chronicle*: "65th Polio Victim Confirmed in Houston in July," 26 July 1945; "Polio Cases Rise," 13 August 1945; "Second Rabies Case in Galveston," 2 March 1946; "Rabid Dog Situation in Houston," 11 March 1946; "15 Treated for Rabies in One Day," "Polio on the Rise in Houston," 12 March 1946; and "245 Year to Date Rabid Dogs in Houston," 10 June 1946. Also the *Texas City Sun*: "Flu Hits City," 24 December 1945 and "Rabies Confirmed," 5 March 1946.

29. Texas State Health Officer Dr. George W. Cox urged control of garbage and rodents. See the *Houston Chronicle*: "Health Officer Warns of Typhus," 1 March 1946; "Major Crimes up 63%," 7 March 1946; "27 Typhus Cases This Year," 29 April 1946; "Boys Home Polio Quarantine," 13 June 1946; and "Covered Garbage Cans Suggested"; also "2nd Rabies Case Confirmed," *Texas City Sun*, 19 March 1946.

Chapter 12

1. "Agency Seeks to Replace Oil Workers Union," *Texas City Sun*, 26 February 1946, and "Oil Workers Defeat Takeover Attempt," *Texas City Sun*, 22 March 1946.

2. "Two City Positions Created," *Texas City Sun*, 5 February 1946.

3. Chief Baumgarten is often described as a volunteer, but according to Mayor Trahan in his torts claims testimony, Baumgarten was a part-time city employee. In addition, there were two full-time equipment drivers who lived with their families at the city's two fire stations. It has also been the practice to report that the entire Texas City volunteer fire department was killed in the explosion of the SS *Grandcamp* on April 16, 1947. Yet, again according to Trahan's testimony, there were between sixty and seventy volunteers, twenty-six of whom were killed. Deposition of Curtis Trahan, 6246.

4. Mabry, *Texas City Diamond Jubilee*, 11; "C of C Wants Dumping on Dike to Cease," *Texas City Sun*, 1 March 1946.

5. "C of C Wants Dumping on Dike to Cease."

6. See the *Texas City Sun*: "Flu Hits City," 24 December 1945, "2nd Rabies Case Confirmed," 19 March 1946, and "Health Emergency Declared," 17 May 1946. By mid-March, two cases of rabies had been confirmed in Texas City. Polio and sleeping sickness were already pervasive in Corpus Christi and San Antonio and beginning to appear in the Galveston Bay area. To be clear, Chagas disease (American

trypanosomiasis) and African sleeping sickness are caused by different insect-borne parasites. Chagas disease is carried by the Triatoma genus of kissing bugs, which feed on nesting vertebrates and favor regions populated with palm trees. The palm trees of Galveston Bay and the infestation of rats on the Texas City dike would be prime habitat for insect carriers of Chagas disease. See "Parasites—American Trypanosomiasis (also known as Chagas Disease)," Centers for Disease Control and Prevention, 11 February 2019, https://www.cdc.gov/parasites/chagas/index.html.

7. "City Approves Bus Service, Sewer Lines, Plan for New Library," *Texas City Sun*, 25 January 1946.

8. "TC Dumping Raw Sewage in Bay," *Texas City Sun*, 3 September 1946.

9. See the *Texas City Sun*: "Texas City Mayor Also Stone Oil Executive," 28 December 1945; "Two City Positions Created," 5 February 1946; "City Charter Approved," 19 February 1946; "25% Tax Surplus Announced: Mayor Johnson Declares Dike to Be Cleaned Up," 22 March 1946; and "Dike Dumping Outlawed," 2 April 1946.

10. See *Texas City Sun*: "Trahan Elected Mayor," 4 April 1946; "School Taxes Raised," 9 April 1946.

11. Sauer, interview by author.

12. Bernice Smith, interview by author.

13. "City Approves Bus Service, Sewer Repairs, Plan for New Library," *Texas City Sun*, 25 January 1946.

14. Meskill, interview by author.

15. The name steel band was a riff on Winston Churchill's "Iron Curtain" speech delivered in March 1946. In the speech, Churchill described the rapidly closing borders of territories occupied by the Soviet Union since the end of World War II. The speech made headlines worldwide, and "Iron Curtain" became a major part of the western lexicon of the Cold War era. Roach's allusion to Churchill's speech would have been lost on no one at the time. William F. Roach, "Texas City Absorbs Industry or Industry Absorbs Texas City," *Texas City Sun*, 8 April 1947.

16. "Texas City Absorbs Industry or Industry Absorbs Texas City."

17. "Health Emergency Declared," *Texas City Sun*, 17 May 1946; "San Antonio and Houston Quarantined," *Houston Chronicle*, 13 May 1946.

18. See the *Texas City Sun*: "Dike Clean-up Impossible," 10 May 1946; "Health Emergency Declared," 17 May 1946; "Clean-up Failing," 4 June 1946; "Clean-up Committees Selected," 18 June 1946; 15 Pt. Plan for Clean-up Outlined," 25 June 1946; "Texas City Passes $297,531 Budget," 12 July 1946; "Open Ditch Drainage Adopted by Commission," 26 July 1946; "City Buys Fireboat," 20 August 1946.

19. Deposition of W. H. Sandberg, 6838–6918. A Department of the Interior report described ammonium nitrate, NH_4NO_3, as "an oxidizer when mixed with TNT in the manufacture of explosives and is one of the best known sources of nitrogen for all crops." Though technically not an explosive on its own, under certain conditions, when introduced to other materials as an oxidizer, ammonium nitrate will contribute substantially to an explosive reaction. Kintz, Jones, and Carpenter, *Report of Investigations*, 4.

20. Laiche, handwritten account.

21. Deposition of Curtis Trahan, 6246.
22. Montegut, interview by author, 1 July 2000.
23. Montegut, interviews by author, 7 November 1999, 1 July 2000.
24. Montegut, interviews by author, 7 November 1999, 1 July 2000.
25. Quoted by Hunter, interview by author.
26. Quoted by Bernice Smith, interview by author.
27. Quoted by Kenneth Mikulik, interview by author, Houston, TX, 25 July 2000.
28. Montegut, interview by author, 1 July 2000.
29. Montegut, interview by author, 1 July 2000.

Chapter 13

1. *Texas City Sun* newspaper reports provide contradictory information about when exactly this strike began. The first mention of the strike, on October 1, 1946, indicates that the docks were already tied up due to the strike. On October 9, however, the same paper announced that the ILA "may strike," which "would close Monsanto and the tin smelter." On October 27, it was reported that the strike had been averted. And finally, on October 31, there is reference to a thirty-day strike. Dick Benedict mentions the strike in his oral history interview with Susie Moncla of the Moore Memorial Public Library in Texas City but does not specify its length. See *Texas City Sun*: "ILA Strike Ties Up Texas City Docks," 1 October 1946; "Longshoremen May Strike," 9 October 1946; "Maritime Strike Averted," 27 October 1946; "Strike Ends after 30 Days—Costliest Strike in History," 31 October 1946.
2. Allen, Green, and Reese, "Strikes."
3. McCullough, *Truman*, 501.
4. "Truman Supports Good Wages, Low Prices," *Texas City Sun*, 8 October 1946.
5. McCullough, *Truman*, 493. According to the US Bureau of Labor Statistics, 18.5 cents in 1946 would be equivalent to $2.40 in 2010. "One Hundred Years of Price Change: The Consumer Price Index and the American Inflation Experience," Monthly Labor Review, Bureau of Labor Statistics, April 2014, https://www.bls.gov/opub/mlr/2014/article/one-hundred-years-of-price-change-the-consumer-price-index-and-the-american-inflation-experience.htm. See also "CPI Inflation Calculator," US Official Inflation Data, Alioth Finance, 30 November 2021, https://www.officialdata.org/us/inflation/.
6. "CPI Inflation Calculator."
7. Dick Benedict, interview by Moncla, Texas City Oral History Project.
8. Dick Benedict, interview by Moncla; see also Curtis Trahan, interview by Moncla, both in Texas City Oral History Project.
9. "Strike Ends after 30 Days—Costliest Strike in History," *Texas City Sun*, 31 October 1946.
10. The summary of the political situation in Texas is from Green, *Establishment in Texas Politics*, 58–67, 108–11.
11. See *Texas City Sun*: "Strike Ends after 30 Days," 31 October 1946; "Truman Ends Most Price Controls," 10 November 1946.

12. "Driving Rains Dampen Eternal Light Dedication," *Texas City Sun*, 11 November 1946.

13. William Roach, "Eternal Light Dedication," speech delivered at the dedication of the Eternal Light war memorial, Texas City, 11 November 1946, typescript in collection of Richard "Dick" Meskill.

14. Lisa May, archivist of the Archdiocese of Galveston-Houston, email to the author, 14 August 2008. Our Lady of the Snows was built in 1938 on the abandoned site of a sugar refinery that fell victim to the Great Depression. When Monsanto established operations in Texas City, it ended up "almost sitting on Monsanto's parking lot." Our Lady of the Snows was actually attached to the parish of Our Lady of Guadalupe in Galveston during Father Bill Roach's time in Texas City. Later it became part of the parish of St. John the Baptist in Alvin (1947–57), then returned to Our Lady of Guadalupe in Galveston (1957–59). In 1959, it became a mission of St. Mary in Texas City. In 1963, it was combined with and absorbed by St. Mary. Eventually, the property was sold to Monsanto.

15. Treviño, *Church in the Barrio*, 12, 120–26.

16. Trahan, interview by Moncla, Texas City Oral History Project.

17. "Oil Workers File Suit for Portal Pay," *Texas City Sun*, 24 December 1946. "Constitutionality of the Portal-to-Portal Act," 1010–12.

18. See *Texas City Sun*: "Oil Workers File Suit for Portal Pay," 24 December 1946; "Manufacturers Warn Higher Wages Will Lead to Inflation and Unemployment," and "Cost of Living Highest Since 1920," both 26 December 1946.

19. Deposition of W. H. Sandberg, 6838–6918.

20. Montegut and Laiche, interviews by author, 1 July 2000. In the Gospel of Matthew, Jesus predicted his own death three times, in verses 16:21–23, 18:22–23, and 20:17–19. Hiesberger, *Catholic Bible*.

21. See *Houston Chronicle*: "Boilermakers Strike at Texas City and Five Other Sites," 27 January 1947; "Fight on Picket Line in Oak Forest," 10 February 1947; "Strikers Turn 2nd Load of Materials Away," 19 February 1947; "Frank Sharp Charged with Carrying a Gun," 25 February 1947; "Bryant and Four Others Indicted for Antistrike Violations," 26 February 1947.

22. "LaGuardia Testifies before Congress," *Houston Chronicle*, 8 March 1947.

23. Montegut, interviews by author, 7 November 1999, 1 July 2000.

24. Hunter, interview by author; Quinn, interview by author, 25 July 2000; "Monsanto Forming a Texas Division Headquarters at Texas City," *Houston Chronicle*, 24 January 1947.

25. See the *Houston Chronicle*: "LA Explosion Kills 15, Injures 158," 21 February 1947; "Big Tragedy Would Catch Houston Short on Nurses," 2 March 1947; "Oil Tanker Explodes," 5 March 1947; "Witnesses Testify in Lyons Creek Explosion," 10 March 1947.

26. Fr. William Saunders, "History of Lent," Catholic Education Resource Center, accessed 21 November 2020, https://www.catholiceducation.org/en/culture/catholic-contributions/history-of-lent.html The word "Lent" may also refer to the month of March. That possibility is interesting because in pre-Christian Roman culture March

was a monthlong celebration of the god Mars. In Roman Catholicism, the Lenten season usually occurs mostly during March.

27. The Catholic season of Lent celebrates the forty-day period Jesus spent fasting and meditating in the desert between his baptism and the beginning of his public life. The period extends from Ash Wednesday to Holy Saturday, the day before Easter. Each Sunday has a particular name and attached theme. In 1947, the six Sundays between Ash Wednesday and Easter were *Quadragesima* (fortieth) on 23 February, *Reminiscere Miserationum* (remember) on 2 March, *Oculi Mei* (my eyes) on 9 March, *Laetare* (rejoice) on 16 March, *Judica Me Deus* (give me God) on 23 March, and *Palmarum* (Palm) on 30 March. William Roach, "Lent," handwritten sermon delivered 23 February 1947, private collection of Richard Meskill.

28. Roach, "Human Relations in a Christian Social Order," typescript of sermon delivered 2 March 1947, private collection of Richard Meskill. Roach often spoke with Dick Meskill about the Catholic Church and its philosophical and moral stand concerning the relationship between management and labor. Roach gave Meskill a few of his sermons and homilies on the subject, as well as the speech he made at the dedication of the war memorial in Texas City. They all have errors crossed out or left uncorrected. Occasionally, handwritten notes and changes appear in the margins. To Meskill, these details accentuate Roach's humanness. Meskill to the author, 11 July 2000.

29. Roach, "Human Relations in a Christian Social Order Are Cooperation Not Conflict," typescript of sermon delivered 16 March 1947, private collection of Richard Meskill.

30. Bernice Smith and Hunter, interviews by author; Montegut and Laiche, interviews by author, 1 July 2000. All witnesses agree on the details of Sr. Diane's vision, Roach's reaction to the vision, and the wording of the unscripted sermon. Likewise each witness mentioned that the sermon was delivered on Laetare Sunday. Though this was one month to the day before the explosion of the SS *Grandcamp* in which Father Bill died, Hunter misremembered the sermon as being delivered on the Sunday before the explosion. That would have been 13 April 1947, the first Sunday after Easter, long past Laetare Sunday.

31. Hunter and Bernice Smith, interviews by author.

32. The tank farm was in Fairbanks, on Texas State Highway 290, between Houston and Cypress. "Fairbanks Tank Farm Burns," *Houston Chronicle*, 20 March 1947.

33. Vincent Schmidt, interview by author.

34. Bernice Smith, interview by author.

35. William F. Roach, "Texas City Absorbs Industry or Industry Absorbs Texas City." Roach's philosophy was deeply rooted in Scripture and other Christian literature, including St. Augustine's *The City of God*. The Parable of the Rich Man and Lazarus (Luke 16:19–31) focuses on the principle that those with means should help relieve the suffering of those without means. Hiesberger, *Catholic Bible*.

36. In Moncla's 1981 oral history interview with Trahan, the former mayor indicates that the race with La Marque to annex the industries happened over the period of a weekend, beginning on Friday and ending the following Monday. However, the mayor

and commissioners of Texas City cast their three-to-two vote on Thursday evening, April 10, 1947. "Industries Annexed," *Texas City Sun*, 11 April 1947.

37. Trahan, interview by Moncla, Texas City Oral History Project. See *Texas City Sun*: "Annexation Debated," 9 April 1947; "Industries Annexed," 11 April 1947.

38. "Fire at Gulf Oil Terminal Headquarters at Clinton," *Houston Chronicle*, 14 April 1947.

39. Bernice Smith, interview by author.

40. Janie Meskill, quoted by Montegut, interview by author, 1 July 2000.

Chapter 14

1. Deposition of Curtis Trahan, 6246.

2. Clarence Anthony Mayville was known to everyone as "Tookey" or "Tooky." Descriptions of Cloma Frederick invariably included that she was "a real character," followed by laughter. Sauer, interview by author; Montegut and Laiche, interviews by author, 1 July 2000.

3. Cloma Frederick relayed this information to Maxine Montegut and Margie Sauer, who quoted Father Bill Roach in interviews with the author on 1 July 2000 and 10 July 2000.

4. Cloma Frederick quoted by Sauer, interview by author.

5. Referred to as "Frank's Café" by many sources, including Harley V. Bowen, general foreman of the Texas City Terminal Railway Company, in his testimony during *Dalehite v. United States*, 346 U.S. 15 (1953). H. B. Williams, safety engineer for Pan American Refining Corporation, used the name "Dockside Café" in Kintz, Jones, and Carpenter, *Report of Investigations*, 11. In *Texas City Remembers*, Wheaton refers simply to "the little water-front restaurant" (3).

6. Ceary Johnson, quoted in Steve Olafson, "Texas City Just Blew Up," *Houston Chronicle*, 13 April 1997.

7. Kintz, Jones, and Carpenter, *Report of Investigations*, 1.

8. According to the Coast Guard investigation, the fire was officially discovered at 8:10 A.M. US Coast Guard, *Final Findings of the Coast Guard, September 28, 1947.*

9. Deposition of Carlos P. Suderman, 1 June 1949, US Department of Justice, Texas City Torts Claims as Consolidated for Joint Trial, RG118, vols. 21–22.

10. Deposition of W. H. Sandberg.

11. Kintz, Jones, and Carpenter, *Report of Investigations*, 1; American Merchant Marine at War, "C2 Type Ships," US Maritime Commission, 26 March 1988, updated 24 June 2019, http://www.usmm.org/c2ships.html; Wheaton, *Texas City Remembers*, 1.

12. Deposition of W. H. Sandberg; Wheaton, *Texas City Remembers*, 12–13.

13. Quoted in Ferling, "Texas City Disaster," 50I; Wheaton, *Texas City Remembers*, 12. In his testimony under oath during the subsequent court proceedings, Bowen quoted Baumgarten as saying merely, "We might need some help." Testimony of Harley V. Bowen, 31 May 1949, US Department of Justice, Texas City Claims as Consolidated for Joint Trial, RG 118, vol. 21.

14. Dick Benedict, interview by Moncla, Texas City Oral History Project.

15. Regarding Roach's presence near the SS *Grandcamp* that day, Monsignor Frank Lagana said, "Whenever there was a fire, the pastor would go and see if he could offer help. There were a lot of fires and in those days the priest always went to see if he could help. There was this fire there [on the *Grandcamp*] and he [Roach] went down there for that reason, because that's what we did, try and help." Lagana, interview by author.

16. Deposition of W. H. Sandberg; deposition of Curtis Trahan, 6246; Janie Smith, interview by author, 26 September 1999. Many accounts state that the entire Texas City Volunteer Fire Department responded that day. But according to Mayor Trahan and other sources, the full force was sixty to seventy members. In *Texas City Remembers*, Wheaton lists a total of forty-eight men in the force (6, 83–84). Most sources place the number of volunteers answering the call on April 16, 1947, at twenty-seven. In "Texas City Disaster," Ferling states that twenty-eight firefighters were on the job and that two were released, resulting in a death toll of twenty-six (50). All other sources state that twenty-seven died. One man, Ben L. Mitchell, was certainly released by Chief Baumgarten to take a radiator to Galveston.

17. Williams, testimony reported in Kintz, Jones, and Carpenter, *Report of Investigations*.

18. Davis, *Explosibility and Fire Hazard of Ammonium Nitrate Fertilizer*. Published two years before the fire onboard the *Grandcamp*, Davis's report lists six physical factors as influencing sensitivity toward explosion: temperature, strength of initial impulse (a force striking the substance), density, packing, particle size, and moisture content.

19. *Texas City, Texas, Disaster*.

20. Kintz, Jones, and Carpenter, *Report of Investigations*.

21. Deposition of Curtis Trahan, 6246; Trahan, interview by Moncla, Texas City Oral History Project.

22. Deposition of Harley V. Bowen, 6363; Wheaton, *Texas City Remembers*, 12.

23. Janie Smith, interview by author.

24. "City Buys Fireboat," *Texas City Sun*, 20 August 1946; Kintz, Jones, and Carpenter, *Report of Investigations*, 14; Stone, *Disaster at Texas City*, 14; Wheaton, *Texas City Remembers*, 13.

Chapter 15

1. Rev. Thomas Carney to Bishop Christopher Byrne, 22 April 1947; Lagana, interview by author.

2. Audrey Carroll, interview by author, Houston, TX, 24 April 1999.

3. Fred Gorzell, interview by author, Hawkins, TX, 26 July 1995.

4. Mary Frances Romano Gorzell, interview by author, Hawkins, TX, 26 July 1995.

5. Catherine Medina, interview by author, Galveston, TX, 18 April 1999.

6. Rita Bouchard Phillips, multiple interviews by author, Houston TX.

7. Curtis Trahan, interview by Moncla, Texas City Oral History Project; deposition of Curtis Trahan, 6246–6320.

8. Benedict, interview by Moncla, Texas City Oral History Project.
9. Wheaton, *Texas City Remembers*, 15.
10. Dick Benedict, interview by Moncla, Texas City Oral History Project. The figures for dead and injured come from Kintz, Jones, and Carpenter, *Report of Investigations*, 1, 14. To this day exact casualty figures are unclear. Col. Homer Garrison stated five hundred people were killed. Garrison, "Texas City Disaster," remarks before the International Association of Chiefs of Police Convention, Duluth, MN, 24 September 1947; on file, Moore Memorial Public Library, Texas City. The *Texas City, Texas, Disaster* report by the Fire Prevention and Engineering Bureau lists 552 fatalities and 3,000 injuries (2). The *Texas Catholic Herald* reported 398 individuals killed, 178 missing, and 63 sets of remains recovered but never identified. Sean Horrigan, "Texas City Explosions Cancelled All Plans for the 100th Jubilee of the Diocese of Galveston," *Texas Catholic Herald*, December 6, 1996.
11. Safety engineer H. B. Williams reported two separate explosions several seconds apart (quoted in Kintz, Jones, and Carpenter, *Report of Investigations*, 13). In his 22 April 1947 letter to Bishop Byrne, Father Carney states he heard two distinct explosions back-to-back when the *Grandcamp* detonated. Texas City resident Fred Dowdy, who happened to be several miles away watching the smoke from the *Grandcamp* when it exploded, witnessed two explosions, one at the ship and another high in the air above it (quoted in Wheaton, *Texas City Remembers*, 18). A report prepared for oil insurance underwriters in New York City states, "A number of witnesses reported hearing two successive explosions." Armistead, *Report to John G. Simmonds*. Another report describes three concussions: "a minor blast shook the ship and seconds later a terrific explosion blew the vessel to bits . . . [then] another earth-shaking explosion followed." American National Red Cross, *Preliminary Report on the Texas City Explosions*. Finally, a Bureau of Mines report stated, "Several competent witnesses heard two blasts." Kintz, Jones, and Carpenter, *Report of Investigations*, 1. Several eyewitnesses perceived only one blast, including Father Frank Lagana, Audrey Carroll, Catherine Medina, Mary Francis Romano Gorzell, and Fred Gorzell, interviews by the author.
12. Benedict, interview by Moncla, Texas City Oral History Project; Kintz Jones, and Carpenter, *Report of Investigations*, 1; *Texas City, Texas, Disaster*, 5–6; Braidech, *Texas City Disaster: Facts and Lessons*, 14–15.
13. Lagana, interview by author; Carney to Bishop Byrne, 22 April 1947. The operator was Thelma Dyess, quoted in Wheaton, *Texas City Remembers*, 17.
14. Deposition of H. O. Wray, US Department of Justice, Texas City Torts Claims as Consolidated for Joint Trial, RG 118, vol. 24; depositions of W. H. Sandberg, Carlos Suderman, and Harley Bowen.
15. Benedict, interview by Moncla, Texas City Oral History Project; Wheaton, *Texas City Remembers*, 13, 15.
16. Carroll, interview by author; Curtis Trahan, interview by Moncla, Texas City Oral History Project; "Texas City Mayor Addresses Complaints about the Red Cross," *Chicago Tribune*, 21 April 1947.

17. Lagana, interview by author.
18. Quinn, interview by author, 7 February 1999.
19. Carney to Bishop Byrne, 22 April 1947. Although the vast majority of clergy present immediately following the explosion of the *Grandcamp* were Roman Catholic priests, at least three Protestant clergy were actively engaged in rescue and recovery that day. Pastor F. M. Johnson, of First Baptist Church in Texas City, spent the day using his own car to drive injured people wherever they needed to go for treatment. Rev. Roland P. Hood, also of First Baptist Church, Texas City, himself injured, nevertheless helped other injured people all day at one of the clinics. Rev. Ervin Jackson, of First Methodist Church, Texas City, was also injured helping in the blast area. Texas State Senate, "Senate Resolution No. 87 by Phillips," April 22, 1947, copy in Archives and Records, Archdiocese of Galveston-Houston, Houston, TX; Stephens, *Texas City Disaster* 87; Wheaton, *Texas City Remembers*, 20.
20. Those first on the scene saw no evidence whatsoever of any organized rescue and recovery effort and no evidence of the presence of groups such as the Red Cross, the Salvation Army, or the military. Lagana, interview by author. In the first hours after the explosion of the *Grandcamp*, Mayor Trahan had tremendous difficulty trying to get much of anything official organized. Working mostly from city hall, but also consulting with Dr. Clarence Quinn at Danforth Clinic nearby, Trahan was at first completely overwhelmed by the sheer magnitude of the disaster. Quinn and others with wartime logistical experience helped the mayor develop an effective response. Still, it took several hours for anyone to assemble and implement any type of logistical plan. Quinn, interview by author, 7 February 1999.
21. Carney to Bishop Byrne, 22 April 1947. Not everyone on the scene was there to help with rescue and recovery. Audrey Carroll said that in her haste to leave the Monsanto office, she left her purse behind. Much later her purse was returned to her, completely empty. The contents had been stolen. The Monsanto office safe, open at the time the *Grandcamp* exploded, had been cleaned out as well. No cash had been kept in the safe, but there were a lot of uncashed checks and employee US savings bonds sold through Monsanto. Carroll, interview by author.
22. Rev. James A. Nelson, interview by author, Houston, TX, 15 February 1999.
23. Quinn, interview by author, 7 February 1999; Lagana, interview by author; Carney to Bishop Byrne, 22 April 1947.
24. Hunter, interview by author.
25. Quinn, interview by author, 7 February 1999.
26. President Ronald Reagan ended this free medical and dental service.
27. "Public Health in Galveston County: A Historical Recollection by the History Council Committee of the Galveston County Health District," Galveston County Health District, accessed 11 January 2021, https://www.gchd.org/home/showpublished document?id=3722.
28. Dr. Clarence Quinn, who was appointed medical coordinator by Mayor Trahan, mentioned the efforts of civilians in Galveston to direct traffic when he wrote his official report to the mayor and city commissioners of Texas City. The report is

published in its entirety in Wheaton, *Texas City Remembers*, 57–59. Fred Gorzell, the seventeen-year-old Kirwin High School student watching a film in chemistry class when the blast occurred, was one of the volunteers directing traffic. School had been dismissed and soon thereafter, Gorzell and his friends were on Broadway, watching vehicles filled with injured people racing by. After one or two instances of near crashes with cars trying to cross Broadway, Gorzell and his friends organized groups to direct traffic at three very busy intersections: Twenty-First Street, Twenty-Third Street, and Twenty-Fifth Street. They redirected cross-traffic to other streets in order to avoid Broadway. The boys were there for several hours before Galveston police took over. Gorzell, interview by author, 26 July 1995.

29. Marine Hospital had 202 beds. Only 28 beds were available when the *Grandcamp* exploded. Father Bill Roach arrived at the hospital with 109 other injured people. He became part of the overflow of injuries placed anywhere space was available. Rhein, notes from an interview by Larry Lee, 17 October 2000; Quinn, interview by author, 7 February 1999; Wheaton, *Texas City Remembers*, 60.

30. Rhein, interview by author; Rhein, notes from an interview by Larry Lee, 17 October 2000; Carney to Bishop Byrne, 22 April 1947.

Chapter 16

1. Quinn, interview by author, 7 February 1999. This observation was confirmed by many others who saw Roach in an open casket during his funeral mass the following day. Wheaton, *Texas City Remembers*, 92; Katherine Hunter and Bernice Smith, interviews by author; Montegut, interview by author, 1 July 2000.

2. Charles Outterside described Roach's appearance to Bernice Smith. Smith, interview by author, Frank's Café collapsed in the explosion, burying everyone inside. Wheaton, *Texas City Remembers*, 3.

3. Wheaton, *Texas City Remembers*, 16. One source reported Roach had suffered a skull fracture. Father John Roach relayed this cause of death to his family in Media, Pennsylvania, when he broke the news by phone. The family in turn told the local paper. McHugh, "Death of a Media Priest,'" *Chester* (PA) *Times*, 17 April 1947.

4. Williams quoted in Kintz, Jones, and Carpenter, *Report of Investigations*, 13–14.

5. Wheaton, *Texas City Remembers*, 5.

6. Garrison, "Texas City Disaster," 17–18; Wheaton, *Texas City Remembers*, 5.

7. *Texas City, Texas, Disaster*, 42; Wheaton, *Texas City Remembers*, 65–66; Stephens, *Texas City Disaster*, 101.

8. Braidech, *Texas City Disaster: Facts and Lessons*, 5–6; Wheaton, *Texas City Remembers*, 3–6; Stone, *Disaster at Texas City*, 84–85, 90; Stephens, *Texas City Disaster*, 101–3.

9. *Texas City, Texas, Disaster*, 40.

10. Based on a $1.00 to $12.18 increase between 1947 and 2021, accounting for inflation and purchasing power. United States. Department of Labor, Bureau of Labor Statistics.

11. *Texas City, Texas, Disaster*, 38–42; Braidech, *Texas City Disaster: Facts and Lessons*, 5–6. Sources give similar but not identical statistics regarding losses and the number

of businesses damaged and destroyed. See Wheaton, *Texas City Remembers*, 4, 6; Stone, *Disaster at Texas City*, 84–85, 90; Stephens, *Texas City Disaster*, 101–3.

12. Wheaton, *Texas City Remembers*, 5, 7, 9, 65.

13. "Texas City Mayor Addresses Complaints about the Red Cross," *Chicago Tribune*, 21 April 1947; Trahan, interview by Moncla, Texas City Oral History Project. In response, Gerald Wesselins of the St. Louis Red Cross office admitted to Trahan that "errors and mistakes" had been made but attributed them all to the general state of confusion created by the disaster.

14. Catherine Medina, interview by author.

15. Wheaton, *Texas City Remembers*, 6.

16. Wheaton, *Texas City Remembers*, 13.

17. Carney to Bishop Byrne, 22 April 1947; Wheaton, *Texas City Remembers*, 7.

18. Kintz, Jones, and Carpenter, *Report of Investigations*, 1.

19. Wheaton, *Texas City Remembers*, 6.

20. Sgt. Don Lynn, "Eyewitness at Texas City," *Tailspinner* (Lackland Air Force Base newspaper), April 25, 1948.

21. Kintz, Jones, and Carpenter, *Report of Investigations*, 2, 16, 17; Wheaton, *Texas City Remembers*, 21, 22.

22. *Texas City, Texas, Disaster*, 40; Wheaton, *Texas City Remembers*, 7; Kintz, Jones, and Carpenter, *Report of Investigations*, 17. Two engineers from the US Bureau of Mines had inspected the elevator at 9:15 P.M. on April 16, twelve hours after the *Grandcamp* had exploded. They found no dead or injured victims and noted that the elevator was not seriously damaged. They did report, however, that the interior of the elevator was extremely dusty from grain shifting during the explosion of the *Grandcamp*. Kintz, Jones, and Carpenter, *Report of Investigations*, 15.

23. Gorzell, interview by author.

24. "Aureole of Heroism Glows above Catastrophe-Stricken Texas City," *Southern Messenger* 24 April 1947.

25. Katherine Hunter and Bernice Smith, interviews by author.

26. Quinn, interview by author, 7 February 1999; "Bishop's Tribute."

27. See *Chester* (PA) *Times*: "Rev. William F. Roach Obituary," 17 April 1947; "Hero Priest Buried in Simple Rites in County," 19 April 1947; Montegut, interview by author, 7 November 1999; *Journey of Faith*, 50.

28. Texas State Senate, Resolution 87, 22 April 1947.

29. Wheaton, *Texas City Remembers*, 6, 9. In *Disaster at Texas City*, Stone states that the Monsanto fires were extinguished by Friday, April 18 (80).

30. Lagana, interview by author.

31. "Bishop's Tribute"; "Solemn Mass for Heroic Texas City Priest," *Chicago Tribune*, 21 April 1947; Hal Boyle, "Texas City Mourns Hundreds of Explosion Dead," Associated Press, 19 April 1947.

32. Stephens, *Texas City Disaster*, 105.

33. Wheaton, *Texas City Remembers*, 107. After the explosions, the Our Lady of the Snows mission was moved to Alvin, TX, eighteen miles west of Texas City. In 1957, the mission

was moved to Galveston for two years. Then, in 1959, it returned to Texas City. In 1963, the mission was combined with St. Mary of the Miraculous Medal. Lisa May, archivist of the Archdiocese of Galveston-Houston, email to the author, 14 August 2008.

34. Stephens, *Texas City Disaster*, 105; Wheaton, *Texas City Remembers*, 90–91, 107. The Texas City Terminal Railway Company would pursue litigation over liability for nine years before its claims were settled. Stephens, *Texas City Disaster*, 100. The railway company sustained $3,000,000 in damage, equating to roughly $36,540,000 in 2021, based on a $1.00 to $12.18 increase between 1947 and 2021, to account for inflation and purchasing power. US Department of Labor, Bureau of Labor Statistics; Henry A. LaGasse, *Description of the Ship Explosion in Le Havre, France on July 28, 1947*, 1–5; US Coast Guard, "Final Findings"; Stone, *Disaster at Texas City*, 90–93. Forty-seven sailors on the SS *Pan Pennsylvania* were injured before the fire was extinguished. "Loaded Tanker Burns at Texas City," *Galveston Daily News*, 18 May 1947.

35. All numbers are from Wheaton, who published a firsthand, eyewitness account the year after the disaster and lists the names of everyone killed and missing. Wheaton, *Texas City Remembers*, 9–10, 107. Other sources give different figures. In *Texas City Disaster*, Stephens estimates a total of 581 killed: 405 identified, 63 unidentified, and 113 never located (105). In *Disaster at Texas City*, Stone sets the death toll at 567 (89). The National Board of Fire Underwriters listed a total of 568 killed, 371 identified, 62 not identified, and 135 missing and presumed dead. The report placed the number of injured at two to three thousand, but the authors acknowledged that as of the date their report was completed (April 29, 1947) bodies were still being recovered and injuries updated. See *Texas City, Texas, Disaster*, 42. On the recovery of bodies from Galveston Bay, see Garrison, "Texas City Disaster," 15.

36. "Many Persons Listed as Dead Are Found Alive," *Galveston Daily News*, 27 April 1947; Robert Shirk, "Texas City on Road to Recovery 6 Months after Terrific Blast," 11 October 1947.

37. Wheaton, *Texas City Remembers*, 10, 107.

Chapter 17

1. "First Suits Filed in Texas City Case," *Houston Post*, 17 April 1948; Stone, *Disaster at Texas City*, 92.

2. Kintz, Jones, and Carpenter, *Report of Investigations*, 21–22. The complete findings were published later that year.

3. *Texas City, Texas, Disaster*, 6; Braidech, *Texas City Disaster: Facts and Lessons*, 8.

4. Braidech, *Texas City Disaster: Facts and Lessons*, 13–15.

5. In *Special Study: Risk Concepts in Dangerous Goods Transportation Regulations*, the National Transportation Safety Board wrote:

> An important aspect of past development of safety measures [from the turn of the twentieth century to 1968] was the relatively low level of research activity required to sustain the unsophisticated level of the safety control activities—both voluntary and regulatory—needed to satisfy the demands of the interested

parties. Until 1968, essentially no research funds were budgeted by the regulators of this transportation. By considering matters at issue on an ad hoc basis for largely single mode use, there was little need for more than arriving at a consensus of expert judgments for the three parties with direct interest in the problem, namely the shippers, the carriers, and their suppliers.

During World War II, two aspects of the approaches described above underwent a change in one of the modes. The regulatory jurisdiction over marine transportation of bulk flammable goods was assigned to the Coast Guard. It then began to exercise the primary initiative for regulatory changes, and to institute meaningful enforcement efforts in this safety area. The nature of the resulting regulations suggests the ad hoc approach and the consensus of experts continued to provide the basis for regulatory changes. (NTSB, *Special Report*, 2–3)

6. Braidech, *Texas City Disaster: Facts and Lessons*, 13–15; LaGasse, *Description of the Ship Explosion*; "Ocean Liberty," Cedre, 16 Oct. 2009, https://wwz.cedre.fr/en/Resources/Spills/Spills/Ocean-Liberty.

7. Kintz, Jones, and Carpenter, *Report of Investigations*, 23; Braidech, *Texas City Disaster: Facts and Lessons*, 11; *Texas City, Texas, Disaster*, 43.

8. Carroll, interview by author.

9. Stephens. *Texas City Disaster*, 107–10; US Department of Justice, Texas City Torts Claims as Consolidated for Joint Trial, RG 118, vols. 21–34; "Last Texas City Reparations Paid," *Galveston Daily News*, 14 April 1957; "Texas City Disaster Relief Act Amended," *Galveston Daily News*, 4 November 1960.

10. "Texas City Disaster Relief Act Amended."

11. "Survivor's Story," *Houston Chronicle*, 13 April 1997.

12. Stephens, *Texas City Disaster*, 104. The *Texas City Sun, Houston Chronicle*, and *Galveston News-Tribune* were among the newspapers collecting relief funds. See "Relief Fund Started for Texas City," *Texas City Sun*, 18 April 1947; *Houston Chronicle*, 21 April 1947; "Texas City Fund Still Soaring," *Galveston News-Tribune*, 25 April 1947; "Bishop's Tribute."

13. See *Galveston Daily News*: "Sellout Crowd Anticipated for Jack Benny–Phil Harris Benefit Show Slated Here Next Monday," 22 April 1947; "Texas City Relief Fund to Be Used for Rebuilding Lives and Homes of Victims," 22 April 1947; "Frank Sinatra Joins Galaxy of Radio and Screen Stars of Texas City Benefit Show," 23 April 1947; "Proceeds from Stars' Party to Swell T. C. Benefit Fund," 24 April 1947. Also see *Galveston News-Tribune*, "Texas City Relief Fund to Be Used for Rebuilding Lives and Homes of Victims," 25 April 1947; Wheaton, *Texas City Remembers*, 74; Stephens, *Texas City Disaster*, 104.

14. "Texas City Ten Years Later," *Galveston Daily News*, 19 April 1957.

15. Stephens, *Texas City Disaster*, 102, 106.

16. "Big Tragedy Would Catch Houston Short on Nurses," *Houston Chronicle*, 2 March 1947; Garrison, "Texas City Disaster," 17.

17. Stephens, *Texas City Disaster*, 103; Braidech, *Texas City Disaster: Facts and Lessons*, 16.
18. Braidech, *Texas City Disaster: Facts and Lessons*, 15.
19. Rachel Stone, "Chrysta Castañeda, Texas Power Grid Failure Could Happen Again," *Oak Cliff Advocate*, 13 September 2021, https://oakcliff.advocatemag.com/2021/09/chrysta-castaneda/. See also Carey W. King, Josh D. Rhodes, and Jay Zarnikau, committee chairs, *The Timeline and Events of the February 2021 Texas Electric Grid Blackouts*, a report by a committee of faculty and staff at the University of Texas at Austin, July 2021, https://energy.utexas.edu/sites/default/files/UTAustin%20%282021%29%20EventsFebruary2021TexasBlackout.pdf.

Chapter 18

1. Montegut, interviews by author, 5 November 1999, 7 November 1999, 1 July 2000; Laiche, interview by author, 1 July 2000.
2. Montegut and Laiche, interviews by author, 1 July 2000.
3. "Roach, John J., Diocesan File," n.d., Archives & Records, Archdiocese of Galveston-Houston; Montegut, interview by author, 7 November 1999; "Monsignor John Roach Obituary," *Texas Catholic Herald*, 27 November 1987; *Journey of Faith*, 48–49.
4. Benedict, interview by Moncla, Texas City Oral History Project; Wheaton, *Texas City Remembers*, 13, 15.
5. Sauer and Meskill, interviews by author.
6. Wheaton, *Texas City Remembers*, 83–84.
7. Montegut, interview by author, 1 July 2000. It was impossible to determine Eddie's identity because neither Sr. Mary William Montegut nor Sr. Mary Catherine Laiche could remember his last name. Wheaton's list the of dead and missing includes sixteen victims with some form of the names Edward, Edwin, or Edmund. There were four men with these first names, eleven with these middle names, and one with a last name. Wheaton, *Texas City Remembers*, 79–82.
8. Sauer, interview by author.
9. Carroll, interview by author.
10. Trahan, interview by Moncla, Texas City Oral History Project.
11. Stone, *Disaster at Texas City*, 36; Stephens, *Texas City Disaster*, 83; Wheaton, *Texas City Remembers*, 92; Bernice Smith, quoted in Mary Ellen Doyle, "Parishioners Recall Death of Fr. Roach," *Texas City Sun*, 16 April 1997. Years afterward, the nuns at the Monastery of the Holy Infant Jesus believed Father Bill had been killed in the explosion of the *High Flyer*. Montegut, interview by author, 7 November 1999.
12. Rhein, notes from an interview by Larry Lee, 17 October 2000.
13. Standard Certificate of Death No. 82129, William Francis Roach, Texas Department of Health, Bureau of Vital Statistics.
14. Benedict, interview by Moncla, Texas City Oral History Project.
15. See "Bishop's Tribute"; "Rev. William F. Roach Obituary," *Chester Times*, 17 April 1947; "Solemn Mass for Heroic Texas City Priest," *Chicago Tribune*, 21 April 1947.

NOTES TO CHAPTER 18

16. Journal entry of Sr. Mary Laurentia, 17 April 1947, Sharon House Journal, pp. 274–75, Society of the Holy Child Jesus, American Provinces Archives, Sharon Hill, PA.

17. "In Memory of Those Who Died—Dedication of Carillon Bells at Local Church Is Scheduled Today," *Texas City Sun*, 21 December 1947.

18. Dorssemont, "Papal Encyclicals," 3–5.

19. Fleckenstein, "'Right to Associate,'" 55–64.

20. "Thomas Merton's Life and Work," accessed 12 December 2021, Thomas Merton Center at Bellarmine University, http://merton.org/chrono.aspx.

21. Fischer, "John M. Corridan, S.J.," 71–87.

22. Keane and McDermott, "The Manner is Extraordinary"; Mullin, interview by author; McHugh, "Death of a Media Priest."

23. Msgr. Owen Campion, "Catholics and Civil Rights," accessed 12 December 2021, Simply Catholic, https://www.simplycatholic.com/catholics-and-civil-rights/.

24. Levy, *Cesar Chavez*, 89.

25. Hunter, interview by author; Montegut, interview by author, 7 November 1999.

BIBLIOGRAPHY

Archives and Document Repositories

Archives and Records, Archdiocese of Galveston-Houston, Houston, TX, rchgh.org/
    "Senate Resolution No. 87 by Phillips." Texas State Senate. April 22, 1947.
Archives of the Monastery of the Holy Infant Jesus, Lufkin, TX.
    Jeremiah, Sr. Mary. "Biography of Bill and John Roach." 1989.
    Laiche, Sr. Mary Catherine, handwritten account of first impressions of Father William
        Roach, n.d.
Archives of St. Philomena Church, Lansdowne, PA.
    Journey of Faith: The History of St. Philomena Church, Centennial Journal,
        1898–1998
Catholic Archives of Texas, Austin, TX.
    "Fiftieth Anniversary Celebration of 'Our Mother of Sorrows Catholic Church,' Burnet,
        Texas." June 9, 1991.
    Maldonado, Vivian B. *Dedication of St. Mary's Catholic Church, Lampasas, Texas.*
        June 18, 1972.
    Vanderholt, Rev. James. "Biography of Father William Roach." 27 May 1999.
Commonwealth of Pennsylvania, Bureau of Health Statistics and Registries, New
    Castle, PA.
Delaware County Historical Society, Chester, PA.
Delaware County Recorder of Deeds, Media, PA.
Lampasas County Recorder of Deeds, Lampasas, PA.

Moore Memorial Public Library, Texas City, TX.

Benedict, Richard. International Longshoreman's Association local union agent and survivor of the Texas City explosions. Transcription of interview by Susie Moncla. Texas City Oral History Project. 1981–82.

Garrison, Col. Homer. "Texas City Disaster." Remarks before the International Association of Chiefs of Police Convention, Duluth, MN, September 24, 1947.

LaGasse, Henry A. *Description of the Ship Explosion in Le Havre, France on July 28, 1947.* US Coast Guard Reserve. Serial Number 501. Reference (a) HQ/D2919582.

Mabry, Meriworth. "The Work Incidental: Was It Worth It?" Unpublished essay, 6 September 1978.

Trahan, Curtis. Mayor of Texas City, 1946–48. Transcription of interview by Susie Moncla. Texas City Oral History Project. 12 June 1981.

Society of the Holy Child Jesus, American Provinces Archives, Sharon Hill, PA.

Texas Department of State Services, Vital Records, Austin, TX.

US Department of Commerce, Bureau of the Census, Washington, DC.

US Department of Justice. Records of US Attorneys, Southern Judicial District of Texas. Texas City Torts Claims as Consolidated for Joint Trial. RG 118, National Archives and Records Administration.

US Department of Labor, Bureau of Labor Statistics, Washington, DC. https://www.bls.gov/.

Interviews by John Neal Phillips

Barrow, Ed. Childhood friend of the Roach brothers. Villa Nova, PA. 10 December 2000.

Bouchard Phillips, Rita. Mother of the author and eyewitness to the Texas City explosions. Houston, TX. Multiple interviews, beginning July 10, 1969.

Carroll, Audrey. Victim of the explosion of the SS *Grandcamp.* Houston, TX. 24 April 1999.

Gorzell, Fred. Eyewitness to the aftermath of the Texas City disaster. Hawkins, TX. 26 July 1995 and 14 February 1999.

Hammett, Jack. Witness to the instability and lawlessness of 1930s Texas. Denton, TX. 20 February 1982.

Hollister, Dana. Parishioner of Rev. William Roach. Lampasas, TX. 29 May 2000.

Hunter, Katherine. Parishioner of Rev. William Roach and friend of Betty Laiche and Maxine Montegut. Texas City, TX. 11 July 2000.

Jones, Nancy. Secretary, St. Mary's Catholic Church. Lampasas, TX. 27 April 2000.

King, Beth. Parishioner of Rev. William Roach. Lampasas, TX. 11 July 2000.

Lagana, Rev. Frank. Seminary classmate of the Roach brothers and eyewitness to the Texas City disaster. Houston, TX. 24 January 1999.

Laiche, Betty (Sr. Mary Catherine). Parishioner of Rev. William Roach and friend of both Roach brothers. Lufkin, TX. 1 July 2000.

Lee, Rev. Larry. Colleague of the Roach brothers. Houston, TX. 1 August 2000.

Medina, Catherine. Eyewitness to the Texas City disaster. Galveston, TX. 18 April 1999.

Medina, Margarite and Mike. Parishioners of Rev. William Roach. Lampasas, TX. 25 July 2000.

Meskill, Richard (Dick). Parishioner of Rev. William Roach and friend of the Roach brothers. San Antonio, TX. 10 July 2000.

Mikulik, Father Kenneth. Fellow seminarian of Richard Meskill and C. F. Quinn. Personal friend of Maxine Montegut, Catherine Laiche, and Father William Roach. Houston, TX. 25 July 2000.

Montegut, Maxine (Sr. Mary William). Parishioner of Rev. William Roach and friend of the Roach brothers. Lufkin, TX. 5 November 1999, 7 November 1999, 1 July 2000, 3 July 2000, and 14 July 2000.

Mullin, Belle. Friendship House volunteer. Jersey City, NJ, 8 August 2000.

Nelson, Rev. James A. Acquaintance of the Roach brothers and eyewitness to the Texas City disaster. Houston, TX. 15 February 1999.

Quinn, Clarence Francis (C. F.). Parishioner of Rev. William Roach and friend of the Roach brothers. Dallas, TX. 7 February 1999 and 25 July 2000.

Rhein, Msgr. George. Seminary classmate of the Roach brothers and eyewitness to the Texas City disaster; present at the death of Rev. William Roach. Houston, TX. 15 August 2000.

Romano Gorzell, Mary Frances. Eyewitness to the aftermath of the Texas City disaster. Hawkins, TX. 26 July 1995.

Sauer, Margie. Daughter of Pete Tarpey and friend of Rev. William Roach. Texas City, TX. 10 July 2000.

Schmidt, Vincent. Friend of Rev. William Roach. Woodlands, TX. 7 November 1999.

Shoch, Eleanor Barrow. Childhood acquaintance of the Roach brothers. Glenn Ridge, NJ. 10 December 2000.

Smith, Bernice. Parishioner of Rev. William Roach and friend of the Roach brothers. Texas City, TX, 4 July 2000.

Smith, Janie. Relative of Texas City volunteer firefighter Ben L. Mitchell. Texas City, TX. 26 September 1999.

Veronica, Sr. Mary. Acquaintance of the Roach brothers. Lufkin, TX. 1 July 2000.

Williams, Barbara. Curator, Drexel University College of Medicine Archives and Special Collections. Philadelphia, PA. 1 October 2003.

Wilson, Emily. Archivist, Mount St. Joseph College. Baltimore, MD. 8 October 2003.

Wittenberg, Joe. Parishioner of Rev. William Roach. Lometa, TX. 10 July 2000.

Newspapers

Chester Times, Chester, PA
Chicago Tribune, Chicago, IL
Dallas Morning News, Dallas, TX
Dallas Times Herald, Dallas, TX
Galveston Daily News, Galveston, TX
Galveston News-Tribune, Galveston, TX
Lampasas Record, Lampasas, TX

Media Times, Media, PA
Philadelphia Public Ledger, Philadelphia, PA
Southern Messenger, San Antonio, TX
Texas Catholic (Diocese of Dallas), Dallas, TX
Texas Catholic Herald (Archdiocese of Galveston-Houston), Houston, TX
Texas City Sun, Texas City, TX
Waco Times-Herald, Waco, TX

Papers, Brochures, and Informally Published Reports

American National Red Cross. *Preliminary Report on the Texas City Explosions*. St. Louis, MO: American National Red Cross, May 1947. Special Collections, Houston Public Library.

Armistead, George Jr. *Report to John G. Simmonds and Company, Inc., Oil Insurance Underwriters, New York City, on the Ship Explosions at Texas City, Texas, on April 16 and 17, 1947 and Their Results*. Washington, DC: n.p. 1 June 1947. Special Collections, Houston Public Library.

Braidech, Matthew M., Director of Research. *The Texas City Disaster: Facts and Lessons*. Report of the National Board of Fire Underwriters. Washington, DC: American Insurance Association, 1948.

Davis, R. O. E. *Explosibility and Fire Hazard of Ammonium Nitrate Fertilizer*. US Department of Agriculture Circular 719. March 1945. Available at https://ia803208.us.archive .org/4/items/explosibilityfir719davi/explosibilityfir719davi.pdf.

Kallus, Rev. Alfred. *St. Mary's Catholic Church Open House, November 29, 1964*. Brochure. Lampasas, TX : St. Mary's Catholic Church, 1964.

Kintz, G. M., G. W. Jones, and Charles B. Carpenter. *Report of Investigations: Explosions of Ammonium Nitrate Fertilizer on Board the SS* Grandcamp *and SS* High Flyer *at Texas City, Texas, April 16–17, 1947*. Washington, DC: Department of the Interior, Bureau of Mines, February 1948.

More Than Brick and Mortar: A History of St. Joseph's Parish, Killeen, Texas. Killeen, TX: St. Joseph's Parish, 1977.

National Transportation Safety Board, US Department of Transportation. *Special Study: Risk Concepts in Dangerous Goods Transportation Regulations*. Report Number NTSB-STS-71-1. Washington, DC: GPO, 1971.

Podbielski, Thad. *Celebrating the Golden Jubilee of the Catholic Church in Central Texas*. Brochure. Diocese of Austin, Most Reverend John C. McCarthy, Bishop, and Our Lady of Lourdes, Gatesville, Texas. Gatesville, TX: Our Lady of Lourdes Church, 1998. Condensed version available at https://ololgatesville.org/history-of-our-lady-of-lourdes.

Texas City, Texas, Disaster, April 16–17, 1947. Report by the Fire Prevention and Engineering Bureau of Texas, Dallas, Texas, and the National Board of Fire Underwriters, New York. Dallas: Fire Prevention and Engineering Bureau of Texas, 1948.

US Coast Guard, US Department of the Treasury. *Explosives or Other Dangerous Articles on Board Vessels, Regulations Governing the Transportation, Storage, Stowage, or Use of Explosives or Other Dangerous Articles or Substances, and Combustible Liquids on Board Vessels.* Washington, DC: US Coast Guard, 9 April 1941, rev. 1 July 1947.

————. *Final Findings of the Coast Guard, September 28, 1947.* Report. Washington, DC: US Coast Guard, 1947.

Published Works

Alexander, Charles C. *The Ku Klux Klan.* Lexington: University of Kentucky Press, 1965.

Allen, Ruth A., George N. Green, and James V. Reese. "Strikes." In *Handbook of Texas.* Denton, TX: Texas State Historical Association, 1976, updated 28 April 2021. https://www.tshaonline.org/handbook/entries/strikes.

Anderson, Gary Clayton. *The Conquest of Texas: Ethnic Cleansing in the Promised Land, 1820–1875.* Norman: University of Oklahoma Press, 2005.

Bailey, Elizabeth. *A History of Leander.* Leander: Leander, Texas, Sesquicentennial Committee, 1984.

Barnes, Kenneth C. *Anti-Catholicism in Arkansas: How Politics, the Press, the Klan, and Religious Leaders Imagined an Enemy, 1910–1960.* Fayetteville: University of Arkansas Press, 2016.

Barrow, Blanche Caldwell, and John Neal Phillips. *My Life with Bonnie and Clyde.* Norman: University of Oklahoma Press, 2002.

Benham, Priscilla Myers. "Texas City, TX." In *Handbook of Texas.* Denton, TX: Texas State Historical Association, 1952, updated 1 July 1995. https://www.tshaonline.org/handbook/entries/texas-city-tx.

Bernstein, Patricia. *Ten Dollars to Hate: The Texas Man Who Fought the Klan.* College Station: Texas A&M University Press, 2017.

"Bishop's Tribute to Heroic Priest." *Southern Messenger.* 24 April 1947.

Brown, Peter. *Augustine of Hippo.* Berkeley: University of California Press, 1969.

Castañeda, Carlos E. *The Church in Texas since Independence, 1836–1950.* Vol. 7 of *Our Catholic Heritage in Texas.* Austin, TX: Von Boeckmann-Jones, 1958.

The Catholic Encyclopedia: An International Work of Reference. 15 vols. New York: Robert Appleton, 1907–12. Accessed 5 January 2022. https://www.newadvent.org/cathen/.

"Constitutionality of the Portal-to-Portal Act." *Columbia Law Review* 47, no. :(1947) 6 52–1010. doi:1118245/10.2307.

Debo, Darrell. *Burnet County History: A Pioneer History, 1847–1979*, vol. 1. Burnet, TX: Eakin Press, 1979.

Dorssemont, Filip. "Papal Encyclicals: The Social Teaching of the Catholic Church." *International Union Rights* 18, no. 4 (2012). www.jstor.org/stable/41936837.

Duquin, Lorene Hanley. *They Call Her the Baroness.* New York: Alva House, 1995.

Evans, Hiram Wesley (Imperial Wizard 1922). "The Catholic Question as Viewed by the Ku Klux Klan." *Current History* 26 (July 1927): 563–68.

Farmer, David Hugh. *The Oxford Dictionary of Saints.* 3rd ed. Oxford: Oxford University Press, 1992.

Ferling, John. "Texas City Disaster." *American History* (February 1996): 49.

Fischer, James T. "John M. Corridan, S.J., and the Battle for the Soul of the Waterfront, 1948–1954." *US Catholic Historian* 16, no. 4 (1998): 71–87. https:// www.jstor.org/stable /25154646.

Fleckenstein, Marilynn P. "'Right to Associate' in Catholic Social Thought." *Journal of Business Ethics* 38, no. 1–2 (June 2002): 55–64. https://www.jstor.org/stable/25074777.

González, Aníbal A. "St. Mary's Seminary." In *Handbook of Texas*. Denton, TX: Texas State Historical Association, 2 November 2001. https://www.tshaonline.org/handbook /entries/st-marys-seminary.

Gordon, Lois, and Alan Gordon. Introduction by Roger Rosenblatt. *American Chronicle: Year by Year through the Twentieth Century*. New Haven, CT: Yale University Press, 1999.

Goulden, Joseph C. *The Best Years, 1945–1950*. New York: Athenaeum, 1976.

Green, George Norris. *The Establishment in Texas Politics: The Primitive Years, 1938–1957*. Norman: University of Oklahoma Press, 1979.

Hackett, Sheila. *Dominican Women in Texas: From Ohio to Galveston and Beyond*. Houston, TX: Sacred Heart Convent, 1986.

Heiland, Louis. Foreword by Commodore John B. Kelly. *The Schuylkill Navy of Philadelphia*. Philadelphia, PA: Drake Press, 1938.

Hiesberger, Jean Marie, gen. ed. *The Catholic Bible, New American Bible, Including the Revised Psalms and the Revised New Testament, Translated from the Original Languages with Critical Use of All Ancient Sources*. New York and Oxford: Oxford University Press, 1995.

Keane, James T., and Jim McDermott. "The Manner Is Extraordinary: The Life of John LaFarge." *America: The Jesuit Review* 199, no. 23 (27 October 2008). https://www .americamagazine.org/politics-society/2008/10/27/manner-extraordinary-life-john -lafarge.

Kennedy, David M. *Freedom from Fear: The American People in Depression and War, 1929–1945*. Oxford: Oxford University Press, 1999.

Kolodzy, Ron. "LaPorte, TX." In *Handbook of Texas*. Denton, TX: Texas State Historical Association, 1952, updated April 7, 2018. https://www.tshaonline.org/handbook/entries /la-porte-tx.

Lampasas History Book Committee. *Lampasas County, Texas: Its History and Its People*. Lampasas, TX: Lampasas County Historical Commission, 1991.

Latourette, Kenneth Scott. *Beginnings to 1500*. Vol. 1 of *A History of Christianity*. New York: Harper and Brothers, 1953.

Levy, Jacques. *Cesar Chavez: Autobiography of La Causa*. New York: W. W. Norton, 1975.

Lipscomb, Carol A. Revised by Tim Seiter. "Karankawa Indians." In *Handbook of Texas*. Denton, TX: Texas State Historical Association, 1976, updated 13 November 2020. https://www.tshaonline.org/handbook/entries/karankawa-indians.

Mabry, Meriworth. *Texas City Diamond Jubilee: A History of Texas City*. Texas City, TX: Texas City Sesquicentennial Planning Committee, 1986.

Márquez, John D. *Black-Brown Solidarity: Racial Politics in the New Gulf South*. Austin: University of Texas Press, 2013.

Marthaler, Bernard L., exec. ed. *New Catholic Encyclopedia*. 2nd ed., 15 vols. Detroit: Thomson/Gale; Washington, DC: Catholic University of America, 2003.

McComb, David G. *Galveston: A History*. Austin: University of Texas Press, 1986.

McCullough, David. *Truman*. New York: Simon and Schuster, 1992.

Miller, William D. *A Harsh and Dreadful Love: Dorothy Day and the Catholic Worker Movement*. New York: Image Books, 1974.

Moorhouse, Geoffrey. *Sun Dancing: A Vision of Medieval Ireland*. New York: Harcourt, Brace, 1997.

Murray, Peter, and Linda Murray. *The Oxford Companion to Christian Art and Architecture*. Oxford: Oxford University Press, 1996.

Palmer, Bruce, and Charles W. Macune Jr. "Macune, Charles William (1851–1940)." In *Handbook of Texas*. Denton, TX: Texas State Historical Association, 1976. https://www.tshaonline.org/handbook/entries/macune-charles-william.

Phillips, Cabell. *The New York Times Chronicle of American Life: From the Crash to the Blitz, 1929–1939*. New York: Macmillan, 1969.

Phillips, John Neal. *Running with Bonnie and Clyde: The Ten Fast Years of Ralph Fults*. Norman: University of Oklahoma Press, 1996.

Ryan, Steven P. "Galveston-Houston, Catholic Diocese of." In *Handbook of Texas*. Denton, TX: Texas State Historical Association, January 1, 1995, updated October 30, 2019. https://www.tshaonline.org/handbook/entries/galveston-houston-catholic-diocese-of.

"Silver Jubilee, St. Joseph's Parish, Killeen, Texas." *Southern Breeze* 9, no. 5 (April 1979).

Sloane, Charles. "Arkansas." In *The Catholic Encyclopedia*, vol. 1. New York: Robert Appleton, 1907. Accessed 5 January 2022, http://www.newadvent.org/cathen/01724a.htm.

Smith, Page. *Redeeming the Time: A People's History of the 1920s and the New Deal*. New York: McGraw-Hill, 1987.

Smyrl, Vivian Elizabeth. "Burnet County." In *Handbook of Texas*. Denton, TX: Texas State Historical Association, 1976, updated 30 September 2020. https://www.tshaonline.org/handbook/entries/burnet-county.

Stephens, Hugh W. *The Texas City Disaster, 1947*. Austin: University of Texas Press, 1997.

Stone, Ron. *Disaster at Texas City*. Fredericksburg, TX: Shearer, 1987.

"Strikes in 1943." *Monthly Labor Review* 58, no. 47–927 :(1944) 5. https://www.jstor.org/stable/41817422.

Treviño, Roberto R. *The Church in the Barrio: Mexican-American Ethno-Catholicism in Houston*. Chapel Hill: University of North Carolina Press, 2006.

Unger, Robert. *The Union Station Massacre: The Original Sin of J. Edgar Hoover's FBI*. Kansas City, MO: Andrews McMeel, 1997.

Wade, Wyn Craig. *The Fiery Cross: The Ku Klux Klan in America*. New York: Simon and Schuster, 1987.

Waskow, Arthur I. *From Race Riot to Sit-In, 1919 and the 1960s: A Study in the Connections between Conflict and Violence*. Garden City, NY: Doubleday, 1966.

Watkins, T. H. *The Hungry Years: A Narrative History of the Great Depression in America*. New York: Henry Holt, 1999.

Weigley, Russell F., ed. *Philadelphia: A 300-Year History.* New York: W. W. Norton, 1982.
Wheaton, Elizabeth Lee. *Texas City Remembers.* San Antonio, TX: Naylor Co., 1948.
Wright, Viva Mae. "St. Dominic's Villa." In *Lampasas County Texas: Its History and Its People.* Compiled by the Lampasas History Book Committee. Lampasas, TX: Lampasas County Historical Commission, 1991.

INDEX

References to illustrations appear in italic type.

Catholic Church: and African American communities, 31; and architecture, 60–61, 63, 65, 73; in Arkansas, 17; and Betty Laiche, 107, 108–9, 118; and Betty Laiche (Sister Mary Catherine Laiche), 204n3, 204n19, 205n7, 205n10, 224n7; and Bishop Christopher Edward Byrne, 27, 28, 30, 31–32, 37, 38, 39, 49, 54, 59, 60, 61, 63, 64, 65, 71, 73, 81, 81–82, 84, 86, 162, 163, 180, 181, 182, 196n30, 198n7, 204n16; and Bishop Nicholas Gallagher, 71; in Burnet, Texas, 54–55, 60, 197n44, 198n44; and Camp Hood facility, 197n44, 198n44; and Cathedral of St. Mary, 162; and Catholic Extension Society, 55, 62–63, 65, 199n16; and Church of St. Christopher, 63, 125; and Church of the Nativity of the Blessed Virgin Mary, 38, 163; clergy of, x, 14, 16, 17, 19, 22, 43, 57, 65, 71, 72, 79, 89, 183, 219n19; and cloistered nuns, 175, 176, 206n4; and convents, 20, 81, 108–9, 175, 192n8; and Diocese of Little Rock, 19, 21–22, 189n23; and Dominican Sisters, 33, 43, 194n11; and Father Cary Fowler, 150, 151, 152; and Father Frank Lagana, 145, 148, 150, 151, 152, 153, 188n32, 204n19; and Father Harris, 153, 155; and Father John LaFarge, 183, 191n17; and Father Nelson, 152–53; and Father Thomas A. Carney, 153, 160, 161, 164, 185n2, 204n16, 204n20; and Good Shepard Church, 51, 196n36, 197n44, 198n1; and Hispanic Catholics, 54, 55, 113, 198n6, 201n34; and Holy Spirit School, 187n19; importance of Mary to, 36, 77, 80, 82, 108; and Latinos/as, 31, 113, 134; Lent season in, 117, 118, 214–15n26, 215n27; and Maxine Montegut (Sister Mary William Montegut), 108–9, 118, 188n32, 204n19, 205n7, 205n10, 224n7; and monks, 59, 81, 83, 200n26; in

Nacogdoches, Tex., 85, 86; national parishes of, 113–14; and nuns, 44, 64, 69, 79, 81–86, 180, 181, 183, 206n4, 207n10, 224n11; and Our Lady of Guadalupe, 214n14; and Our Lady of Lourdes, 63, 19; and Our Lady of the Snows, 113, 134, 151, 164, 170, 214n14, 221–22n33; and Our Mother of Sorrows, 60, 73, 124, 198n44, 201n34; and popes, 182, 189n22; and relationship between labor and management, 215n28; religious images of, 44, 45, 65; response to 1947 blast, 160; Reverend Michael J. Leahy in, 72; and Sacred Heart Cathedral, 30, 176; and Sacred Heart Church, 65, 176, 197n44; schools of, 32, 33, 34, 43–44, 46, 56, 192n8, 194n11, 199n16; and seminaries, 14, 17–18, 19, 21–22, 23, 24, 25, 26, 27, 31–35, 37–38, 40, 48, 63, 76, 107, 152, 162, 163, 181, 199n16, 204n19; and services in alternative spaces, 42–43, 53, 54, 62, 71, 198n6; sexual abuse in, 181; and Shrine of the True Cross Church, 72, 145, 148, 151–52, 159, 160, 204n20; and St. Christopher's Church, 197n44, 201n42; and St. Mary's Catholic Church, 61, 194n11, 214n14; and St. Mary's in Lampasas, 195n22, 197n44, 198n1; St. Mary's Parish in, 40, 41, 42, 43, 44, 48, 49, 53–54, 55, 56, 60, 64, 65, 72, 196n31, 199n7; and St. Mary's Seminary, 181; and St. Philomena Catholic Church, 9, 11, 12; and St. Teresa of Ávila, 65, 184; in Texas City, Texas, 88–89, 104, 113; and Vatican, 27, 34, 44, 181, 183, 206n14. See also Catholicism; names of individual churches and clergy; Texas City, Texas

Catholicism: animosity toward, 42, 45, 186n12; and Catholic Charities, 172, 176; and Catholic schools, 5–6, 7, 8, 9,

Hunter, Katherine, 91–92, 119, 153, 184, 192n10, 206n12

International Longshoreman's Association, 88, 90, 110, 111, 177, 209n6
Interracial Justice: A Study of the Catholic Doctrine of Race Relations (LaFarge), 183

Jackson, Ervin, 163
Jester, Beauford, 112, 156, 172
Joseph, Saint, 40, 55, 64–65, 77

Karankawa people, 29, 67–68, 203n2
Kelly, Grace, 38
Kelly, Jack, Jr., 38
Kelly, John Brendan "Jack," Sr., 8, 9, 10, 13–14, 38, 57, 188n30
King, Beth, 44, 45, 50, 196n36
Ku Klux Klan: anti-Catholic sentiments of, x, 20, 21, 23–24, 44, 46, 85; in Arkansas, 191n16; Atlanta, Ga., headquarters of, 20; and Basil Edward Newton, 20; and confrontation with Father Bill, 52; and immigrants, 44; and Lampasas, Texas, 44; and leader Reverend Harry Knowles, 20; and mask-wearing, 44, 45, 195n13; nationwide popularity of, 20, 194n10; and political action, 20–21, 46, 194n10; propaganda of, 23; targets of, 44, 45–46, 194n10; and violence, 45–46

labor movement: and African Americans, 16; and Catholic Christian movement, 182; and César Chávez, 184; and Farmers' Alliance Number One, 51; and Irish labor movement, 186n12; and job descriptions, 97; length of workweek, 94, 95, 98, 99–100, 111, 211n26; and National Labor Relations Board, 101; and National War Labor Board, 95; and Philadelphia, 5; and

politics, 110–11, 182; and Share Croppers Union (SCU), 24, 191n18; and strikes, 94, 95, 96–97, 98, 110, 111, 112, 115, 116, 142, 144, 148, 210n10, 210n11, 213n1; and Texas City, Texas, 15, 88, 94, 97, 98, 117; and unions, 16, 24, 88, 90, 94, 96–97, 98, 99, 101, 110, 111–12, 114, 115, 116, 177, 182, 184, 209n6, 210n10, 210n11; and United Mine Workers, 96, 210n10; and wages, 15, 16, 20, 94, 95, 96, 97, 98, 99–100, 111, 112, 114–15, 182, 211n26; and workers' living conditions, 15, 16; and working conditions, 20, 94. *See also* International Longshoreman's Association; Lewis, John Llewellyn
Lafitte, Jean, 29, 67, 68
Laiche, Al, 69, 70
Laiche, Betty, 69, 70, 72, 75, 76–79, 89. *See also* Catholic Church; Laiche, Sister Mary Catherine
Laiche, Sister Mary Catherine, 118, 175–76
Lee, Larry, 58, 63–65, 89
Leo XIII (pope), 182, 184
Lewis, John Llewellyn, 96
Longhorn II, 130, 136, 147
Luna, Julio, Jr., 138
Luther, Martin, 44, 45
Lykes Brothers Steamship Company, 139, 148

Marine Hospital, 153–54, 155, 159, 178, 180, 220n29
Maurin, Peter, 57, 191n17, 200n20, 200n22
McCarthy, Glen, 83
Medina, Catherine, 146, 159–60
Merton, Thomas, 58–59, 63, 182, 183, 200n26
Meskill, Cora Tarpey, 75, 89, 122, 153, 205n5
Meskill, Dick, 75, 89, 162, 214n13, 215n28, 229
Meskill, Richard, 75, 76, 77, 89, 90, 91. *See also* Texas City, Texas

Roach, William Francis (Father Bill)
(*continued*)
65; and Pennsylvania, 115, 186n13;
Pontifical Requiem Mass for, 162; poor
diet of, 33–34, 37; and priesthood
studies, 12–13, 14, 15, 16–18, 21–23, 25,
26–27, 32, 33, 34, 37–38, 71, 72, 76, 184,
187n25; rectory of, *126*, 184; and Ruhl J.
"Pete" Tarpey, 89–90, 92, 94, 177; and
Saint Joseph, 40, 55, 64–65, 77; and
Saint Catherine of Siena, 108, 184; and
Saint Mary's in Lampasas, 71; and
Saint Mary's Parish in Texas City, 65,
70–80; and Saint Mary's Seminary, 63;
and Saint Philomena Catholic Church,
9, 11; sense of humor of, x, 6, 12, 23, 34,
35, 49, 64, 66, 119, 205n4, 205n9;
sermons of, 1, 75, 86, 89, 215n27, 215n28,
215n30; and service for victims of
explosions, 164; smoking of, 1–2, 37, 47,
51, 75, 76, 79, 135–36; social awareness
of, 24, 25, 57, 118, 181–82, 184, 200n22;
spirituality of, ix–x, 11–12, 14, 15, 17–18,
30, 31, 34, 35, 36–37, 51, 52, 65, 76, 77,
79–80, 84, 86, 184, 202n51, 205–6n12,
205n9, 215n35; and Texas City, 70, 71,
72, 80, 81, 89–91, 94, 106–7, 113, 114, 129,
140, 144, 153, 173, 174, 196n31, 207n7,
214n14; and Texas City explosions, x,
xi, 2; and Texas State School for Boys,
63; and Thomas Merton, 58, 59,
200n26; as toddler, *123*; transportation
of, 49–50, 62, 64, 89, *131*, 157, 164,
192n10; and visit to monastery, 118
Roach, William Francis (father):
character of, 6; and death of Helen
(first wife), 3; gas station of, 4, 8, 9, 12,
26, 163; and requiem mass for Father
Bill, 163; and Roach twins, 187n25; in
Sharon Hill, Pa., 4, 5, 7; and sons' first
mass, 38
Romano, Mary Frances, 146, 217n4
Roosevelt, Franklin Delano, 38, 57, 65, 96

Sandberg, Walter "Swede," 87, 88, 106, 139,
140, 144. *See also* Texas City, Texas
Schmidt, Father Frederick A., 54, 197n44,
198–99n7, 201n34
Schmidt, Vincent, 119, 191n11, 215n33
Sinatra, Frank, 171, 223n13
Sinclair, Upton, 24
Smith, Alfred Edgar, 21, 199n8
Smith, Bernice, 119, 121, 206n2, 207n7,
207n17, 208n15, 212n12, 213n26, 215n30,
215n31, 215n34, 216n39, 220n1, 220n2,
221n25, 224n11
Smith, Lawrence, 119, 192n14
Smith, Rita, 121–22
Soto, Hernando de, 19
Spain, 27, 29, 68, 192n6
SS *Grandcamp*: and airplane deaths, 147;
and ammonium nitrate fertilizer, 141,
142, 143, 148, 166–67; Captain de
Guillebon of, 138–39; cargo of, 136, 138,
140, 141–42, 147–48; and Curtis
Trahan, 179; docking of, 121; explosion
of, x, *130*, 130, 131, 132, 133, 136, 145, 146–
48, 151, 152, 153, 155, 157, 163, 166, 167,
169, 170, 177, 178, 179, 180, 211n3, 215n30,
218n11, 219n19, 220n29, 221n22; and
Father Frank Lagana, 145, 217n15;
and Father Nelson, 152; fire aboard,
138–44, 145, 156, 217n15, 217n18; and
lawsuits against government, 166; and
Longhorn II, *130*; and Texas City, *129*,
136; and Warehouse O, *131*; weight of,
138; zinc in hull of, 168
SS *High Flyer*, 139–40, 148, 149, 152–53,
160–62, 166, 180. *See also* Texas City,
Texas
SS *Ocean Liberty*, 169
SS *Pan Pennsylvania*, 165, 222n34
SS *Wilson B. Keane*, 143, 148, 161, 162, 165
Standard Oil, 69
St. Dominic's Villa, 43–44, 46, 50, 194n11
Steeds, Floyd, 88
Steinbeck, John, 25

Texas City, Texas: and ammonium nitrate
fertilizer, 87–88, 106, 115, 121, 138, 140,
158–61, 167–69; and annexation of
industries, 104–5, 114, 115–16, 117, 119–21,
177, 215–16n36; and Betty Laiche, 104,
106, 126; black and Latino/a
neighborhoods of, 120, 151, 159, 164, 170;
buildings of, 94, 97, 157; and Campbell's
Bayou, 68; and Carl Nessler, 170;
Catholics in, 71, 75; charter of, 103, 120;
and deaths from 1947 explosions, 165,
166, 169–70, 217n16, 218n10, 220n2,
222n35, 224n7; and Dick Benedict, 129,
130, 131, 136, 137, 139, 140–41, 144, 147,
148, 149, 177, 180, 218n10; diseases in,
102, 103, 105, 115, 156, 157, 211–12n6;
educational system of, 104, 165;
elections in, 103, 110; expansion of, 121,
171; explosions in, x–xi, 93, 94, 99, 105,
129, 130, 133, 134, 136, 141, 146–49, 152,
155, 156; and explosions of 1947, x–xi,
129, 130, 133, 133, 134, 136, 146–49, 150,
152, 155–58, 160–65, 168–69, 170, 171, 172,
173, 174, 175, 176, 178, 188n32, 195n22,
218n10, 218n11, 220–21n11, 220n2,
221n23, 222n35; and Father Bill Roach,
48, 74–75, 79, 86, 89, 119–20, 137, 147,
162, 182; and Father Thomas A. Carney,
218n11; Fire Department of, 99, 101, 102,
136, 139, 140, 141, 143, 144, 157, 171, 177,
211n3, 217n16; and flaring, 173; founding
of, 68; and Galveston, Texas, 145–46,
151, 163; garbage problem in, 102, 103,
105; housing crisis in, 97, 112; and
hurricanes, 68, 69, 70, 72, 102, 104;
industries in, 68–69, 70, 76, 96–97, 98,
104–5, 106, 115, 116, 119, 120, 121, 144, 148,
157–58, 171; jobs in, 70, 98; labor issues
in, 90, 94, 96–97, 98, 101, 111; and
Lampasas, Texas, 136; location of, 67,
68; map of, 137; and Maxine Montegut,
104, 106, 107, 126; and Mayor Curtis
Trahan, 103–4, 105, 111, 114, 115–16, 117,

120, 121, 133, 143, 146, 147, 156, 158, 159,
164, 170, 178–79, 211n3, 215–16n36,
217n16, 219n20, 221n13; and Mayor
E. A. Johnson, 97, 103, 112; and oil
refineries, 68–69, 70, 94, 96, 97, 98,
99–100, 119, 137, 156, 158, 162, 164; and
oil workers' strike, 96, 98, 99–100, 110,
112; oil workers union in, 101, 114,
211n26; and Pan American Refining
Corporation, 104, 141–42, 156, 203n7;
Pete Tarpey's house in, 128, 137;
population of, 67, 69, 70, 171; as port
city, ix, x, 66, 68, 69, 70, 90, 93, 99, 104–
5, 106, 110, 121, 136, 138, 157, 165, 167, 168,
171; and Red Cross, 159, 160, 219n20,
221n13; relief fund for, 170–71, 223n12,
223n13; and rescue and recovery from
blasts, 156, 158–60, 219n19, 219n20,
219n21, 222n35; and Richard and Cory
Tarpey Meskill, 75, 89, 122, 153, 162,
188n32, 205n5, 205n9; sailors retreat in,
90–91, 107, 113, 164, 184; Salvation Army
in, 159, 219n20, 219n28; sewage problem
in, 102–3, 114; and SS High Flyer,
224n11; and St. Mary of the Miraculous
Medal, 101, 107, 116, 121, 125, 128, 129, 135,
137, 141, 164, 181, 204n19, 204n20,
222n33; and St. Mary's mission, 214n14;
and St. Mary's Parish, 65, 70–73, 116;
and taxes, 103–4, 114, 120, 121; and
Texas City Terminal Railway
Company, 121, 136, 138, 140, 141, 148–49,
158, 161, 164–65, 177, 216n5, 222n34; US
Army base in, 69; and victims of
explosions, 164, 165, 169–70, 179, 181,
211n3; Walter Sandberg in, 148–49, 161,
168; and war production, 70; and
zoning laws, 97. See also Disaster Relief
Act for Texas City; Mexican Petroleum
Company
Texas City Refining Company, 68
Texas City Sun (newspaper), 96–97, 103,
114, 119, 210n23, 210n24

CPSIA information can be obtained
at www.ICGtesting.com
Printed in the USA
BVHW050046030922
646139BV00006BA/477

9 780806 190709